SOCIAL WORK PRACTICE WITH
OLDER PEOPLE

[A POSITIVE PERSON-CENTRED APPROACH]

RORY LYNCH

SAGE

Los Angeles | London | New Delhi
Singapore | Washington DC

Los Angeles | London | New Delhi
Singapore | Washington DC

SAGE Publications Ltd
1 Oliver's Yard
55 City Road
London EC1Y 1SP

SAGE Publications Inc.
2455 Teller Road
Thousand Oaks, California 91320

SAGE Publications India Pvt Ltd
B 1/I 1 Mohan Cooperative Industrial Area
Mathura Road
New Delhi 110 044

SAGE Publications Asia-Pacific Pte Ltd
3 Church Street
#10-04 Samsung Hub
Singapore 049483

Editor: Alice Oven
Assistant editor: Emma Milman
Production editor: Katie Forsythe
Copyeditor: Jane Fricker
Proofreader: Bryan Campbell
Indexer: Elske Janssen
Marketing manager: Tamara Navaratnam
Cover design: Jen Crisp
Typeset by: C&M Digitals (P) Ltd, Chennai, India
Printed in India at Replika Press Pvt Ltd

© Rory Lynch 2014

First published 2014

Library of Congress Control Number: 2012954789

British Library Cataloguing in Publication data

A catalogue record for this book is available from the British Library

ISBN 978-1-4462-0183-1
ISBN 978-1-4462-0184-8 (pbk)

In memory of Diarmuid Lynch

CONTENTS

ABOUT THE AUTHOR

Rory Lynch is a lecturer in social work at Robert Gordon University, Aberdeen. He comes from St. Johnston, County Donegal in the Irish Republic and has lived and worked in Aberdeen for forty years. During this time he has developed and worked in a range of agencies from single homelessness, substance misuse and latterly mental health services. He has published on a variety of themes related to older people including sociology and social work; need, risk and protection and social policy for social work within a Scottish perspective.

Rory currently teaches within the School of Applied Social Studies with a specific remit for coordinating the teaching on older people and social work across a range of courses but specifically on undergraduate courses. He also teaches human growth and behaviour within the university on undergraduate and distance learning courses and has a specific interest in object relations. He is currently in the process of developing a user-friendly text on this subject for social work students.

INTRODUCTION

The structure of this book is very much driven by some of the radical changes that have taken place within community-based support, care management, the political context and more recent downturns within the economy of the United Kingdom. The book also sets out to explore and define the nature of modern social work training within the recent Professional Capabilities Framework for Social Work and the impact this has on training and service delivery. Just as importantly, the text seeks to focus on those ethical and value-driven aspects of working with older people. While the author would not support the view that values and ethics of themselves are under attack in the modern world, it is true that financial and resource stressors will impact on service delivery and how the needs of older people are met. Most of the chapters of the book will focus on these themes and a consideration of what it is to be an older person in the twenty-first century. This book will appear at a time when there are real concerns as to how older people, without adequate resources, will manage in areas of nutrition, heating and a wider social engagement with families and local communities. Students of Maslow (1987) may wonder what the wider implications for personhood and belonging are when the basics of human existence may be under threat for some individuals. The text is permeated throughout by case studies, exercises and questions to ponder.

The author has also attempted here to define the changing nature of the older person and **Chapter 1** focuses on this within the context of the transition of growing into older age with an emphasis on law and policy. This is as opposed to youthfulness, which is more readily grown out of. The chapter addresses how older people may become hidden in full view where expressed needs are denied or not acknowledged. Older people may become increasingly worried about their perceived lack of input into society. This is particularly at odds with those older people who are still working post-retirement as well as carrying out voluntary, caring and kinship roles. Lord Birchard, former head of the benefits agency, has not helped the current debate by suggesting that retired individuals should commit to community services to reduce the burden on the state, or have their state pensions reduced (Morris, 2012). A starting premise therefore for any consideration of social work with older people is that older people are not an adjunct to the state but are the state itself. When this politically driven premise is considered as a rational debate as opposed to a consideration of the lack of resources, then older people may have cause to worry. From a social policy perspective this has to be considered within the context of the UK's gross domestic product (GDP), which is one of the highest in Western Europe.

Chapter 2 is concerned with values and ethics and how social work practice can remain professional and moral within what is considered the 'rightness' of actions.

These considerations may be at a time when resources are limited and practitioners may be forced to make decisions based on this premise. Essentially, this chapter is related to need and its resolution within a context of inclusivity and engagement. The chapter seeks to explore those wider dimensions of personal values as well as a consideration of that more philosophical aspect of what it is to be. The author suggests that without this consideration the needs of all vulnerable groups may not be met. This chapter also considers something of the 'tyranny' of youth, although caution needs to be exercised here to ensure that youthfulness and older age are not seen as conflicting opposites. This is more related to a mutuality of respect and an acknowledgement of the psychological forces at work across the life course. These are not only stages that need to be worked through but hopefully in a collaborative way.

Chapter 3 addresses the range of skills necessary to consider and engage with the needs of older people. This is not a static set of skills and will need to reflect the changing impact of ageing itself across the generations. The focus here will be on listening, engaging and not assuming, as part of a more personalised agenda. Even the most careful professional interaction can develop into a 'professional knows best' at a time of stress on finances and resources generally. This is explored here within the new social work standards and again the chapter has a strong emphasis on ethics and values in relation to a meaningful and successful communication with all older people. At the heart of this understanding is that older people are not a homogeneous group. They are as different and diverse as any equivalent group of younger people or people from different cultural or ethnic backgrounds and should be engaged with in a way that reflects this diversity.

Chapter 4 explores community care from its inception, what it potentially sought to achieve and a critique of what this can mean in reality. The reader is encouraged to consider the history of this and, more importantly, how a community-based focus may not always meet the needs of older people. This can relate to individual choice, a lack of support networks, inadequate resources and social isolation. The chapter also addresses a range of assessment models with a critique of their value and particularly those themes that drive care management. The author cautions against an unthinking use of the language of the marketplace at the expense of the language of support and liberation. Older people are not commodities.

Chapter 5 focuses on mental health and well-being, which is, in the author's view, one of the most significant areas of current practice with older people. This comes at a time when older people may experience the double trauma of the ageing experience allied with poor and declining mental health. When disabilities become compounded then there is a greater potential for discriminatory practice. The consideration within this chapter is, how will the more complex mental health needs of older people get addressed if the main debate is on older people and their collective drain on the national purse? This is compounded by cuts in National Health Service provision, where there has been a real decrease in spending of 3.1% within the 2011–2012 budget for older people's mental health services (Boffey, 2012). So this chapter takes a much more focused approach to well-being in terms of individual psychopathology as well sociological forces of construct, ageism and stigma generally.

Chapter 6 explores the complex area of dementia. While the chapter on mental health focuses on wider issues of well-being this chapter on dementia resides as much within a focus on human rights as a diagnosis of illness. Again there is a strong ethical focus here with that implicit understanding of the uniqueness of individuals. This chapter addresses the wholeness of the person and how this may support both social work understanding and intervention. A consideration of Kitwood's (1993, 1997, 1999) 'personhood' is critical here to facilitate individual experience and need within an ethical and human rights perspective. The chapter concludes with a range of practical skills to consider when working with those older people diagnosed with dementia.

Chapter 7 identifies how assessment is at the heart of any effective communication and intervention with older people. A quality assessment will consider all the relevant expressed detail of an older person's life and needs. This chapter addresses the theoretical framework for assessment and intervention, with a strong focus on the 'process' of engagement. While it is not a conflict it is certainly the case that where the rules of engagement are defined then there is a likelihood for a more successful outcome! Too often practitioners become caught up within an outcome-driven focus when the actual liberating aspect resides within the simple engagement with the older person. Given the importance of this assessment, the author has worked through this aspect within practice to speculate on how older people may feel and respond to it. This chapter has also not shied away from issues of emotional pain, however difficult these may be to evaluate. The author believes that without entering into this world of potential trauma it is ultimately not possible to engage with the personhood of individual older people.

Chapter 8 explores gerontology, the science of ageing. The author has integrated key themes of the demographic of ageing and the research basis for this. This also addresses significant issues of how ageing itself is a social construct, influenced more by social policy than individual capacity for coping. A significant emphasis here is on practitioners being able to 'read' the meaning of what older people may be trying to express using the theoretical underpinning knowledge contained within this chapter. This specifically seeks to engage with those themes that make for the likelihood of a more successful psychological ageing across the life course. There is a specific focus here on how areas of psychological development (or dysfunction) may be missed if older people are deemed to withdraw as a natural consequence of ageing itself. This refocusing will helpfully encourage both workers and developing practitioners to view those more individual dimensions of older people's functioning across the life course.

Chapter 9 addresses the meaning of care and what this means within a more formalised residential setting. While older people may have to engage with the challenge of transitions to a new environment, this is made less easy where there is a lack of choice and inclusion. The media depiction of the scandalous treatment of older people in care also needs to be acknowledged here and how this may frighten older people. A key feature of this chapter is that there is no natural correlation between ageing and vulnerability. This is something that is more likely to reside within the eye of the beholder as well as being reinforced within negative media reporting and unsympathetic social policy. A significant feature of this chapter is the destructive force of disempowerment. When the citizenship of the older person is removed then what is left may equate more to incarceration than care. This is addressed more fully within the section on privacy and the nature of institutions. An important feature of this chapter is a consideration of end of life care and the importance of addressing this within the continuum of life itself.

Chapter 10 seeks to formalise the relationship between evidence-based practice, research and professional development. Modern social work practice acknowledges that the research base will support new and developing practice and that this should have a positive impact in working with older people. The premise for this is that working in any area or with any specific group will not remain static over time. With an increasing awareness of the role older people have in deciding their own futures it is important that there is a secure research base to support our understanding of what these needs are. The research-practitioner is a facilitator therefore who seeks out the views and opinions of older people. This encompasses a consideration of collaborative practice where there is a mutuality of learning. This can be carried out at the personal or agency level where the end remit should be a direct emphasis on developing practice or supporting policy directives. A note of caution is to ensure that where social work itself becomes the focus of research the older person is not lost with the process. There also needs to be a dialogue on who owns research (the individual or the agency) and how these research findings are utilised. Also, the author identifies a more radical feminist perspective within the research-practitioner focus. This is to ensure that when roles and expectations are being assessed, socially constructed inequalities and power differentials are acknowledged. This is particularly the case given the significant numbers of women who live into older age.

So, in conclusion to this chapter, the author hopes that any reader will become more engaged with that totality of working with older people. It is also hoped that more practitioners view this as a significant area of practice and that there is a rejuvenation of how working with older people is valued in a modern world.

1

HISTORICAL CONTEXT, LAW AND POLICY

Learning Outcomes

This chapter looks at:

- How older people are perceived within a structural context.
- Retirement, poverty and the future of an ageing population.
- The legislative and policy context of ageing and how this may be socially constructed.
- The role of the family and carers in supporting older people's needs.
- What does the future hold for older people, particularly within the context of major financial upheavals within the UK?

Introduction

Old age and ageing is something of a moveable feast. While individual older people may seek to answer specific questions of 'who am I?', policy makers and legislative developers may take the more pragmatic response of 'what are you?' This divergence of the existential aspect (Thompson, 1992) and how older people are engaged with and represented through policy and legislation may be increasingly at odds in a society where older people are referenced as net 'takers' as opposed to 'contributors'. I intend in this chapter to address these issues through a historical perspective of old age and ageing itself and how policy and legislation is developed for older people within a postmodernist society. This will include an examination of Fook's (2003) multiplicities of 'knowing' and how there is an increasing focus on the research-practitioner and the roles of the practitioner through experiential working in knowledge and skills development. This will also include a significant emphasis on the roles that carers and service users may play and how they may influence future policy and legislative practice through the processes of inclusive and ethical social work engagement. Concurrent structural themes and a focus on the 'serenity' of older age can also be misleading within practice as this may have more to do with the perceived invisibility of older people than an acknowledgement of their real, expressed need. Rogers (1980) refers to his increasing anger in old age with more extreme ranges of emotions and sensations and that sense of the intuitive/existential/spiritual matrix that he defined as the new 'frontier of knowledge'. It does not take a huge intellectual leap to acknowledge that these finer philosophical points of existence may hold little sway when it comes to the functional aspects of how policy is derived to meet those fundamentals of existence as defined by Maslow (1987), in the current era.

World view of the older person

At the risk of stating the obvious, the longer a person lives the older he or she becomes, and the more the individual becomes identifiable as an older person. This is important in the context of the perception of ageing and its changing focus through the ages. In pre-industrial societies the choices may have been stark where an inability to contribute to food production may have had dire consequences. Similarly, cultures that prized the wisdom of age may have both venerated and supported the older person as a repository of experience and knowledge across the age of that society. These concepts of ageing are not new and in a postmodernist society practitioners need to consider the paradox of ageing as exemplified by Dewey (1939) where he suggested that as a society we value maturity but deprecate older age.

Concurrent with this is the sense that while younger people may be denigrated purely because of youth, this is a condition that they will inevitably grow *out of*. It is a period of transition (Garstka et al., 2004), whereas old age is a stage that is *grown into* and may deny older people a consideration of what is the social truth and reality of their circumstances. There is in fact no real evidence to indicate that older people make increasing demands on the welfare system or that they make unreasonable demands on that system (Bury and Holme, 1991). What there is evidence for is that older people may not be treated as equitably as other members of society when it comes to accessing services such as pensions, health care, housing and the social attitudes that prevail in relation to this group (Hughes, 1995).

Exercise

- Write down four key words or phrases that you associate with old age.
- Can you assess these words/phrases in the context of ageing and ageism?
- Where do you think your attitudes to older people and ageing come from?
- Can you contextualise these thoughts/opinions within a theoretical framework?

How do we define an ageing population?

McIntyre (1977) identifies how older age has been perceived as a 'social problem' by policy makers, where there is a tendency to frame the needs of older people within the language of dependency and crisis. As practitioners we cannot deny the reality of the increasing demographic of ageing. Almost 16% of the population is over 65 years of age and almost 2% are over the age of 85 years, with a perceived significant increase in the ageing population generally through improved medical and health care. It is all too easy to lose sight of the real discourse that should be taking place in relation to ageing and a consideration of how this is socially constructed and where older people need to be supported and encouraged to take more control over their lives (Tulle and Lynch, 2011).

It is certainly not helpful to draw any comparative analysis between chronological ageing, retirement (again constructed) and the ageing process itself where people age at different stages and with different experiences of the ageing process. This sociological consideration is important if we are to recognise that it is not the inevitability of ageing that creates poverty and dependence but poorly constructed policy that relates to insufficient benefits provision (Walker et al., 1993).

This over-focus on the 'cost' of ageing fails to address the bigger picture of the contribution that older people have made within society as well as the actual contribution they currently make both within the wider economy and caring roles within the home. Indeed, a perceived lack of resources to meet older age benefits can also be interpreted as the reduction of contributions from increased unemployment and employers who have managed to persuade employees out of the pension system (Naegele and Walker, 1999). This, coupled with the modern societal values of individualism, and even body image, can have a detrimental impact on the practitioner. He or she may subtly absorb these values and deny that sense of individualisation within a more homogeneous overview of the older population.

A world standard of care

The Care Minister Paul Bustow, supported by his Labour shadow Liz Kendall and a group of agencies including Age UK and the Royal College of Nursing, has recommended a 'dignity code' that all staff would sign up to within care settings for older people. This is to ensure that older people are not 'spoken down to or denied their dignity' (Bingham, 2012). While any policy decision that raises the profile of the older person and a wider public awareness is to be lauded, I do wonder what role existing legislation has to play? (I refer here, for example, to the Care Standards Act 2000, the guidelines published in the mid-1990s by the Department of Health Social Services Inspectorate for standards within care homes for older people and the Human Rights Act 1998.) The danger is that the waters can become somewhat muddied here by reactive policy as opposed to a reinforcement of existing strategies for older people.

?   Reflective Question   ?

- Do you consider dignity an aspect of social work ethical practice or a feature of human rights? Discuss.

Retirement

There is no logical reason why people should retire when they reach an older age, although some older people will want to devote energies to areas and interests they may feel they have missed out on during the course of their lives. Some older people may also feel that they have done their bit and it is now time to take stock of themselves, their relationships and what the future may hold. Historically, it was perceived within a capitalist ideology that older people would be effectively more expensive to maintain within the workforce. This stance had more to do with an ingrained ageism and an erroneous thinking that an older workforce would be less productive (Walker, 1992; see also Loretto, 2010). Dean (2009: 9) suggests this is not the case and more enlightened companies such as B&Q have recognised the value of employing older people 'because of their enthusiasm for the work, much lower absenteeism and their greater rapport with customers'.

Enforced redundancy

At the same time, any formal sense of enforced retirement has more to do with social constructionist thinking and is a product of a post-capitalist society where making older people redundant effectively frees up work opportunities for younger people (Phillipson, 1982). This will also have the effect of ensuring the hoped for beginnings of a new tax-paying cohort of people, who in their own time may become superfluous to economic need. The Employment Equality (Age) Regulations 2006 follow the European Directive on age discrimination and make it unlawful for an employer to treat someone less equitably because of their age. Unfortunately, the UK government decided on a 'default' position by making it mandatory for men and women to retire at 65, thus negating the possibility for older men and women to work on beyond this age except in exceptional circumstances (R on the Application of *Age UK* v. *Secretary of State for Business, Innovation and Skills* (2009) EWHC 2336).

In the meantime the state pension age for both men and women will increase to 65 years by 2020 with an additional sliding scale of increases through until approximately 2050 (Age UK, 2011a). The government identifies this as a means of ensuring there will be enough taxpayers within any age cohort to ensure there is funding and resources available to meet the needs of those more vulnerable in society. This would also take account of any potential decrease in the population up to that date.

Retirement and employment

Paradoxically, as forces impact on older people to ensure they retire, often at an age that is not of their choosing, the projection for the future is that we will need over 13 million more workers to make up for a shortfall in retirements and new and more advanced methods of working (UK Commission for Employment and Skills projections for 2007–2017). Since these figures have been published there has been a dramatic downturn in the economy generally, with over 1 million young people now out of work. The focus for the future will be the dichotomy that exists between a competitive market for employment generally that may disadvantage older people and the potential downturn in taxpayers to fund the needs of older people in the future. Interestingly research carried out by Walker and Maltby (1997) within a European perspective clearly showed that both younger and older respondents were opposed to any idea of people retiring in their fifties to make way for a younger generation. This has probably more to do with a consensus view that those who have devoted their time to both personal and career development should not be stigmatised or penalised by this application.

At the same time as this debate continues there is evidence within the UK to show that while employers may seek to retain employees past retirement age, not least to ensure transferable skills do not devolve to another competitor, there is little evidence to indicate that companies are actively recruiting new older people (McNair et al., 2007). The worrying feature for the future however is that a younger generation may blame and stigmatise an older generation for taking for granted that which they struggle to achieve.

Exercise

- What do you consider retirement to be?
- What do you consider the positive and negative aspects of retirement?
- What are the key features (either resources or support) that you think older people would value in retirement?

Poverty and older people

In his seminal work on poverty Townsend (1979) recognised that any discourse on poverty had to have a consideration of those wider inequalities that exist within society. He suggested that an emphasis on the disparity that existed between the haves and have-nots would give a better picture of the demographic of wealth distribution and structural inequality and poverty. What is clear is that, where there is a significant level of pre-existing discrimination and poverty, even small adjustments to the income of older people will have a significant impact (Smale et al., 2000). Walker (1981) suggests that since information on older people has been collected 'systematically' there has been clear evidence that older people have been one of the largest groups who habitually experience poverty. They have been identified as the group more likely to be poor than any other sector of society. The authors of the Poverty and Social Exclusion Survey (2006) have suggested that between 32% and 62% of all older people households will experience some degree of poverty (Patsios, 2006).

Indeed, Scharf (2009) identifies that an average under-claim of benefits by older people of £28 per week may not appear significant but may have the capacity to move someone from a basic subsistence level to an increased quality of life. While the Welfare Reform Act 2008 went some way to addressing this issue by identifying where direct payments could be made, this needs a reinvigoration to find those older people who are eligible, particularly within the current financial climate.

Already we see that within the benefits system there is evidence that older people are depriving themselves of the basic necessities of life to cover amenities such as food and heating. Age Concern evidenced that despite government support one in five of older people are denying themselves food to pay for heating costs (Lewis, 2010). This is reinforced through the work of the National Pensioners Convention, who have criticised the government for the poorly publicised Warm Home Discount policy to support heating costs for older vulnerable groups. This is particularly significant where the Office for National Statistics has shown that there were over 25,000 excess deaths alone in 2010. It may not be possible to state definitively that inadequate heating was the cause. However, if there is consistent evidence that older people are depriving themselves of food to pay for heating then this has to be a significant factor at the very least (Murphy, 2011).

Concurrent with this Townsend (1979) recognised that where political ideology held sway that this would potentially have a negative impact on the poverty of disadvantaged groups. He speculated that an emphasis on these policies of inequality 'tend to misrepresent the shape of the wood, and in endeavouring to account for it, fail to account for the trees' (Townsend, 1979: 45). Essentially what is being said here is that policy engages often with homogeneous and generic groups at the expense of the lived experience of the individual. While some theoreticians may postulate that older age is a time for revisiting those areas of interest or ambition that may not have been fulfilled at an earlier stage of life, de Beauvoir (1972: 499) suggests that society 'allows old people leisure only when it has removed the material means for them to enjoy it'.

National wealth

The UK has one of the highest rates of gross domestic product (GDP) in Europe and in 2008 this was measured at approximately £24,000. As of March 2012 the UK has the seventh most buoyant economy in the world. At the same time it has one of the highest rates of older age poverty. Research (Pensions Commission, 2005; Zaidi, 2006) indicates that of the 25 European Union countries the UK has the sixth highest rate of potential poverty among older people. This is particularly the case among older women who may not have accrued enough pension rights over the course of their working lifetime and who may also have a higher life expectancy, thus ensuring they will live in poverty for longer. The issue then becomes not one of providing for subsistence living but the more philosophical aspect of what equality is and what it confers to a complete and inclusive society.

In the same way that children can grow out of childhood they may also grow out of poverty through employment and education opportunities. The same is not true of older people. They may enter old age with a reduced income and it is extremely unlikely that these circumstances will improve over the course of that older age (Scharf, 2009). Essentially, this is not specifically an issue just about the range of benefits and the rather piecemeal approach to making up inadequate resources with top-up benefits. This is more related to the wider concept of social justice and whether, in one of the wealthiest countries in the world, we can countenance the idea that older people may be living in poverty.

Background to Poverty

Given that Britain is a very rich country, it has a poor record compared to other developed western countries in providing adequate pensions for older people and the capacity to address poverty among this demographic. If this is a consistent theme across all governments then this is evidence of a more *systemic* failure. The historical background is grounded within several factors, not least of which is a tacit under-standing of the inevitability of reduced resources and poverty in older age (Walker, 1990). This tends to reinforce that notional sense that only those involved in the means of production are to be valued within society, whereas the sagacity of experi-ence has little or no market value. This limited understanding of what is meant by 'productivity' does not take account of those other areas of support and expertise that older people can provide: kinship care, volunteering and support for need within their local communities. At the same time there is a significant class-base to older people poverty, where those with adequate resources can have a greater range of choices as to where and (just as importantly) how they live. Those without these resources may find themselves becoming increasingly impoverished, marginalised and ghettoised (Phillipson, 1993; Phillipson, 2007).

Pension inadequacy

So why are pension incomes often so inadequate? The main factor here is not the amount that is spent on overall benefits within any fiscal year. This tends to result in a points scoring exercise of statistical one-upmanship where the actual need of older people may be minimised or lost altogether. The main area of concern is where the link between older age pensions and earnings was broken in the 1980s and instead index-linked to prices. For instance, in 2000 the linkage between the state pension and the Retail Price Index (RPI) resulted in a 75 pence a week pension increase and this triggered a significant backlash from politicians and those representing the inter-ests of older people (Cann, 2009).

When there was an increase in wages over this period (1980s) with a reduction in overall prices then it was not surprising that the overall value of the state pension fell and continues to do so at the present time where there have been significant increases in energy and food prices. The nettle that ultimately has to be grasped is one where there is an acceptance that the state pension is set too low and that this needs to be addressed. As I write, and as I approach older age myself, I see the issue more clearly as one of a greater distribution of wealth, a greater percentage of the gross national product (GNP) set aside for pension benefits and ultimately an increase in taxation. No one who is not politically naïve would see this as a potential vote winner for incumbent governments now and in the future. The current debate on capping the payments that older people should provide for their care costs is a starting point for debate. This figure started out at £20,000 but is now expected to rise to £75,000 within the current fiscal year. A more questioning approach might suggest this is a 'double-whammy' where the people who are the poorest and have paid the most over a lifetime are being asked to stump up again.

Whatever the outcome of a more radical approach to pension provision in the future, the demographics indicate that by the year 2015 approximately 22% of the population will be of pensionable age (OPCS, 1991).

Again, while ageing itself is something of a moveable feast, the pension age is somewhat the same. Future ideology may have to contend with a complex range of issues, from an extended retirement age and the availability of employment in a declining economy to how the general morbidity of health among older people will develop in the longer term.

Exercise

- What do you spend your money on as opposed to what you actually need to spend your money on?
- What are the fundamentals of everyday living and how much of your income do you spend on this?
- What proportion of income do older people spend on food and heating and why are these costs so significant in older age?

The politics of ageing in the UK

The welfare state in the UK was forged in the aftermath of the Second World War and included the Beveridge Report (1942) with its commitment to the alleviation of want, disease, idleness, squalor and ignorance. The report sought to protect some of the most vulnerable groups in society (widows, those who had become ill or unemployed) from poverty. The report recommended that a contributory social security system be adopted and this would involve contributions from workers, employers and the state (Hill, 2003). This was predicated on the understanding that there would be full employment within the UK with an attendant rate of contributions to the national social security pot to meet payments to these identified groups in the future.

Interestingly, when Beveridge (1942) formulated these benefits they were designed to meet a 'subsistence' level of living without having to resort to supplementary means-testing to top up any existing benefits. Unfortunately, this has largely not been achieved because of the implications for government expenditure and the potential impact on lower wages within the UK. A knock-on effect of this is the difficulties some older people have in accessing benefits they are entitled to and monies that remain unclaimed within any fiscal year. It is estimated that between 30% and 40% of older people of pension age fail to claim their Pension Credit. Overall it is estimated that over £5 billion may go unclaimed during each year of means-tested benefits (i.e. benefits that are set aside based on the approximate known number of older people who would be expected to claim identified benefits) (Department for Work and Pensions, 2008a).

The whole focus of those inequalities that exist within ageing can be difficult to address. Some may interpret these inequalities as self-inflicted and related to a perceived fecklessness or lack of preparedness of older people for their future. Others will clearly focus this within an understanding of structurally oppressive considerations. Walker (2009: 141) attempts to define the nature of these inequalities as those 'that either transgress a distributional notion of social justice or damage the health and well-being of those at the bottom of the stratification hierarchy'. He postulates that there are a significant number of pre-existing determinants ranging from childhood to middle age that can have a direct and detrimental impact on an older person. Key areas of significance within an individual's mid-life are employment history, marital status, gender, ethnicity and health history. These can have the effect of contributing to the means of provision for a financially secure old age with access to good health and services or the alternative of poverty and a more limited capacity for health and access to those services. Again it is important that there is not any natural correlation of ageing and health as significant numbers of older people experience good health or at least health needs that are not any more demanding than any other sector of the community. Grenier (2007) suggests that a consideration of older people's needs based on a purely biomedical approach with a focus on infirmity and necessity will have the effect of undermining the 'autonomy' of older people and limit their access to health services and other resources. A significant irony is the advent of the National Health Service and Community Care Act 1990 with its emphasis on community-based services and, more importantly, a complete rejection of any form of care deemed to be institutional. The subsequent lack of support and accommodation for older people within hospital settings and the closure of local authority care homes led to an explosion within private care provision and the current debate on how care needs will be paid for in the future (Dalley, 2000).

? Reflective Questions ?

- Why are older people the only significant group of people within society who are asked to pay for their own care?
- Does this rule apply to children or pregnant mothers?

State pensions

The National Insurance Act 1946 introduced a state pension scheme funded by national insurance contributions that guaranteed a flat rate and below subsistence level pension for those on lower incomes. This allowed (in principle) for employees to make additional contributions to be accrued towards a final pension figure. This was at a time when men were the main earners within families and there was little acknowledgement of the role that women played either within the home or within often part-time and low paid work within pension provision (Ginn and Arber, 1999). There is something of the apocalyptic in the language frequently used to refer to the demographics of the ageing population and how this will be economically sustainable in the future. The World Bank and the International Monetary Fund (IMF) support this view, but as Cunningham (2006) so eloquently posits these agencies could hardly be described as 'politically neutral' within this debate. This is particularly where the promulgation of free market economics is deemed to be the saviour of pension provision for the future. The irony of this view will doubtless not be lost on those who are at the bitter end of current pension and service provision cuts as a result of an out of control marketplace overly focused on a worldwide inflated (although currently crashing) property market. Vincent (2003) goes further by suggesting that there is a deliberate attempt to 'demoralise' the public as to the sustainability of future state pension provision to enhance the role of the private sector.

Private pensions

Wolff (2011) speculates that individuals can never be sure what in fact they are purchasing in relation to private pensions. Pensions may be mis-sold due to commission considerations and the purchaser may not even be sure that the pension vendor will still be in business when the time for payment comes. Certainly by the 1990s a three-tier system of pensions had evolved where those with good public sector pensions to top up the state pensions were doing quite well financially. Those on lower pensions, through low paid or interrupted work and child care considerations, would need to access means-tested benefits as it is for those in the middle income bracket with modest and potentially declining private pensions. The debate was and is, how to create a balance between meeting the needs of an increasing number of poor older people and how to ensure that a reasonable level of pensions can be maintained in the future (Hill, 1997).

What does the future hold? Interestingly, Age UK has recently had a cool response towards the idea of an Older Person's Commissioner for England on the premise that older people need to start to represent their own views and become their own force for change (Brindle, 2012). There is still some way to go here and Age UK's charity chief, Michelle Mitchell, suggests that she does not foresee an 'army of older people' taking to the streets in the near future. Whatever the outcome of this, it will be less clear to policy makers and to the general public that a high level of scaremongering in relation to the ageing population will inevitably have disadvantageous repercussions for older people. Research by Manton et al. (1995) evidences that there may be a shorter period of what is referred to as 'compression of morbidity' in the very old. This compression means that older people may experience life changing illness or disruption over a shorter period of time because of increases in health awareness and care. However, this 'morbidity' may be exacerbated by a range of interrelated aspects of health where poor physical and mental health may be heightened by poor access to support services and social isolation (Pilgrim, 2007).

World view of ageing

There is a direct correlation between poor mental health and the capacity for older individuals to maintain emotional relationships with others.

This means effectively that very old people are ill and have greater care needs for a shorter period when they are very old and consequently could/would not be a dramatic drain on any country with high levels of taxpayers and a working population. Perhaps the secret is a more proactive response to ageing and a reiteration to the general public that they are not being unfairly disadvantaged through taxation (or otherwise) but they are in fact investing in an inevitable future. Perhaps this is a consequence of a more individualistic culture and a more general fear of the ageing process itself.

Legislative and policy context in a changing world

I have often asked social work students what their thoughts are in relation to specific legislation for older people (i.e. the use of 'older people' within specific pieces of legislation) as opposed to the more generic 'adult'. Students often speculate that there should be as this would identify very specific areas of age and ageism directed at this cohort and provide added protection and support. It can often be frustrating for developing practitioners to consider that an excess of legislation will not of itself confer protection. Conversely, it may draw additional attention to a group who have committed no act other than accumulate years and buy into that wider ageist debate where age is expected to confer frailty with a concomitant inability to contribute to society (Grenier, 2007; Walker, 2009).

So what is the legislative context of support for older people? The background to any legislative or policy context has to include a consideration of ethics and human rights and how this relates to value-driven social work practice. There also needs to be an awareness of what 'capacity' means, particularly within the framework of mental health. If an older person has capacity and refuses assistance then there may be a limited range of opportunities to engage in this person's life. Conversely, where there is a lack of capacity then it is unethical to seek the consent of that person for any intervention (Naylor, 2010). The issue of capacity is extremely important when there are adult protection considerations and particularly where research shows that approximately 4% of older people over the age of 66 are abused or neglected every year. The highest number of abused older people is among women, who may live longer, have poorer mental health and be incapacitated for longer (O'Keeffe et al., 2007). This level of abuse (possibly underreported) has to be viewed within the experience of older people generally, who may not be used to interference from outside agencies and who may have retained a fierce independence throughout their lives.

The emphasis therefore will be to ensure that practitioners have a minimal and least restrictive approach to clients' lives with a concurrent respect for the individualism and privacy of the older person (see the Data Protection Act 1998). On a practitioner basis this will be underpinned and defined by the British Association of Social Workers (BASW) Code of Ethics (Mantell and Scragg, 2009). Related legislation such as the Human Rights Act 1998 and the Disability Discrimination Act 2005 will also have a considerable impact when considering the needs of vulnerable older people. The Human Rights Act 1998 is under considerable strain at the moment from politicians who feel that it confers too many 'rights' on some individuals, although this is generally couched in the language of the worst case scenario. Unlike many other aspects of social work practice human rights are absolute and the clue to this is in the wording!

There is no specific legislation in place within England and Wales to support investigations into adult abuse or exploitation and a range of related legislation will have to be considered. In Scotland, the Adults with Incapacity (Scotland) Act 2000 is widely considered to need a greater emphasis on 'capacity' as opposed to 'incapacity' as this relates more closely to modern considerations of the personalisation agenda where older people themselves are the focus of attention (Social Care Institute for Excellence, 2010).

The National Health Service and Community Care Act 1990 s.47 provides for practitioners to carry out an assessment of older people's needs, where the commissioning services will put in place support services to ensure that older people are free from abuse and abusive environments. At the same time there is the capacity for compulsory removal from home under the National Assistance Act 1948 s.47 for anyone who is suffering from chronic disease, is incapacitated or living in an insanitary environment. Tellingly, the Act allows for the removal of an older person to a hospital or care setting in the event he/she is not receiving adequate care within the home. The problem here is where the older person who is being abused may be the owner of the home and where the victim effectively becomes penalised. In Scotland the Adult Support and Protection (Scotland) Act 2007 allows for the removal of the perpetrator and, as far as possible, for the older person to maintain their independence within their own home.

Exercise

- Can you identify the positive aspects of a care setting for older people?
- What are some of the potential flaws in community-based services in meeting the needs of older people?

There is an ongoing debate throughout the UK on the rights of those with a mental illness. The same governing principles of the 'least restrictive' apply when interacting with the lives of older people with a mental illness. The Mental Capacity Act 2005 and the Mental Health Act 2007 provide the statutory basis for ensuring that the voice of those with a mental illness is heard. There is some way to go here as there is still considerable stigma associated with mental illness (Larkin, 2009).

While it is inevitable that people will grow older there is no associative linkage with mental illness other than dementia, and practitioners have to consider the very real stressors that will prevail with older people who may already be struggling with poor health and end of life considerations. For those who may spend their final days within a care setting, the Care Standards Act (CSA) 2000 set the standards for social work training as well as establishing the Commission for Social Care Inspection (CSCI; now the Care Quality Commission) to register and monitor social care services and specified the National Minimum Standards for care homes. The CSA 2000 s.80 also allows for the Protection of Vulnerable Adults List (POVA) to ensure that vulnerable older people are protected from staff who have been dismissed for misconduct.

The Safeguarding Vulnerable Groups Act 2006 provides a direct contact register for those who have been deemed a risk to children and vulnerable adults and is accessible to those seeking to check on the status of potential employees. As can be seen there is considerable legislation in place in relation to vulnerable adults. It is within this focus that we should consider the current debate on providing 'dignity' for older people and how this appears to have become lost within pre-existing legislation and policy.

The Equality Act 2010 came into force in October of that year and is currently superseding all anti-discriminatory legislation within the UK. The law sets out clearly the individual characteristics that are protected as well as the behaviour that is deemed unlawful. The key areas that are protected are age, disability, gender reassignment, marriage and civil partnership, pregnancy and maternity, race, religion and belief, sex and sexual orientation. Students would do well to consider the latter two areas here and the fact they are *not* the same thing. More importantly, there is clear provision within the 2010 Act for service users. This encompasses rights of membership, political activity, transport, reasonable adjustments, removing barriers and how to counter discrimination generally. The Act also provides guidance on rights for employers, workers, service providers as well as guidance on equal pay. The focus here is on the new Codes of Practice for the Equality Act 2010 which have taken over the former Equality Commission's role, although some of the previous documentation will still be useful in the context of historical perspective as well as examples of practice. The Equality Act 2010 can be accessed in its entirety on the Home Office website (www.homeoffice.gov.uk/equalities/equality-act).

There is also a significant range of related and relevant policies in relation to the protection and support of older adults. While not definitive, you can find a more comprehensive list within the Home Office website and Her Majesty's Stationery Office website with its specific remit for publishing all UK-wide legislation (www.tso.co.uk). For those students working and studying in Scotland, relevant documents can be found on the Scottish government's site (www.scotland.gov.uk/publications).

A Range of Legislation and Policy

Carers (Recognition and Services) Act 1995

Carers Strategy (Caring about Carers) 1999

No Secrets: Guidance on Developing and Implementing Multi-agency Protection of Vulnerable Adults (Department of Health, 2000)

In Safe Hands (National Assembly for Wales, 2000)

Care Homes Regulation 2001 Reg 37

Carers (Equal Opportunities) Act 2004

Safeguarding Adults (2005)

Carers at the Heart of 21st Century Families and Communities (Department of Health, 2008)

Equality Act 2010

Care Quality Commission (CQC) (www.cqc.org.uk) regulates all health and adult social care services in England. It also addresses the concerns and the protection of anyone detained under the Mental Health Act 2007. The following documents can be accessed on the CQC website: Community Mental Health Survey 2012 and the Mental Health Act Annual Report 2011–2012.

Changing role of the family

While there may be an emphasis within current literature on the difficulties that older people experience in straightened times, there are positive aspects to ageing. There is an increasing reintegration of older people within the family unit throughout the UK as they provide a kinship caring role for grandchildren or partners (Hothersall, 2006). There is also the issue of reciprocity where families are more likely to reinvest in the care of older people who have themselves invested in the support of the family unit over the years.

However only 5% of older people live with a family member throughout the UK and the advent of community care has meant that there is a greater likelihood that older people will stay within their own owner-occupied tenancies or care settings (Patsios, 2006). This has to be balanced by the awareness that there may be a degree of confusion within local authorities of the roles that family, professional and volunteers may play within support services for older people as resources diminish. An inevitable consequence of the devolution of families and sole occupancy is that there will be a greater likelihood of isolation for older people. Riddell (2007) suggests that not all older people will grow old 'gracefully' and a vulnerable older person, isolated from the cohesion of friends and support services, may legitimately assume that they have therefore become 'disgraceful' with all the connotations of stigma and labelling that that may entail. The Better Life (O'Hara, 2012) initiative by the Joseph Rowntree Foundation (JRF) set up a five-year project in 2009 to assess the needs and raise the public profile of older adults with a range of high support needs. This group of older people has the added disadvantage of being older and with complex care and support needs that are exacerbated by a lack of resources.

For those older people who are cared for at home the primary carers tend to be children or partners and this raises complex issues of how older people themselves will cope in the future when providing care and support for equally old or older family members (Social Exclusion Unit, 2005).

Role of carers and caring

It is likely that in the future the family may not be the mainstay of meeting the needs of older people. There may be a dual focus here of families fracturing in a geographical sense in the pursuit of employment in an uncertain world. Families can also become disengaged through divorce where the children may feel less obligation to look after a parent in older age (Vincent et al., 2006). At the same time there has to be an awareness of the considerable stress families may be put under when coping with financial pressure and the potential for psychological trauma when coping with adverse financial and living conditions. Research by Lyonette and Yardley (2003) indicate that there are a variety of reasons why carers take on this role: a sense of obligation; the perceived disapproval of others if carers do not take on this role; and a means of reiterating a profoundly held sense of personal duty.

Resourcing care

It is clear that the value placed on meeting the needs of disadvantaged groups is generally evidenced by the amount of resource spending devoted to that particular group of people. Indeed, as practitioners, we could speculate that in a modern age the degree of funding is commensurate with the accord individuals and groups are afforded in society. Cunningham and Cunningham (2012) suggest that even where older people access residential care the focus is pre-eminently on meeting care needs. Even within care packages at home, the same thinking tends to apply rather than supporting and advocating for that older person to have as full a participation within the wider community as possible. This over-focus on care needs has the potential for what Martin-Matthews (2000) refers to as an 'apocalyptic' view of future care. This is more likely to occur because of the changing demographics of the family and the speculation that where this is the case there will not be a family member available or willing to provide this care.

Lloyd (2009) suggests that approximately 10% of people over 50 were providing some form of care for a parent, sibling or partner in 2004. The greatest number of these providers were women and this level of care increased over time, particularly when it related to spousal care. Indeed, Finch and Groves (1980) put the case clearly and in a less ambiguous way when they stated that care in the community effectively means care within the family, and family care generally means care by female members of the family. This raises significant issues in relation to gender neutrality when assessing what is equitable in the expectation of who provides future care for older people.

> Advice for Carers- A practical guide, Age UK – Improving Later Life, July 2011.

Future directions in policy for older people

It is becoming increasingly difficult to assess the future role of policy in meeting the needs of older people. The economic downturn is likely to increase stressors within families and the nature of the support these families may be able to afford to older people in the future. What is clear is that a personalisation agenda, properly followed through, is welcomed by older people as is any initiative that gives a voice to their needs and concerns. This can extend to the Partnership of Older People Project (POPP) which ran in 29 local authorities within England from 2006 to 2009. The purpose was to bring together local groups to address issues of concern such as isolation, healthy living and delayed discharge among the older population and was very much a feature of the personalisation agenda. The findings indicate that poverty and a lack of awareness of support services were the two most important aspects of older people's lives (Windle et al., 2010).

Also, research into the sexuality of older people (Musingarimi, 2008; Ward et al., 2008) indicates that this may be a serious area for consideration, particularly at a time when there are increasing attempts to address sexual identities. Cronin (2006) identifies that 'heteronormative assumptions' are the focus of most debate on sexuality and older people and may leave a significant number of older people significantly disadvantaged through loneliness and isolation. Groups such as the Gay Greys (Age Concern, 2008) and the Grey Wolves draw wider attention to unacknowledged needs – although the vulpine analogy will not be lost on those who struggle with the accusations that they have taken more than their fair share as part of the baby boomer generation!

What is certain is that current radical changes in health and social care are predicated on resources that are already too limited to meet the identified demographic need (Wanless, 2006). Increasing awareness of personalisation issues and access to benefits and services will place further pressure on existing resources that are proposed to meet longer-term needs. There is only so far anything can be stretched before it ultimately snaps. The more that policy makers assert that it is the reorganisation of services that is key to meeting future needs the more likely it is that the central focus of poor resourcing will be missed.

Lymbery (2010) refers to the political rhetoric of dismissing previous policy for the care and support of older people. There is then something of that sense of *year zero* in formulating new policy with a concurrent lack of continuity from the past. Saying is not doing and constant formulating of new policy directives may say more about meeting political ideology than meeting the needs of older people. While there is still the ongoing debate on whether policy is being developed to meet the needs of citizens (Clarke et al., 2007) (with all the rights associated with this) or consumers of services, it is clear there is still some way to go.

Essentially, as long as older people are at the end of the queue for services and resources there is unlikely to be a consensus opinion on how the needs of older people will be met in the future. The Health and Social Care Act 2012 currently wending its inexorable way through parliament is a case point. While the chairman of the British Medical Association refers to the potential here for 'fragmentation of health care', the Bill has other anomalies that may mitigate against the future well-being of older people: a lack of free personal care for older people within the proposed legislation as currently exists in Scotland and an abolition of patient watchdogs through the Community Health Council (CHC). The *Guardian* editorial of 5 March 2012 reiterates the ongoing fears of vulnerable groups within a market economy when cooperation and collective practice is a proven means of meeting their needs. In conclusion, and somewhat worryingly, the editorial suggests the Bill 'continues to place an unbalanced duty on the regulator to stamp out anti-competitive practices, but not practices which undercut co-operation'.

Conclusion

Any conclusion has to address a range of issues related to what has worked with older people in the past and an awareness of the impact of ideologies as opposed to the identified wishes of older people. These ideologies deny the rights of older people over time within the maelstrom of political divide. It is therefore clear that more of an all-party approach is required with something of the nature of social working itself with its emphasis on value-driven practice. While older people themselves should be allowed to identify what it is they want for a secure and fulfilling older age. I fear within the divide that currently exists between a more neoliberal focus and the pragmatism of a cradle to grave approach that there is unlikely to be this consensus. If there is one significant feature of older people and the changing demographic of ageing, it is that older people will inevitably wield more power in the future through the ballot box. An increasingly educated population may be less inclined to 'make do and mend' in the same way that previous generations have accepted.

Recommended Reading

Cunningham, J. and Cunningham, S. (2012) *Social Policy and Social Work: An Introduction*, Transforming Social Work Practice series. London: Sage/Learning Matters. Very good sections on autonomy and the social policy of ageing.

Hill, M. (2003) *Understanding Social Policy* (7th ed.). Oxford: Blackwell. A scholarly text that covers all the relevant areas of policy from health, social security and employment.

Johns, R. (ed.) (2011) *Social Work, Social Policy and Older People: Thinking Through Social Work*. Exeter: Learning Matters. A very concise historical account of the role of policy in meeting the needs of older people with a specific focus on why social workers need to understand social policy.

Larkin, M. (2009) *Vulnerable Groups in Health and Social Care*. London: Sage. Includes a very readable and informative chapter on 'older people'.

2

VALUES AND ETHICS

> ## Learning Outcomes
>
> This chapter looks at:
>
> - Ethics and values and the perception of older people and ageing generally.
> - Moral philosophy and what we may consider and know about the 'rightness' of actions.
> - Professionalism and the understanding and role of social work.
> - Structural oppression and ageism and how cultural and societal norms influence and reinforce discriminatory practice.
> - Cultural diversity and perceptions of difference and deviance.
> - Sexuality and gender and myths of ageing, experience, needs and rights.

Introduction

The purpose of this chapter is to explore a consideration of ethics and values as part of that inclusive continuum of effective social work understanding. There is a focus here on the differences between ethics and values and how these may be viewed (Beckett and Maynard, 2005; Hugman, 2005; Reamer, 2006). This will extend into the more fundamental aspect of how social workers perceive the 'rightness' of their actions from a moral philosophy perspective, and how they can meet needs (Bytheway, 1995, 1997; Cann and Dean, 2009) at a time of increasing demands on resources. Implicit within the nature of ethical practice is an understanding of the nature of professionalism itself (Lishman, 2009), and how this relates to interprofessional working with that emphasis on collaboration and inclusive practice (McLean, 2007; Ovretveit et al., 1997). In an increasingly diverse and multicultural society there is an onus on practitioners to engage at a meaningful level with the lived and shared experience of groups who may identify with different cultural norms (Rowson, 2006) that may not be valued by the wider society. This cultural and structural aspect of potential discrimination may also extend to a more personalised sense of individual sexuality (Biltgard, 2000; Bywater and Jones, 2007; Pugh, 2005), and how this is viewed by external agencies.

Ethics and values

While ethics may relate to that sense of what is moral and good in the world this may prove problematic within the personal, cultural and structural (PCS) aspects of how and by whom this is defined. The wider context of ethics resides within a commitment to moral and global issues of human rights and social justice (Statham and Kearney, 2007). Ethics can also be defined as *morals* in respect of what is acceptable within society and resides within the realms of moral philosophy with its emphasis on what is *good* and what is *right* and consequently what can be characterised as 'unprofessional' within the wider panoply of professional practice. Within the focus of social work practice the terms 'ethical' and 'moral' are often used interchangeably although for the purpose of this section, I will refer to ethics throughout.

In essence, ethical awareness relates to that sense of the uniqueness of all persons irrespective of their gender, disability, sexual orientation, ethnicity and age. It is all too easy to become inured to the sense of loss and physical and emotional pain of disadvantaged groups purely because they may be perceived as having the greater part of their lives behind them. In an age when image may hold more sway than substance and where there are increasing pressures on people to appear youthful, then this again may mitigate against old age itself. Old people may be characterised as a group whose bodies are perceived as dysfunctional and whose physicality may be considered as out of place with modern times and its fascination with youth and agelessness (Williams and Bendelow, 1998).

A true understanding of ethics is that greater awareness of the specific and individual needs that older people have in the same way as a younger person or, just as importantly, social work practitioners themselves (Older People Steering Group, 2004). It is both a truism and philosophical imperative for social work practitioners to address inequitable approaches to and with older people which are at the heart of discrimination itself and the ethical and value dimensions of working effectively with this group of individuals (Banks, 2006).

CASE STUDY

Angela Brown is 72 has been referred to the social work department as she has been charged with causing a disturbance while intoxicated through drink. She comes from a travelling family and has found it difficult to manage a settled existence after spending most of her life on the road. She presents as very withdrawn and appears to have difficulty in expressing herself or to offer up any explanation for her behaviour. As a social worker you are finding it increasingly difficult to engage with Angela and her apparent unwillingness to take part in any support activities. You are at something of a loss and feel that you may not have the skills or understanding to work with this very challenging case.

Reflective Questions

- What impact may Angela's previous lifestyle have on her capacity for coping now?
- How might you gain information and knowledge that could support your work with Angela?
- What role may discrimination play in the life of Angela?
- Where would you go for support to increase your confidence and skills in working with Angela?

Note

I hope you can see here that this image of Angela may buy into a negative stereotype of travellers themselves and, more importantly, the role that structural oppression can play in the lives of those who are already disadvantaged. Can you also define here how a consideration of the role of the PCS model (Thompson, 2006) could be evaluated within the lived experience of Angela's life?

Values

The definition of 'values' tends to focus more on that set of issues and practice skills that social workers should refer to as the underpinning ethos in meeting those more universal ethical and moral aspects of professional practice (Beckett and Maynard, 2005; Hugman, 2005; Hugman and Smith, 1995). Social work itself is one of the most value-based occupations in terms of its reflection on practice, attention to the rights of individuals and a facility for critically evaluating the structural roles of oppression and discriminatory practice (Payne, 2006b). In terms of practice, social work ranks with medicine as one of the most value aware professions. It is what defines the core of who we are and how we address the needs of vulnerable clients and all citizens. Intrinsic to our understanding of values is that they are not an 'add on' during working practice but a fundamental core of our human understanding; nor is it possible to completely disaggregate our personal values from our decision-making processes (Reamer, 2006).

Individual beliefs and cultural awareness

Strongly held personal belief systems may accord with who an individual is but if they are used as a focus to discriminate against difference and the individual capacity of older people to live their lives in the way they choose then they may reinforce discriminatory practice rather than liberate. This may be the case where a social worker has very strong religious or political views which supersede the more traditional and radical value base of social work practice. (Milner and O'Byrne, 2009; Parker and Bradley, 2010). This is particularly the case where practice is culturally blind to the individual needs of service users. This has the effect of homogenising a specific culture into a series of accepted and acceptable norms, frequently based on a white ethnocentric understanding (Parrott, 2010). Ironically, this homogenising of culture relates closely to the way older people may also be perceived.

The context of values may have changed over the years from those more traditional values of Biestek (1961) to accommodate a wider context of the holistic aspects of clients' lives within a more emancipatory focus. These liberating aspects may include wider themes of respect, protection, social justice and the inclusive aspect of a rights-based approach to meeting the individual needs of the older person (Dominelli, 2003). This social justice has as its benchmark the understanding that resources should be allocated on a basis of need rather than merit. This more emancipatory understanding may be increasingly at odds with an understanding of the nature of older people, individuality and capitalism itself (Pease and Fook, 1999).

It is incumbent upon developing practitioners to assess how these rights and risks can be assessed within a framework of cultural diversity where the social work professional, and social services generally, may not be the first point of support contact for carers and family members.

Existential understanding

A philosophical insight into what it means to be a human being and a person is a starting point for any discussion on ethics and values. This ultimately has to be considered in the context of the lived reality of older people's life experiences. The coming together of those philosophical debates on existence should lead to a greater awareness of who we are as practitioners and a fundamental understanding of how all individuals interact with their environment and impact upon it. Whatever the personal experiences of older people, an ethical and value-driven understanding should encourage workers to consider the wider paradigm that we are all bonded by the suffering of others. This understanding is the central focus of our appreciation of value-driven social work and our understanding of the importance of self-determination, human rights, welfare rights and privacy (see Articles 8 and 14 of the European Convention of Human Rights enshrined within the Human Rights Act 1998 with their emphasis on privacy and the right to family life and the right not be discriminated against).

One of the most significant writers on social work values was the American, Felix Biestek (1961), who promulgated seven principles that should be considered when working with clients within the voluntary engagement of professional practice:

- Individualisation
- Purposeful expression of feelings
- Controlled emotional involvement
- Acceptance
- Non-judgemental attitude
- User self-determination
- Confidentiality (Biestek, 1961).

All of these facets may impact on social work with older people where a client's wishes (inclusion) and need for self-fulfilment may be at odds with service provision (needs led versus resource driven) and the knowledge, understanding and skills of the social work practitioner. The ethical dimension of the role of practitioners here is critical in addressing whether they are agents of support or agents of state control.

Exercise

- You might like to consider these more traditional and emancipatory values and write down a list of how these relate to your experiences of knowing or working with older people. Concentrate on the uniqueness of the individuals and the significant events in their lives that have formed them at a social and psychological level.

Structural influence

Inherent to this consideration of social work values is the political structure within which they are applied. This cannot be seen exclusively in the context of absolutism given the very differing political ideologies that exist throughout the world. Society may have a very different idea about how individuals and families should lead their lives as opposed to people who may be more concerned with rights of self-determination (Reamer, 2006).

Within Britain today the main unit of support is still the family. With the inception of the recent coalition government there has been a refocusing on the family as an institution. There is an expectation that it is imbued with the characteristics of self-help and self-support. But these may not be sufficient to address the wider needs of older people at a time of economic decline when there is additional pressure on the family unit (Barrett and McIntosh, 1994). It is important, therefore, that students and practitioners are able to differentiate between political ideology and the responsibility of a caring society to meet its obligations. Again this relates to social justice as opposed to the minutiae of political ideology.

Social construct of ageing

This is further compounded by that social construction of ageing and later life where we may perceive ageing within a more static and unchanging focus. This potentially negates an historical realisation that old age and ageing is constructed through social and cultural processes (Tulle and Lynch, 2011).

Increasingly the family may be seen as both the repository of affectional bonds but also the environment where dysfunction and abuse may occur. Older people may be increasingly isolated from friends, family and the wider community as a result of increasing stress within families, particularly at a time of economic recession. This may be exacerbated if there is a commensurate decline in physical and mental health and a concurrent impact on the coping capacity, stress and financial capabilities of the wider family unit.

Jill Franklin is 79 and lives in a very run-down flat in the centre of town. She lives on a basic state pension and has never married and mainly worked in low paid and low status employment over the course of her working life. Jill suffers from recurring chest infections because of the damp conditions in her flat and has been hospitalised with double pneumonia. A social worker has been assigned to her case to assess her care needs for the future, although Jill is insisting that she is 'perfectly able to look after myself'. The social worker feels that Jill would be much better off in a care setting and has suggested this to Jill who is horrified by the suggestion and states that 'care homes are for old people'.

?   Reflective Questions   ?

- Can you identify any instances here where personal values could conflict with ethical social work practice?
- Do you think that Jill's gender may have a bearing here on how she is being assessed and if so, how?
- What do you think are the range of social work skills required within a value-based and ethical consideration of Jill's case?
- Can you identify practice here that may be unethical?

Values, ethics and moral philosophy

What is right and what is wrong has been something of a negotiable issue across the centuries. What is considered reasonable behaviour nowadays such as co-habitation outside marriage and having children through this relationship would have been considered morally reprehensible a century ago. Indeed, it is the nature of humanity itself and the 'rightness' of actions that we need to consider here in relation to how we engage with vulnerable clients of whom older people may be a part.

While there are undoubtedly deeply held political and religious belief systems that influence how people behave in relation to others, through a preordained set of rules or principles, we have to consider a wider philosophical aspect of morality. This working ethic of partnership with older people also has a philosophical dimension. Hugman (2005) defines partnership as that democratic role service users and carers have in determining the nature of what that partnership should be.

I propose here to briefly address two philosophical theories: the deontological and utilitarian position. This should encourage students and practitioners to consider even everyday events within a philosophical framework as a means of encouraging understanding and human rights.

Deontological approach

Deontological thinking is a development of the work of the German philosopher Immanuel Kant with its progenitor in the Greek word for 'duty' and already this should give you some idea of the focus of this approach (Beckett and Maynard, 2005). It postulates that there are moral absolutes (something we must do) in the context of how we address the needs of others, such as an appreciation of the uniqueness of all persons purely because they are persons (Crisp, 1995; Davis, 2000).

Intrinsic within this thinking is that all persons are worthy of respect regardless of the role they may be perceived to have within society.

Utilitarianism

The utilitarian position, associated with both Jeremy Bentham in the eighteenth century and the nineteenth-century philosopher John Stuart Mill ([1861] 1998), postulates that rather than viewing an action as right or wrong it should be viewed more in the context of the impact it has on the wider population. In effect, can an action that mitigates against the needs of an individual but meets the wider need for the majority of the population be considered as moral (Clarke, 2006)? This is referred to as a *consequentialist* approach where the consequences of actions have to considered in the moral context of the action itself. It is 'a moral doctrine that the right action in any situation is the one that will produce the best overall outcome, as judged from an impersonal standpoint which gives equal weight to the interests of everyone' (Scheffler, 1988: 1).

The question for social work practitioners is how can we evaluate the 'rightness' of our actions beyond what we may perceive to be intrinsically right, i.e. from a moral philosophy perspective (Cohen, 2003)? If we take as the premise for effective practice that all clients are worthy of respect because they are persons, then how do we understand decision making that may have a negative impact on vulnerable clients (Hugman, 2005)?

You are a social worker in a care home for older people. The local authority has suggested that there are monies available to redecorate the home with a particular emphasis on creating en-suite bedrooms. This will have the effect of increasing the capacity for clients to access bathrooms but would cut down on the number of bedrooms within the care home. The net result is that some clients who have lived in the home for many years will be encouraged to move out against their wishes.

CASE STUDY

? Reflective Questions ?

- How would your consider your knowledge of the values and ethics of this situation within practice?
- How could you define this issue within a deontological and utilitarian context?

Values and ethics in practice

This is quite a complex area that needs an evaluation of the personal and professional aspects of ethics and values in practice. Our personal values may be distinct to ourselves and have developed over a lifetime but may be at odds with what is considered as professional practice. This is where the philosophical aspect and reflective practice (Schon, 1987) should converge to hopefully make for a better level of understanding and practice generally.

What is a professional?

A professional is someone who belongs to an occupation that is underpinned by a higher education focus, has a range of esoteric knowledge (generally known to the profession and not the wider public) and has a set of governance of its activities. The regulatory body for social work and social care in England, the General Social Care Council (www.gscc.org.uk/about.htm) (in Scotland the Scottish Social Services Council; www.sssc.com) with its Code of Practice for Social Service Workers and the Code of Practice for Employers of Social Service Workers), has a responsibility for ensuring that codes of practice and responsibility are both formulated and adhered to and that effective social work education and training is delivered. The debate is still ongoing as to whether social work fulfils all those criteria for professionalism given that it is the delivery of service rather than the gaining of knowledge that is significant here. This is particularly the case where we may choose to access a doctor but we may not choose or wish for the services of a social worker. In fact, it may be the case that clients engaging with social work services may do so on an involuntary basis. Nevertheless, the effectiveness of the client–worker relationship has to be based on the professional identity and knowledge of the practitioner in addressing the positive aspects of clients' coping (Saleebey, 2009).

There is also an issue as to whether professional social work practice can ever be 'neutral' in that it is subscribed by and underpins the current political ideology whose power base may unwittingly be that of oppressor in meeting wider societal and structural aspects of need (Howe, 2002).

Gender and social work values

Within this context we also have to consider something of a feminist approach (Wharton, 2005) and its attempt to analyse that dichotomy that may exist within the 'caring' professions and what this actually means. Ungerson (1990) debates the difference between 'caring for' others and 'caring about' others and the confluence of those ideas within a consideration of the social construct of gender particularly and the changing focus of older age within society (Marchbank and Letherby, 2007).

Paternalism

It may be considered within a more paternalistic environment as an absolute that women are expected to take on these more caring and nurturing roles but at a significant cost to themselves both financially and emotionally. Practitioners need to consider whether this fits within a consideration of a wider global value and ethical awareness. The former (caring) may mean a more hands-on approach in the provision of actual care including feeding, bathing, personal care and ensuring that both physical and emotional needs are met. A significant feature of the caring 'for' and 'about' others is that the latter often has significantly more professional cachet whereas the 'caring for' is often an undervalued, poorly paid and resourced occupation. This is a particularly significant debate when we consider the role that women in general and particularly older women may be expected to take on in the care of dependent family members and also through kinship care in the nurturing and support of a new generation. This is at a time when they may have expected to withdraw more from the stresses of life. There is a need to consider the focus on patriarchy here from a feminist perspective that suggests patriarchal systems ensure that society is constructed to meet the needs of men and disadvantage women (Yuill et al., 2011). A significant feature of this is the way that women may be impoverished in older age through fractured work experience and poor pension rights.

Structural oppression and gender

What do we mean by structural oppression? This is where those wider forces within society of social divisions, class and the power inherent within these systems mitigate against any specific group. The iniquity of discriminatory practice in relation to older people generally may be understood at the personal, cultural and structural level (PCS) (Thompson, 2006), but there is evidence to show that women may be more disadvantaged than men within these power structures in the realms of employment, pensions and the expectation that they will take on caring roles as defined within a more paternalistic focus.

Gender

At the same time we have to have a clearly defined understanding of what gender is and what is the difference between gender and sex. While the sex of an individual may be determined at birth, gender is less of a fixed determinant. Gender refers more to those cultural, psychological and social aspects of a person's lived experience that are reinforced through cultural stereotyping, power imbalances within society and patriarchy in particular (Sheach-Leith et al., 2011). The seminal question for developing social work practitioners is why it is taken as a predetermined norm that women will be more natural carers for children purely because of their biological capacity for bearing children (Sands and Nuccio, 1992). At the same time, a denial of the complexity of gender with its ascribed roles leaves developing practitioners open to becoming part of a wider structural oppression as opposed to increasing their understanding of what maintains and sustains an inequitable society.

While older men undoubtedly experience oppressive practice within the realms of retirement, social roles and the means to sustain themselves into a 'decent' old age, there is strong supporting evidence within the context of poverty, pensions and quality of life to show that women may be more disadvantaged. By 'decent' I mean that if older people cannot have what the wider population takes for granted to sustain a decent lifestyle, that they are in effect denied these resources, then implicitly they may be left with an abiding sense of indecency (Galbraith, 1999). There is a certain irony that in a country identified as one of the richest in the world – the IMF identified the GDP of each citizen as $36,500, placing it above most other European countries – there are substantial pockets of poverty and deprivation particularly among older citizens and this is exacerbated within more socially deprived areas (Scharf, 2009; Scharf et al., 2002).

The difference between anti-oppressive and anti-discriminatory practice

It is the case that these terms may be used interchangeably, but there are some significant differences that need to be considered in the context of ethical practice with older people. Anti-discriminatory practice has a legal focus, in that it guarantees to engage with vulnerable groups through the delivery of effective social work practice and assessment that conforms to these legal requirements (see the Equality Act 2010). Anti-oppressive practice has at its heart the understanding that oppression is more related to power inequalities within society within a PCS framework. Oppressive practice reinforces negative stereotypes of older people and older age itself at a time of decline rather than at a time of growth and engagement (Braye and Preston-Shoot, 1995). Consequently oppressive practice should be considered as a primary consideration for any intervention that addresses ethics and values of practice.

Gender and poverty

This is particularly the case among women with their increased longevity and over-representation within the older age demographic. Evidence suggests that inequality of resources primarily impacts on women and older people belonging to minority ethnic groups and that over 2 million pensioners survive on an income that is below 60% of the average income (Department for Work and Pensions, 2008b). Developing practitioners have to consider the impact this has on older people (and particularly women) to engage fully with the benefits and support of the wider community. There may be more concerns with issues of access to medical services, transport and quality of nutrition than those wider issues of belonging and feeling that they have a valued role within society (see Maslow, 1987).

Isolated old age

Older people in rural communities may be doubly disadvantaged by a lack of services, amenities and that sense of loneliness and isolation that is more likely within these areas. Pugh and Cheers (2010) suggest that values and ethics are contingent within work in isolated areas that includes a capacity for working with individuals and families, local organisations and communities. These should be underpinned as part of a wider appreciation of anti-oppressive practice and significant political network-ing to ensure needs and best social work practice are met. The actual skills required are an appreciation of the needs of differing cultures and the capacity for engage-ment with, and an interest in, rural communities.

Ageism

Ageism is the multifaceted aspect of how older people may be disadvantaged through negative stereotyping and language, policy and practice that excludes older people and a broader sense of stigmatising older people purely because of an accumulation of years. This may be exacerbated within public perception at times of financial and emotional stress and through a cultural fear of the nature of ageing itself. We fear most what we do not understand (Bytheway, 1995; Stuart-Hamilton, 2006). The paradox of ageist behaviour is that the ageist becomes what one fears the most – becoming old. This can result in older people being viewed exclusively in the context of their disabilities as opposed to their abilities, with a concurrent diminution of their wider role of experience and support within society. This may be further exacerbated when we consider race, class and gender as well as that more psychological aspect of having a sense of usefulness and belonging (Lymbery, 2007). If the needs of older people are couched exclusively in terms of their dependency then it is likely that this will increas-ingly result in older people being perceived as vulnerable and needy.

The ageing body and practice

We live at a time when style and the presentation of image are prized over content and endeavour and where fame itself becomes part of a self-fulfilling identity. Images of youthfulness and body image (Cranny-Francis et al., 2003) permeate all aspects of television, advertising and even politics with its emphasis on the presentation style and the sound bite. If perfection of form is a sign of health, sexual allure and success then the stigma of declining vigour, ill health, disability and ageing must confer to older people feelings that they may not meet acceptable standards of presentation, health and attractiveness (Williams and Bendelow, 1998). Given the high numbers of younger students accessing social work degree courses it is inevitable that individuals will subsume something of this analogy of 'decrepit' ageing in their own thinking with a subsequent impact on an ethical and value aware social work practice (Schwartz and Simmons, 2001).

The young's perception of old age

It may be an inevitable consequence that younger people will internalise these themes of physical presentation and youthfulness as a benchmark for success. This may be at the expense of a future consideration of older age and the impact that physical decline may have. Research by Garstka et al. (2004) indicate that when groups of younger and older respondents were asked to evaluate images of a range of differently aged photographs for their perceived social status that something interesting happened. The younger respondents characterised the photographs of the older people as having the same social status as very young children, thus giving a whole new focus to the old adage of the 'second childhood'. Interestingly, when youth was denigrated within the study there was not the same sense of distress, as youth by its very nature, will grow up and away from the opprobrium and experience of youth itself into an older age.

Exercise

- What contact do you have with older people other than through the medium of your work?
- Do you consider growing old and what this will be like?
- Where do you think your ideas of ageing come from?
- What are your images of old age?
- Do you fear growing old and can you say why?

Disengagement theory

This may be reinforced further within a consideration of disengagement theory. This theory (Cumming and Henry, 1961) suggests that it is a natural consequence of ageing itself that older people may choose to devote less time to activity pursuits and more to a reflective aspect of their lives. Disengagement may be part of a wider continuum where friends have died or children have moved away. Conversely, it may also involve multiple losses in terms of individual roles and engagement with the wider community (Victor, 2005). This has some potentially serious consequences for social work practice. Older people may become marginalised within practice if the assumption is that this withdrawal is a logical and inevitable consequence of ageing itself. Practitioners may then miss the more underlying pathology of exclusion and social isolation because of the perceived interpretation that this disruptive ageing is a natural consequence of old age (Macionis and Plummer, 2008).

However, it may also be related to a dysfunction that has existed across the life course and which has brought the older person to an isolated and lonely old age (Erikson, 1995). The focus of ethical and value social work therefore is not to assume that disengagement is a natural process but that it may be an indicator not only of a deeper dysfunction, but a dysfunction over the life course. An inability to consider this may further disempower an older person and potentially lock them into a cycle of despairing old age reinforced by ill-informed social work practice.

The ethics of care

There are also ethical considerations of the role of the family and carers and how we as professionals engage with this. Older people can be both carers and cared for. As carers they will provide an invaluable service to the next generation imbued with experiential knowledge and a capacity for support. From a value-based social work perspective this may present some problems, not least of which is the assumption that older women should now take on an extended caring role for the next genera-tion. This could be at a time when they may have wished to withdraw from these more rigorous aspects of their lives to devote time to other interests or reflection on the past and what the future holds. This has to be balanced with the real trauma experienced by families in caring for and maintaining the independence (Gillies and Edwards, 2006) of older sick and disabled family members at a time when support services and state benefits may be inadequate to meet their care needs.

Jill Roberts is 86 years of age. She is becoming increasingly forgetful and her GP has suggested she may have the onset of vascular dementia. She has lived with her daughter since her husband died and has had an integral role in the care and support of her grandchildren and regularly provided babysitting services as the children grew up. Her occasional loss of sense of direction and specialist diet to support other physical disabilities has placed an increasing strain on the family budget and coping generally. The family has contacted the social work department to say that they are unable to cope and are requesting she be considered for a place in a care home setting.

CASE STUDY

? **Reflective Questions** ?

- Do you think the family should be responsible for the future care needs of parents and grandparents in old age?
- Do you think that older people who have experienced poverty and have saved over the course of a lifetime should be expected to pay for their care in old age?
- How might the needs of the family be met here to ensure there is an ethical awareness of the needs of everyone concerned?
- Who might be considered as part of any assessment of care for the future?

Ethics and generational understanding

There should be an awareness of ethnic and cultural diversity that includes older people in the context of anti-discriminatory practice as well as a deeper understanding of the meaning and impact of ageism, racism and lack of cultural sensitivity generally. Interestingly, in a Europe-wide study by Walker and Maltby (1997) there was clear evidence that two-thirds of the older people researched stated that they had little or no contact with younger people below the age of 25. Conversely, older people questioned thought that their peers would choose to associate more with people of their own generation, so contact with the young, or lack of it, may be by choice. Where there is a strong ethical dimension is within the area of pension provision, now and in the future, for an ageing population. While there is clear evidence of an ageing demographic over the next 25 years this may be a fairly crude way to address issues that are more related to the *social contract*.

This 'contract' between the various groups within society is to ensure that the creation of wealth of itself does not become the primary indicator of success but the totality of an environment that addresses the needs of all citizens. It is therefore important that there is a greater level of intergenerational contact between the young and the older population to ensure that there is the capacity for the debate on meeting needs. A lack of clarity in this regard, where older people are forced into the role of passive recipients of care while being characterised from a narrow ageist perspective, will further disenfranchise older people from the capacity to influence decision making in relation to their future welfare (Ginn and Arber, 1999). The simple premise here may be that where there is an absence of *inclusion* then *exclusion* may be the norm for older people. The relationship of the young and old is therefore pivotal as part of the awareness of being and becoming.

Ethnic awareness and ethics

If any ethnic majority is considered as the norm within any society then, by definition, ethnic 'minorities' will be perceived as different and potentially deviant. This 'deviance' may extend to any individual or group of individuals who do not share those common cultural characteristics of the dominant group within society (Macionis and Plummer, 2008). It is all too easy therefore to view minority groups as somehow being more 'needy', with a concurrent focus on their exclusion, marginalisation and a potential lack of contribution to the needs of society generally. Ethnic identity can then be categorised within an understanding of social exclusion, a changing and evolving cultural and religious focus, developing communities and the role that these factors have in the evolution of new and developing structural identities (Modood et al., 1998; Rowson, 2006).

At a fundamental level, ethical ethnic practice may have as its progenitor the basics of good communication itself (Lishman, 2009). A starting point is the premise that practitioners recognise the dichotomy that frequently exists between valuing diversity and the realities of older people as a stigmatised group. This is further characterised within the domain of 'over-accommodative communication' (Williams and Nussbaum, 2001), where practitioners behave in a patronising way to older people. This is characterised by use of a shrill or overly loud speaking voice and an over-simplification of language. This may be identified within the realms of conflicting practice, for instance within care settings for older people, where older people are constantly 'checked' under the banner of effective health and safety (Bowles et al., 2006). Bloustein (1964) suggested that a person open to this level of public scrutiny would lose that sense of individual uniqueness that all people possess and become a compliant and conventional being, unable to engage with his or her personal identity at a cultural and structural level. This should also be viewed from a human rights perspective, where the right to privacy is already enshrined.

Ageist practice

Empirical evidence suggests that social work practitioners themselves may hold ageist views irrespective of their level of experience and training (Allen et al., 2009). There is evidence to suggest that proximity to older people seems to equate to a deeper engagement with the lives of older people. However, a dichotomy seems to exist between valuing wisdom while denigrating old age itself (Stuart-Hamilton, 2006).

Exercise

- What communication skills would you have to consider when working with older clients?
- How might your understanding of the needs of ethnic and cultural diversity impact on your use of self and social work skills?
- What resources might you make use of to inform ethical ethnic practice?
- Where might you gain support and knowledge from in addressing issues of ethnic and cultural diversity?

Personalisation and person-centred practice

There is an increasing emphasis throughout the UK on personalisation, where public services can be used to meet the more individual needs of presenting client groups. Essentially, the personalisation agenda moves away from the more pragmatic aspect of direct payments through the Community Care (Direct Payments) Act 1996 and individual budgets (Glendinning et al., 2008) to a more inclusive role for older people. Rather than being characterised as the recipients of services older people will now actively engage with the process of change itself. Personalisation is much more focused on inclusion and empowerment in meeting individual need and away from a more bureaucratic response of a 'one size fits all', although there is evidence to suggest that this may disadvantage older people who find the process of managing these budgets to be difficult and stressful.

There is also an inevitable tension that will exist within the discourse of personalisation and the resource-driven implications of meeting need in a time of austerity. Galpin and Bates (2009) raise the interesting proposition that when choice and person-centred practice related to personalisation are viewed exclusively in the context of "consumer rights" (customer satisfaction) then those more fundamental aspects of human rights may become compromised. The reality is that not all older people may wish to or be in the position to manage these personal budgets and in the process be denied those services that the wider population may take as their right: access to health, quality nutrition, social inclusion and the capacity for continuous development through the life course.

Ethical awareness of sexuality in old age

One of the great myths of ageing is that older people are largely sexless (Lefrancois, 1999). This thinking may buy into that consideration of the body as a metaphor for success in the modern world. It is not uncommon that professionals negate the individual sexuality of older people as part of a consideration of risk assessment and safety and the question that must be posed is, whose needs are really being met here? While it is inevitable that there may be a decline in those more physical aspects of sexuality, there is little evidence to show that there is a decline in levels of intimacy across the ageing population (Schlesinger, 1996). There is currently something of a national debate on the baby boomer generation in terms of their contribution to modern society. They have been characterised as a homogeneous group who have taken advantage of the structural opportunities (pensions, education, housing) afforded them through generations of labour and political demands for fair treatment. It is an irony that those very opportunities which have now been passed on to a future generation of benefits, health care and education have further characterised older people as net 'takers' rather than 'contributors' to the state. This is also the generation that experienced a sexual awakening and freedom for the first time in the post-war period and it is unlikely that older people generally will wish to be considered as sexless or lacking in affectional bonds by the wider public and the social work profession particularly. Social workers may then be castigating an already disadvantaged group of people within the wider community either through embarrassment and lack of information or individual lack of consideration based on fear of ageing itself (see Disengagement Theory).

Negative connotations of sexuality

It may be safer, from a disengagement structural perspective, to characterise older people within the confining language of the 'elderly'. Again this has all the negative connotations and characteristics of a homogeneous group slouching towards the inevitability of older age and death itself as part of a wider ageist attitude (Bytheway, 1997). Older age is more structurally defined as either a static state or a doorway to a more inevitable state of dependency and decline. The reality of older people's needs generally, and specifically in the area of sexuality, is that *they are what we will become*. This more philosophical consideration of what it is to be is at the heart of a more humanistic approach bounded by the understanding of respect for persons through person-centred working (Rogers, 2002) and an understanding of fundamental needs and rights such as sexuality. This may be further exacerbated in the case of women where socially constructed gender based on patriarchy and control may emphasise the structured links between sexuality and reproduction and identify older women as a group unable to fulfil their reproductive function (Hanmer, 1997). In a wider context there is an argument to be made that because of the disrupted working lives of women caring for children and their subsequent impoverishment in older age that poverty itself may be the price of this fertility.

Labelling of deviance

It is inevitable that these ascribed characteristics of deviance and exclusion will be taken on by older women as part of their own 'label' and further exclude them from inclusion within their own community (Bywater and Jones, 2007).

This 'labelling' process tends to become self-perpetuating. The older person may begin to characterise him or herself in the context of this perceived deviance (older sexuality) which then further reinforces this labelling (Payne, 2005). If this is the focus of heterosexuality and older people then how more difficult will it become in relation to older lesbian women and gay men? Significant studies such as Gay and Grey in Dorset (2006) and the National Service Framework for Older People (DH, 2001b) identify, respectively, actual and perceived levels of discrimination across the respondents' lived experience and an identification of minority groups that exclude specific reference to gay older people.

Older lesbians and gay men

As professional practitioners we should acknowledge the diversity of older gay people in the same way that we acknowledge the diversity of older people generally (Pugh, 2005). The Civil Partnership Act 2004 and the Equality Act 2010 have gone some way to raise awareness within the wider population of the need for a more ethical approach towards this discriminated group and their right to self-determination. This is undermined however by a media depiction that focuses on gender-specific nomenclature that raises issues of the nature of the construction of gender and patriarchy itself. It is as if the state of partnership of individual gay men and women is considered but only in a heterosexual context. The ethical challenge for legislators, professionals and carers is to recognise the real trauma that older gay men and women experience where that very aspect that defines them as individuals is denied them (Age Concern, 2008). Scotland, at the time of writing, is legislating for full marriage rights for gay couples as a clear focus on the absolute nature of human rights.

Conclusion

Hopefully this chapter will have provided clarity on values and ethics in the context of ageing and ageism and the nature of the professional role in meeting the needs of older people. This should provide some points for consideration on the 'rightness' of action and, through the exercises within the chapter, where one's individual core values emanate from. Finally, it has emphasised how practitioners need to be mindful of and engage with those more fundamental needs of older people in the context of care, ethnicity, cultural diversity, inclusion and sexuality.

 Recommended Reading

Age UK (2011b) *Lesbian, gay or bisexual, Planning for later life*. Age UK. A comprehensive overview of the needs and concerns of these disadvantaged groups with a clear emphasis on acceptance, benefits and human rights.

Beckett, C. and Maynard, A. (2005) *Values and Ethics in Social Work: An Introduction*. London: Sage. A comprehensive read with a solid emphasis on professional context and power and ethical practice.

Cann, P. and Dean, M. (eds) (2009) *Unequal Ageing: The Untold Story of Exclusion in Old Age*. Bristol: The Policy Press. Encompasses wider areas of exclusion in old age and the more philosophical aspects of the ageing process.

Thompson, N. (2006) *Anti-Discriminatory Practice* (4th ed.). Basingstoke: Palgrave. This seminal text addresses the personal, cultural and structural aspects of discrimination for disadvantaged groups in an accessible and coherent way.

3

SKILLS IN WORKING
WITH OLDER PEOPLE

Learning Outcomes

This chapter looks at:

- Ageism and ageist attitudes and how these should be considered and addressed within an inclusive and collaborative practice.
- Preparation for engagement with older clients and what should be considered here within a context of ageism, ethnicity and choice.
- Communication skills and how the National Standards for Social Work (Scotland, Wales and Northern Ireland) and the new Professional Capabilities Framework (England) could be addressed in the context of verbal, non-verbal and written communication.
- Assessment skills and how collaborative and interprofessional practice supports client need and professional development within a context of student education and knowledge.

Introduction

Older people are not a homogeneous group, in that they have a unique set of life experiences that impact and inform their individual sense of identity. Indeed, it is contingent on any consideration of social work skills that issues of language and its potential for oppression is addressed. This is particularly the case in relation to describing older people as the 'elderly', which denies individuals their sense of uniqueness across the life course (Tulle and Lynch, 2011). Any failure to consider these life events in the context of a holistic, individual lived experience may result in the older person being viewed solely in terms of their age, disability or potential loss of coping (Ray and Phillips, 2002). If this is the case then how is it possible for practitioners to engage in an empathic and ethical practice that focuses on the individual coping capacity and potential for development in older age? This is likely to be reinforced where an older person experiences discrimination and ageist attitudes through the quality of services provided or a wider societal perception of the older person as frail and vulnerable (Phillips et al., 2006). Incumbent upon professional practice is an appreciation that while ageing and death are natural physical processes these are experienced differently by all older people and these experiences are as diverse as the range of older people themselves (Bytheway et al., 1990).

Structural ageing

A professional consideration of work with older clients should address personal and structural aspects of ageing as well as the more pragmatic aspect of the sources and use of power. This will be reinforced here by a consideration of Fook's (1995) assertion on the relationship between social work and social justice at a time of uncertainty within a 'Big Society'. While this sense of scale may attempt to address the wider presenting needs of those with disabilities as well as older people it also has the potential for promoting a sense of invisibility of those groups who may lack the power or resources to have their views heard and acted upon. This may result in older people becoming hidden in full view. There also needs to be a discourse on the nature of psychological development through the life stages and the impact this can have on both adult behaviour and a potential for resilience and coping in an uncertain time for older people. Even within the assumed repository of support and affection within the family, Lowe (1993) has speculated on the mutual entrapment that children and parents can experience in old age where each may feel subsumed within the process of caring and being cared for. This may be at a time when the older person struggles to make some sense of order out of the totality of their lived experience as a precursor to death itself. It may also be that it is the *fear* of ageing that is more traumatising and problematic here than the reality, where only one person in every eight over the age of 80 develops some form of dementia (Knapp and Prince, 2007). The wider paradigm is, then, what are the practice skills that need to be considered within effective engagement with older people and what underpinning theory at the personal and societal level needs to be addressed?

The Range of Skills

The starting point of any consideration of social work skills is the training base and what this brings to professional practice and I will address this further within the sections on the National Occupational Standards (NOS) (Scotland and Wales) and the new Professional Capabilities Framework (PCF) (England) that are currently being developed within social work training. Integral to this is an underlying and supporting ethical and value base (see Chapter 2) that places the older person at the centre of any intervention in as collaborative and inclusive a manner as possible. While I will consider areas of communication and assessment within this chapter this is not a comprehensive overview and the following skills areas also need to be considered within any working practice with older people:

- User's perspective and professional understanding of how the older person interprets their situation and condition.
- Mental health – see Chapters 5 and 6.
- Safety and how the practitioner is able to assess and interpret the older person's awareness of neglect and risk.
- Medical and health background and how older people and practitioners can work together to define abilities, coping and overall health. This also relates to working together to ensure that the older person has every opportunity to contribute and communicate and engage effectively within any intervention that may impact upon them.
- Relationships and emotional well-being (see Chapters 2 and 5) where the emotional and sexual needs of older people are considered within a framework that includes carers and professionals while respecting the rights, privacy and individual integrity of the older person.
- Personal and environmental care where the day-to-day needs of hygiene and health (oral, aural, foot care) are both considered and met. The same care and attention needs to be considered when considering the living environment. How many times as professionals have we experienced agencies providing a good quality of care but where odour control, decoration and the overall ambience is lacking or missing altogether (Department of Health, 2002a)?

Explicit within these considerations is an awareness of the nature of ageism and how it will be extremely difficult to meet these person-centred standards if the starting premise of engagement is that older people are perceived as 'problematic'. Rather what needs to be emphasised here are those core skills that all social workers should possess for effective practice, such as encouraging older people to take control of their own lives, challenging inequitable social structures, informing personal and collective practice through evidence-based practice (EBP) and managing the complexities of an evolving and changing social environment in a new age of austerity (Lymbery, 2005).

It is just as important to consider the hubristic nature of unprofessional practice. This can be used by practitioners as something of a check list for their own assumptions when working with older people. While the ideal is a person-centred and collaborative approach to practice, the reality is that as practitioners we are all flawed in terms of our own personal value base and interpretation of the world. This will, of necessity, impact adversely on the older client unless there is a consistency of critical evaluation of individual practice (Craig, 2004; Powell, 2008). This is the nature of what reflective practice is really about. So what are the areas we should address and confront?

- Assuming we know more about the client than the client's expressed wishes.
- Being overly expert and using obscure social work language as a protective function; also hiding behind procedural complexity.

- Making decisions that do not consider the views and expressed wishes of the older person and their carers.
- Viewing the social work role as more important than the views of the carers and service users, where targets and conclusions may become more important than the process of engagement.
- Failing to consider the ethnic and cultural aspects of the older person's life within a white Eurocentric focus (Dominelli, 2002).

Lymbery (2007) characterises effective collaboration and interprofessional practice as the 'Holy Grail' of effective practice. Coupled with this is a need to be an informed, confident and knowledgeable practitioner who is prepared to acknowledge the individual traits, skills and concerns of other practitioners and respect these. Miller and Freeman (2003) go further and characterise the skills of preparation, planning, information sharing, strong management and support systems (administrative and management support) as pivotal to any effective interprofessional focus. The keynote for any successful practice is therefore that sense of rigorous commitment by all interested and influential participants. Concurrent with this is a willingness to accept and give up personal and agency power in equal measure to effect a positive outcome. This is the heart of person-centred and interprofessional practice.

Preparation for intervention

A starting point for any effective intervention with older people is a consideration of the lived experience of individuals as opposed to the interests of dominant groups (Thompson, 2003b), which goes hand in hand with anti-oppressive (Dalrymple and Burke, 1995) and anti-discriminatory practice (Thompson, 2006) with its focus on addressing inequitable power. This should also be considered within a structural and personal level and the meaning of chronological ageing: any notion of an older person purely in the subtext of an accumulation of years is likely to lead to discriminatory practice with its focus on diminishing powers and skills (Crawford and Walker, 2008; Johns, 2011). Phillipson's (1982) Marxist perspective identifies the capitalist need for a healthy and effective workforce that drives social policy and may further disadvantage the older person in a cultural and structural sense. Alternatively the older population, with its perceived non-productive emphasis, is likely to have a marginal impact on structural forces generally and a sense of enforced passivity.

Needs of black and ethnic minorities

While old age and ageism may be significant factors for the older person these may be compounded by additional areas of discrimination in relation to cultural and ethnic definition. Language is always one of the first ways that society attempts to address discrimination against minority groups. Essentially people are disadvantaged by oppression that constricts the natural wishes and development of individuals (Nabors et al., 2001) and a feature of this is how groups and individuals are described and defined within society. Interestingly, Parekh (2000) avoids the use of the word 'ethnic' because of its very specific meaning of shared culture and religion, and also the word 'minority' with its connotation of marginalisation and a concurrent lack of importance as a group. The focus here is to avoid language that further stereotypes a national sense of dysfunction purely because of differences in ethnicity, a potential lack of voice and old age itself.

Exercise

- Write down a list of the key words, phrases and areas of practice you think you would have to consider or address when working with black and ethnic minority groups. Compare these to the nine key capabilities from the Professional Capabilities Framework (PCF) or to the National Occupational Standards (NOS) later in this chapter.

Use of self

There needs to be critical reflection not just of the effectiveness of the use of self but how societal structures themselves may reinforce discriminatory practice. As Stanley and Wise (1990) so succinctly refer to in their discourse on the interpretation of the functional aspects of social work, this should include a sense of its *transformational* nature in addressing discrimination, poverty, injustice and inequality within a structural and societal context. Concomitant with this is the overarching sense of what Rogers (2002) referred to as 'unconditional positive regard' as part of a person-centred approach to practice with older people. This is not to suggest that 'regard' and 'liking' are the same thing but that the totality of the older person's life experience, both good and bad, has to be acknowledged within that more holistic understanding.

Albert Daly is 88 years of age and has recently moved to a care home near where he formerly lived. He has a large dispersed family who are unable to visit him regularly due to geographical location and their own family commitments. Albert served as an artillery sergeant in the last war and remained in the army when the war ended rising to the rank of gunnery sergeant before retirement. His work meant that he had to relocate often with his family. In his retirement he had an active life gardening and becoming a member of the community council. He is currently feeling isolated and very low in mood and has expressed a feeling that he is now 'past his sell-by date'. You are a trainee social worker and you have been asked to meet with Albert to assess how he is feeling and whether there is anything you can do to support him in his new home.

CASE STUDY

> ? Reflective Questions ?
>
> - Can you identify any specific areas of preparation you would consider when entering into any engagement with Albert?
> - What do you think are the underlying value and ethical aspects you should consider within any interaction or intervention with Albert?
> - What do you think the benefits are of learning more of the specifics of the lived experience of Albert's life and how might you go about this?

The reluctant client

I hope you can identify here that any engagement at this level may involve a good deal of stress for an older client, particularly if he or she has come to the attention of support services at a time of vulnerability. Core to any debate on the nature of the voluntary–involuntary client exemplar is a reflection on the variety of interpersonal skills that may be required to meet need, irrespective of how the client may have accessed services. This can be compounded by feelings that fundamental issues of poverty, personal care, mobility and a general sense of inclusion and engagement with the wider society may be under threat. The uniqueness of individual experience therefore cannot be underestimated, particularly when it is evaluated within a consideration of oppression and societal aspects of gender, poverty and class and the particular psychosocial circumstances of that lived identity. Interestingly, where life satisfaction is assessed as a feature of successful ageing this is much more related to the older person's perception of their own coping and life skills than any more objective awareness of societal perception (Boyd and Bee, 2009; Gana et al., 2004). This understanding is particularly important when addressing the needs of older people who have experienced trauma at an earlier life stage and where this trauma is still unresolved in older age. Schreuder (1997: 18) suggests that 'in every traumatic experience there was an abrupt disruption of existential continuity'. Essentially he suggested that people would lose their sense of security and coping (equilibrium/homeostasis) both on a personal and familial level and in some circumstances this would never return. This dislocation of the older person in space and time could then be explained away by disengagement theory rather than as a feature of individual trauma. The skilled practitioner will be able to recognise this or at least consider the potential reasons for a lack of engagement by the older person. Again this has to be balanced by that fundamental right to privacy as enshrined within the articles of the Human Rights Act 1998.

It is incumbent on all social workers to develop a knowledge and sense of understanding of ageing and its pernicious effects both on the feelings of older people specifically and on the potential for value-driven and ethical social work practice generally. This has to be evaluated within a changing social climate where the vulnerability of older people may be the dominant perception. While cultural and structural norms may mitigate against the needs of older people through that paramount western ideology of image and youthfulness, there is rarely any thought of how the changing demographics will ensure that older people have a greater say in the future politics of the UK. Politicians beware!

Communication and skills development

The National Occupational Standards (NOS) for Social Work and the Code of Practice for Social Care Workers have helped develop a more consistent approach to what core social work and social care standards should be. The National Occupational Standards for Social Work identify six key learning roles to evidence social work competency and these as well as a consideration of structural disadvantage should be the benchmark for engaging with any older client. While the following National Occupational Standards for Social Work still apply in Scotland, Wales and Northern Ireland, the recently developed Professional Capabilities Framework (PCF) for Social Work is coming into force in England at the time of writing.

The six key roles identified by the NOS are as follows:

Key Role 1: Prepare for, and work with individuals, families, carers, groups and communities to assess their needs and circumstances.

Key Role 2: Plan, carry out, review and evaluate social work practice, with individuals, families, carers, groups, communities and other professionals.

Key Role 3: Support individuals to represent their needs, views and circumstances.

Key Role 4: Manage risk to individuals, families, carers, groups, communities, self and colleagues.

Key Role 5: Manage and be accountable, with supervision and support, for your own social work practice within your organisation.

Key Role 6: Demonstrate professional competence in social work practice.

These roles characterise the range and depth of social work skills that are required and are also contingent on the practitioner's own capacity to develop over the course of the professional lifetime.

New standards for social workers in England

The new Professional Capabilities Framework (PCF) for Social Workers in England has developed the following standards for practice across a range of different stages and professional development. The entry level capabilities for accessing a social work degree include the following:

1 Professionalism: Identify and behave as a professional social worker, committed to professional development.
2 Values and ethics: Apply social work ethical principles and values to guide professional practice.

3   Diversity: Recognise diversity and apply anti-discriminatory and anti-oppressive principles in practice.
4   Rights, justice and economic well-being: Advance human rights and promote social justice and economic well-being.
5   Knowledge: Apply knowledge of social sciences, law and social work practice theory.
6   Critical reflection and analysis: Apply critical reflection and analysis to inform and provide a rationale for professional decision making.
7   Intervention and skills: Use judgement and authority to intervene with individuals, families and communities to promote independence, provide support and prevent harm, neglect and abuse.
8   Contexts and organisations: Engage with, inform and adapt to changing contexts that shape practice. Operate effectively within own organisational frameworks and contribute to the development of services and organisations. Operate effectively within multi-agency and interprofessional partnerships and settings.
9   Professional leadership: Take responsibility for the professional learning and development of others through supervision, mentoring, assessing, research, teaching, leadership and management. (www.collegeofsocialwork.org).

Assessment of the nine core areas or domains

These new standards utilise these nine core capabilities across a range of knowledge and personal and professional development leading on to how students are supported in their learning and development in their post-qualification year. The PCF assesses these nine core capabilities across a range of developing professional standards (also known as *areas* of practice or *domains*) including:

- Entry level capabilities
- Readiness for practice capabilities
- End of first placement level capabilities
- Qualifying social worker level capabilities (see also Health and Care Professions Council (HCPC) Standards of Proficiency for Social Workers)
- Assessed and supported year in employment (ASYE) level capabilities
- Social work level capabilities (www.collegeofsocialwork.org).

CASE STUDY

Amanita has come to the attention of the local housing association as her neighbours have become concerned about her unkempt appearance and her general social isolation. She comes from an extended Indian family who visited her until recently when there was a family dispute related to an arranged marriage. Amanita has chosen to oppose this marriage as it concerns her favourite granddaughter who is also opposed to the marriage. Amanita is on a basic state pension and it is clear that she is not eating properly and she has already stated to a neighbour that she is 'very lonely'. She has also indicated that she is fearful for her own safety although she has consistently refused to give any specific details of why this is. The people who have contacted the housing association and subsequently the social work department have insisted that they remain anonymous. You have been asked to assess Amanita's needs taking into consideration the different *domains* of practice (PCF) and the stage of study and experience you may currently be at.

? Reflective Questions ?

- How could you support and promote your professional identity?
- How does an ethical understanding support working with diversity and promoting individual rights?
- What is the role of legislation and policy in your professional development?
- What are the benefits of a wide range of social work interventions in effective practice?
- How do you view the development of your professional skills in the promotion of learning for others?

All of these capabilities, irrespective of the stage of study of the student, should be viewed as interdependent and not separately. This removes the students from a more module-based approach to learning where assignment tasks may be the main focus of attention. The reality is that there has to be an emphasis on a continuum of learning that encompasses a working knowledge of policy, theory, knowledge base, ethics and diversity, organisational contexts and leadership to inform professional practice. '*Progression between levels* is characterised by people's ability to manage complexity, risk, ambiguity and increasingly autonomous decision making across a range of situations' (www.collegeofsocialwork.org).

Continuous professional development (CPD)

Social work is not a finite science but a skills-based occupation that will inevitably depend for its success on continuous professional development (CPD). These standards are defined within the Social Work Reform Board's (SWRB) standards on 'Developing a coherent and effective framework for the continuing professional development of social workers' (Department of Education, 2010). These constitute the following standards that should support social workers to:

- Demonstrate that they maintain and improve their skills.
- Extend and deepen specialist skills and knowledge.
- Acquire knowledge and understanding of, and contribute to, research which informs evidence-based practice.
- Develop as leaders and managers both within their own organisations and within the social work profession.

- Become more confident, emotionally resilient and adaptable to the changing demands of social work.
- Play an effective role in developing other social workers (e.g. as practice educators, mentors for NQSW).
- Become the next generation of social work academics and researchers where appropriate.

Concomitant with these CPD standards is a more formal structure of the role that employers play within social work training. There has been something of the 'ne'er the twain shall meet' aspect between employers and social work education in the past. This potential divergence of purpose may deny employers, social work educators and practitioners the opportunity for a supported employment and that sense of being able to develop as an effective worker. The Social Work Task Force (SWTF, 2009) in its final report on 'Building a safe, confident future' recommended that there should be clear standards set out for social work employees and what they could and should expect from their employers in terms of support and development. As well as this, the report highlighted the very significant role that professional supervision plays in supporting an effective and confident workforce.

If we characterise the professional as someone with that sense of esoteric knowledge, then implicit within this is a sense that this has to be a part of a continuum through the professional life course (Thompson, 2009). This focus on CPD is analogous to how older people can be viewed in the context of their uniqueness, previous experience and potential for future capacity and coping, with an emphasis on personal integrity, equality of opportunity and the more expansive focus on social justice (Thompson, 2003a). If empowerment is at the centre of our work with older clients then we have to be clear what we mean when we refer to empowerment. Foucault (1980) refers to that 'normalising power' underpinned by social work practice but subscribed by governmental and structural norms. If these norms are based on attitudes and consideration of the needs of older people that are inherently oppressive then there is a fine line between the emancipatory aspect of practice and the potential for control through the medium of professional practice itself. The very word 'empowerment' has within it an understanding of power being *given* as opposed to an assumption that this is a human and civil right and a starting point for any consideration within practice (Parker et al., 1999). Indeed, older people can be characterised as one of the most disempowered groups within society. Poverty may be an underlying paradigm for wider areas of disadvantage within housing, health services, negative stereotyping and the sense that older people are perceived as a drain on public finances (Thompson and Thompson, 2001). This may be allied to the perception of the homogeneous nature of ageing as opposed to the individual, experiential and heterogeneous nature of what older people are in reality.

Communication

The core skills of communication and information sharing, professional and interprofessional practice, a developing knowledge base through research and evidence-based practice and critical evaluation of use of self within a value-based practice are to the heart of effective practice. Communication skills, by their very nature, are not characteristics we are born with but aptitudes we hone and develop over the course of a lifetime and are analogous to the life skills developed over the course of an older person's life. The focus of effective communication, therefore, is the ability to 'read' a situation with that sense of reflection of self and the older person's environment and to recognise the additional pressures of work and stress that may impact adversely on effective engagement (Thompson, 2002). The practitioner needs to be able to reflect on practice and have a professional capacity for thinking and defining the nature of the problem as distinct from any more linear application of knowledge and theoretical skills. In effect, this is what Schon refers to as moving from a position of reflection 'on' action into reflecting 'in' action (Schon, 1987) with a consideration of analysis, assessment and personal judgement.

Communication skills

At the heart of any intervention with older people will be a focus on the verbal and non-verbal skills of the practitioner (Lishman, 2009). This is not to deny the importance of written communication but there may already be a significant amount of documentation relating to the older person in the public domain. This will include contact with a range of agencies from medical to support and welfare. The focus here on verbal and non-verbal considers the dichotomy that may exist between this range of documentation and whether this is a true reflection of the needs of the older person. We have already speculated that older people may only access social work services *in extremis* and it is therefore fundamental to any successful outcomes of expressed needs and wishes that the older person is afforded the time, respect and opportunity to fully explore these.

Ageing and communication

Dreher (2001) suggests that communication with older people can be influenced by both social and physical changes. In the former, older people may trade something of their personality to gain whatever benefits of security may be present, particularly within a care setting. In the latter, older people may become judged by their physical presentation of appearance and voice. Dreher suggests that giving a concern a 'name' goes some way to helping to identify, characterise and help to resolve any specific problem for an older person. The payoff here is the potential for a mutuality of respect between the older person and the practitioner and an acknowledgement of the individual humanity of both.

Also contingent on any successful outcome will be a consideration and evaluation of any more specific needs of the client in terms of visual, aural or speech impairment. A failure to engage effectively with older people from ethnic backgrounds may be further compounded where there is a need for interpreter skills. Here preparation, in terms of neutrality and confidentiality, will have to be evidenced. This is an area that should be considered within the current discourse on the nature of multiculturalism itself. While this may present some additional difficulties, not least in resources or access to interpreter services, it should not be referred to as a last resort when it is obvious from the outset that the older client is experiencing difficulty in communication.

Any understanding of positive and effective communication has at its heart the capacity to listen and interpret what the older person is *really* saying. While a primary focus of all good social work interventions is listening, I would go further and suggest that *hearing* may be more important, given that workers can listen and not hear but generally not the reverse. Practitioners also need to consider the anxieties that can bear down on their own sense of practice and coping and consider something of the 'approach–avoid' axis in analysing verbal communication (Koprowska, 2008). This focuses on those positive 'approach' aspects of verbal communication where practitioners actively engage by communicating openly, providing information and actively listening to the client's perspectives. This is in opposition to those more 'avoid' aspects where practitioners, through their own unresolved anxieties of lack of professional identity, overly focus on information gathering, use closed questions that elicit little useful information and are overly protective of the self and the agency at the expense of the client's views and wishes.

The core skills of effective communication are:

- Verbal communication: This has to be a *focused conversation* to ensure that the purpose of the intervention is met. An unfocused approach without clear purpose may result in a conversation that is mutually satisfying but not one that meets presenting needs. The practitioner also has to be aware of the more psychosocial aspects of the client, both in the context of how life forces have impacted on current coping and how the older person may fit into an engaged personal and community-based focus. The *level, pace* and type of *language* used are also important. Anxious practitioners may hide behind that more esoteric social work language while at the same time disadvantaging clients from taking a full role in the identification of need. At the heart of any communication therefore is a reiteration and consideration of the nature of power itself and the capacity of the professional to critically evaluate his or her own impact on any intervention (Higham, 2006). The very word 'intervention' may have a strong emphasis (as in empowerment) on the power dynamic that exists between an older person and the social worker and Dalrymple and Burke (2006) have suggested that a more relevant description should be 'interaction'. This allows more for that sense of collaboration and engagement and has as its focus a consideration of the capacity for listening, hearing and anti-oppressive practice generally. 'Intervention' tends to suggest a focus on the inequitable balance of power that will inevitably exist between the social worker and the client. This is significant when we consider that interactions with clients may not have finite beginnings and endings but are more likely part of a continuum of mutual learning, support, trust and identification of real need through engaged collaboration (Doel and Shardlow, 2005).
- Non-verbal communication: This may indicate how both the professional and the client are feeling rather than what they actually say. A practitioner should be aware of her or his individual *sense and use of self, presentation style mode of dress, ease of facial and eye*

contact, relaxed demeanour and *capacity for placing the client at ease* (Thompson, 2003b). The social worker should also be able to read the subtlety of any non-verbal language that the older person is expressing, particularly where this is at odds with what the client appears to be saying. If an older person is asked a question in relation to his or her independent living skills and the client indicates he or she is coping well but evidences very agitated body language this may mean a variety of things. Either the older person is threatened by any further loss of independence or has real fear of a lack of coping and what the future may hold. At a more fundamental level the older person may be tired or may not like the intervention of someone into their life whom they barely know. At the heart of any interaction is the premise that the professional is 'invading' the territory of the older person and the critical feature here is to manage those skills that are more likely to lead to a successful outcome.

Practice skills in communication

A skilled practitioner will be able to pick up the subtext here and by careful and considerate questioning encourage an older person to express these anxieties by concentrating on the values of good practice and an assertion and guarantee of the safety of the environment. Argyle (2007) suggests that where there are problems related to the feelings of inclusion of the client and the levels of irritability of the practitioner within communication, it is the non-verbal messages sent out that have the greatest significance. Symbolic communication will also play a part in how an older person will feel that he or she is being treated with respect, dignity and a sense that their needs are as important as that of any other client. This symbolism can reside within a lack of attention to the client's surroundings, space and environment (ergonomics) which are either lacking in cleanliness, invaded or hazardous. It may send out a quite contradictory message to the older person of their sense of worth than the practitioner's expressed sense of support.

The ethical aspect

The surprising aspect of substandard services for older people is not just that they exist but that older people endure them and why this might be. The ethical dimension of advocacy therefore has to be grounded in the older person as an active citizen with all of the rights that entails and the practitioner's ability to communicate these needs to the older person and a wider society. This ethical dimension is critical when we consider the nature of dignity itself, which tends to be viewed as a subtext of rights when the opposite is the case. Older people have rights 'because they have dignity. In an ethical sense, then, dignity is prior to rights. We respect the rights of others because we first recognise their dignity' (Sulmasy, 2008: 25). This sits favourably within that philosophical dimension of what it is to be a human being and the rights inherent within this premise.

As a part of effective communication, then, the social worker will have to consider additional aspects of diminishing mental and physical health and capacity; class and cultural considerations; inadequate life resources as well as those real fears of loneliness and of what the future may hold (Lishman, 2009). Communication skills do not reside in isolation; they permeate and cross boundaries of practice, client groups and other skills. They are at the heart of effective engagement whose practice leads to a sense of professional role, identity and expertise for the social worker and a sense of liberation for the older people where they are able to express strong emotions and fears in a mutually supportive environment. The practitioner should be self-aware and self-reflective within this process. All professionals will carry some anxieties related to their life experiences that may adversely impact on working with certain clients or areas of practice such as sexual abuse or substance misuse.

CASE STUDY

Jane has been a qualified social worker for three years and has recently started a new job in a care setting for older people. She had a traumatic childhood characterised by a father who drank heavily and who bullied Jane from an early age and who also physically assaulted her mother when drinking. Jane felt unable to help or support her mother and left home as soon as she could to avoid this abusive relationship. Her father died from an alcohol-related illness although Jane had no contact with him in the two years before his death. Jane has now been asked to work with Jim, a man in his seventies, who has had a lifetime of alcohol misuse and has lived in the care home since his family are no longer willing to support him at home. Jane has been asked to try and negotiate family contact with Jim who is increasingly lonely and isolated within the home. Jane is experiencing a wide range of emotional and stressful feelings during her communication with Jim and is feeling a physical pain that she cannot explain.

?   Reflective Questions   ?

- Can you speculate on the type of feelings Jane will be experiencing?
- Where do you think these feelings come from?
- How do you think these feelings may impact on Jane's capacity to communicate with Jim?
- What could Jane do to help resolve the issues of these strong feelings to sustain her working practice and professional development?
- What does Jane need to do to gain support and ensure she has an effective and professional communication with Jim?

These are not uncommon feelings within social work practice and should focus practitioners on what they can realistically achieve, where their support and development comes from and a realisation that social work does not exist in a microcosm but is part of an engaged and inclusive world practice.

Silence

A very effective skill in the tool kit of practitioners is the use of silence. This is very significant within the panoply of actual and developing professional skills as it indicates the confidence of the practitioner to work in an inclusive and empathic way. This also allows space for the older client to reflect on what it is he or she wants to say. It also supports the older person to disaggregate those more peripheral (but nonetheless distressing) concerns that may get in the way of the real need to be identified.

Egan (2007) has characterised the facets of *inadequate listening* in the way the practitioner may be feeling at that time, personal anxiety, difficulties in relating to the client or an over-identification with the client or a lack of empathy with the lived experience of the older person. If there is a high level of anxiety or lack of confidence in the practitioner's role then silence can prove to be very threatening (Kadushin and Kadushin, 1997).

Silence can be utilised by the client to indicate anxiety, annoyance, reflection or that he or she has said everything they want to. One person's silence may be another's eloquence and it is the professional capacity for interpreting these silences that will give ultimate meaning to the interaction.

Written communication

Social workers are committed to the preservation of client privacy and confidentiality and need to be aware of the characteristics of effective information gathering and report writing. This confidentiality is characterised by Biestek's (1961) focus on the ethical and value-driven aspects of protecting clients from undue public scrutiny as well as interacting in a way that is respectful and non-intrusive. There have been significant advances in the way that current social work files are stored within an electronic database and the numbers of practitioners who may have access to this information (Healey and Mulholland, 2007). Practitioners should be aware of the appropriateness of what is contained within these databases, particularly when they are accessed by third parties, as the tone, content and accuracy of information can have a significant effect on how the assessment and needs of an older person are characterised and evaluated. From my own experience in working in learning disability I came across an assessment of a client who had been referred to as 'annoying' that was yellow with age and had been written during her time in a large psychiatric unit 30 years before. This document was at the front of her personal file and undoubtedly coloured if not influenced how new members of staff related to her. Consequently, and unsurprisingly, this discriminatory practice effectively labelled the client, who lived up to this label as the only means she felt she had to exercise some control within herself and her environment. What appeared to be inexplicably aggressive behaviour could then be viewed within the context of labelling and finding any means of communication, however dysfunctional, in an effort to be acknowledged and heard.

? **Reflective Questions** ?

- What do you think should be the starting point for any interview or interaction with an older person?
- What do you need to know about your own presenting style and how are you able to critically evaluate this?
- Why should you avoid questions that elicit a 'yes' or 'no' response and when might these questions be appropriate?
- What roles do empathy and an ethical approach to working with older people have within any interaction?

Risk assessment

It is not the role of professional social work practice to assume an automatic connection between older age and risk. The older person may be perfectly capable and content to live independently and engage with his or her community and social networks even if external agencies automatically assume a lack of coping and isolation. The National Occupational Standards for Social Work and the Professional Capabilities Framework identify the range of skills that social work practitioners should have and among these is the facility to assess need. As in *empowerment* and *intervention* practitioners have to critically evaluate the actual meaning of *assessment* in the context of personal and professional skills and the collaborative process of assessment 'with' as opposed to an assessment 'of' an older person (Doel and Shardlow, 2005). Again there is a significant ethical focus here where assessment carried out within the narrow confines of agency protocol may address a declining range of services. This may be distinct from social work need and more importantly the older person's wishes. It is not uncommon in trainee social worker reports to read statements such as 'I assessed the client's needs and decided that ...' , without any real integration of the *process* of this interaction or the power imbalance that tends to reside within any interaction with social work clients.

The following question is one that may be missed at a time of increasing pressure on resources, particularly within the capacity for meeting the current and future care needs of older people.

? **Reflective Questions** ?

- Is it morally or ethically defensible to assess clients' wishes and needs knowing that the resources to meet these outcomes are not available?

Need and risk

Need and risk are not the same thing. While need may be evidenced as part of a more inclusive awareness with the older person as the sole arbiter of individual circumstances, risk should be addressed in a wider framework of the older person's concerns, strengths, rights and personal and structural resources (Lloyd and Taylor, 1995). This is integral to that enduring debate on the consideration of civil and human rights.

Assessment

Areas of Assessment Requirements When Working with Older People

Community care assessments (National Health Service and Community Care Act 1990, s.47)

Mental health assessment for admission to hospital or guardianship (Mental Health Act 1983, s.2,3,4,7)

Single assessment process – NHS Plan (Department of Health, 2000b) and the National Service Framework for Older People (Department of Health, 2001b)

Carer assessment – Carers (Recognition and Services) Act 1995

Assessments can take many forms although there are core skills that relate to a greater possibility of a successful outcome. Among these are:

- A clear idea of what the assessment is related to and hopes to achieve; analysing the information received to take an effective and appropriate course of action.
- A clear indication of how the practitioner will progress this information within the specific of action planning and review.

While the contextual aspects of how to proceed with an assessment may be clear to the social work practitioner it is the *process* within which this interaction takes place that is important here. This is particularly the case when the different models of assessment are taken into account. Smale et al. (1993) have identified three models of assessment, the *questioning*, *procedural* and *exchange*. While it is implicit within social work practice that practitioners will have to gain detailed information using a questioning model, it is also the area where discriminatory practice is most likely to occur. A *questioning* approach may have an over-focus on information gathering as opposed to those more psychological coping aspects, feelings and social work awareness of the long-term developmental issues of a client's present needs. The practitioner here is more likely to hold the power within this relationship and consequently this has the capacity to limit the involvement of the service user. The *procedural* model has the potential for similar attitudes in that the assessment may be completed to meet agency needs and resources where the individuality of the older person's experience may become subsumed within the procedural process itself. The *exchange* model fits well within any interaction with older people. While practitioners should not negate the importance of information relating to an older person's circumstances in terms of support, finances, community integration and emotional well-being, this has to be addressed within the understanding that the older person will be the best judge of what he or she needs (Watson and West, 2006).

Risk across the life course

The practitioner should also consider the *accumulation of risk factors*. Davey Smith (2003) postulates that the earlier life experiences of children may have a profound effect on that person as an older adult. The accumulation of life disadvantages from insecure nurturing, poverty and a lack of access to life opportunities such as secure employment and education may lead to an older person who has not been able to accumulate the necessary personal and resource capital to survive in old age. It is therefore incumbent upon the social work practitioner to assess any risk within the structure of what social work can provide and the coping and capacity skills of the client. This understanding also supports a rationalisation of the differential between risk and partnership. The resolution of risk may reside within the realms of professional practice, whereas the partnership aspect defines the older person as the repository of the knowledge and information to help support and sustain his or her individual needs (Watson and West, 2006).

The interprofessional context

What is Interprofessional Practice?

While professionals have to consider their own views and value base and the role that clients play in effecting successful outcomes, the same is true of the interprofessional role. While the multidisciplinary focus may be on meeting client need while preserving professional autonomy, interprofessional practice has an implicit sense that practitioners will work collaboratively to meet a common goal and also give up something of their professional power to meet this goal.

Within this focus there are key areas of knowledge, ethical practice and skills that social workers can bring to any collaboration. The ethical focus is particularly important as it is this that characterises social workers as a distinct professional body. Within this resides the capacity for challenging practice that falls below a professional standard. A significant starting point is that, irrespective of the different values that professionals may have, there is a mutuality of respect both for the expertise of the practitioners and what they can bring to any interaction with older people. Given the very different power differentials that can and do exist within interprofessional practice, a good starting point is for the constituent members of any team to clarify their potential for contribution and how this relates specifically to service delivery for the client (Irvine et al., 2002). This can mean defining the terminology used, individual skills, effective lines of communication and how the confidentiality of the service user is respected (Ovretveit et al., 1997). This is important within any focus on working with older people, where assumptions about the capacity of the older person to contribute to this process may vary within any team due to issues of understanding, power and the real meaning of collaborative working. Social work is ideally placed to take an overview of the lived experience of the older client and to address psychosocial issues, social inclusion and justice, needs and wishes and counter discriminatory practice based on ageist thinking and practice. Current social work practice has as a benchmark the very real contribution that service users and carers can make to this process. This should focus the professional's thinking on the presenting needs of an older person rather than as part of some broader speculative assessment on the physical or psychopathological potential of that client. Beresford and Croft (1993) have considered a *consumerist approach* and a *democratic approach* as integral to the role that service users and carers sustain within their involvement in services that impact upon them. The former attempts to increase the amount of choice and inclusion that service users and carers have within these services, whereas the latter relates more to that more esoteric area of social inclusion and, more fundamentally, to social justice (see Chapter 2). Essentially, this latter position relates more to structural and personal power and how disadvantaged groups such as older people may lose or be discouraged from using this power as part of the decision-making process (Warren, 2007).

The key characteristics of any successful interprofessional practice are:

- Knowledge of professional roles
- Willing participation
- Confidence
- Open and honest communication
- Trust and mutual respect
- Power (Barrett et al., 2005).

CASE STUDY

You are a social worker member of an interdisciplinary team comprising GP, community nurse, occupational therapist and home care supervisor brought together to discuss the case of Jane Lorimer. Jane is 84 years of age and has recently had a fall in her house and broken her leg. She has experienced poor health for a number of years and has severe mobility problems due to advanced arthritis. Jane is currently in hospital and there are very differing views among the members of the team as to how Jane's future needs should be assessed and met. Jane is due to be discharged in two weeks.

Given the characteristics of what makes for effective interprofessional practice can you consider the following questions?

? Reflective Questions ?

- Why is it important to define the specific roles of the participants and how might you go about this?
- How could the members of the team ensure that Jane is included in all aspects of the decision-making process?
- Why might some participants be more unwilling to engage in the interprofessional relationships than others?
- What makes for a professional identity and how could this progress the work of the team?
- What strategies could be put in place to ensure an effective communication and to ensure that all participants have their views considered?
- Why are issues of power so important within interprofessional practice and how does power relate to professional identity?
- How are the roles of the service user and carers to be addressed?
- Who should chair this meeting and why?

While this may postulate more questions than answers, a capacity to consider, if not answer, these questions should focus on the very specific role that social work plays in meeting needs and where there is an active consideration of the role of the older person.

Conclusion

A consideration of the older person as an individual with specific needs and experiences accrued over the life course is integral to effect a successful engagement and outcome. The core skills of preparation for working with older people and specific skills of communication are significant in ensuring that older people recognise that their individuality, wishes and needs are being addressed and not subsumed within a wider professional-organisational context. In effect, it is not enough to say that we will engage with older people but we have to state clearly how we propose to do this, who will contribute and how this is delivered in an inclusive and collaborative way with the older person.

 ## Recommended Reading

Higham, P. (2006) *Social Work: Introducing Professional Practice*. London: Sage. This text addresses issues of professional identity as well as more philosophical aspects of moral competence and a more psychological aspect across the life course.

Koprowska, J. (2008) *Communication and Interpersonal Skills in Social Work* (2nd ed.). Exeter: Learning Matters. This is a comprehensive read that addresses the finer detail of communication and is strong on inclusive practice, collaboration and value-driven working.

Thompson, N. (2003) *Communication and Language: A Handbook of Theory and Practice*. Basingstoke: Palgrave Macmillan. This complex publication extrapolates the finer details of communication and interpersonal engagements with a strong focus on postmodernism and relevant case studies.

4

COMMUNITY CARE

Learning Outcomes

This chapter looks at:

- Background to community care and its historical perspective.
- Community care legislation and related policy and how this may be interpreted in meeting older people's needs.
- Care management and a range of assessment processes and methods to raise awareness of the multiplicity of approaches to addressing need.
- Safeguarding adults and the protection of vulnerable adults and what this range of protections may be.
- Self-directed support, individual budgets and personalisation and their role within support, inclusion and the promotion of anti-discriminatory practice and independent living skills.

Legislation and policy: background

Services for older people have frequently been characterised as something of a 'Cinderella service' as they have historically been last in the queue for the allocation of resources. There has been a clear prioritising of specific groups in need where child protection issues have been in the ascendance since the raising of public awareness beginning in the 1970s with the Maria Colwell and other related cases. Concurrent with this has been that sense that a lower priority and 'unglamorous' group such as older people may also be in receipt of services that are less focused on a professional engagement and where unqualified staff may be the norm rather than the exception. Ironically, the writings of Townsend (1964, 1981) identified the same historical themes when reviewing the institutional nature of residential care settings as well as the structured dependency of older age where poorly qualified and motivated staff, more redolent of the views and attitudes of the poorhouse, were the norm.

The concern over the demographics of abuse and an ageing population has brought into focus how services for older people will be managed in the longer term. The Griffiths Report (1988) on *Community Care: An Agenda for Action* fed into the Department of Health's (1989) White Paper on community care and ultimately the National Health Service and Community Care Act 1990. An increase in private nursing care and the Department of Health and Social Security (DHSS) guidelines that allowed easier access to social security funding to acquire these services heightened the awareness and concerns of the potential financial implications of covering these costs in the longer term. It is true to say that while this burgeoning private sector was in accord with neoliberal political aspirations, it was at odds with governmental commitment to a more domiciliary care focus. Students and practitioners might like to consider the implications for the future care of older people where care and profit come into conflict.

The Griffiths Report (1988) suggested that there needed to be more clarity as to the responsibility of local authorities in meeting the needs of older people and that current policy of funding through the social security system was wasteful. Also, there were concerns as to whether older people in care settings would be better supported within a more community-based support system. He also suggested that there should be more collaborative working between private, local authority and voluntary agencies to develop support systems to meet these needs. This fitted very much with the governmental emphasis on free market economies, where the private and independent sector would be stimulated through competitive tendering to provide cost-effective support. These policy initiatives had as their foundation the ideological stance that these services would ultimately be more cost-effective than the more bureaucratic public services (Hughes, 1995).

Key Objectives of the Griffiths Report

- Promote inclusive practice and self-determination for services users and carers. The service user would now become a consumer with all the rights that that confers within a more market-driven economy and a focus on value for money.
- Ensure that as far as possible older people should be supported within their own homes where the support services would be provided within the wider community.
- Target resources for those identified as most in need to avoid duplication of services.

At a wider level Griffiths suggested that there needed to be a more strategic governmental approach and the resourcing of support services should be focused within collaborative local authority provision. This also reiterated the more political dimension: local authorities would move from provision to *enabling* service provision within a mixed economy of care and with an emphasis on prudent financial management.

National Health Service and Community Care Act 1990

The 1990 Act was fully implemented in April 1993 and one of the major changes was the way that funding for residential and nursing care would be managed in the future. A key characteristic of this was that anyone seeking to access these services would now have to be assessed through the local authority and the guidelines laid down within the 1990 Act. This care management aspect was introduced as a focus of the new legislation and arranged packages of care to ensure that as far as possible older people would be able to remain within their own homes rather than having to access residential care or become hospitalised. This care management focus has been at the centre of considerable political debate as to how it fits within the process and function of value-driven and ethical social work practice.

This focus on the consumer and consumerism is at odds with the reality of the experiences of older people in need. The dichotomy here is that expressed need may be at odds with the decision-making powers of social workers and what they may ultimately define as need. There is also the debate as to whether a two-tier system will evolve where older people with better resources will effectively have a better range of services and choice, while those with limited resources may have to face the reality of less choice and poorer quality of care (Phillips et al., 2006). The larger political and ethical question as to whether the care of older people generally should be at the behest of market forces as opposed to a more inclusive and engaging system tends not to figure prominently within current economic and policy debate. There is also evidence from the current rhetoric on inclusion, choice and personalisation that is somewhat at odds with governmental and media scaremongering about the 'problem' of older age and its resourcing. Practitioners will need to become increasingly more politically aware if they are to fulfil an engaged and empathic as opposed to a controlling role in meeting the needs of older people.

Recent Legislative and Policy Initiatives

Caring for People (1991) – the emphasis here is on an awareness of the potential long-term and enduring physical and mental ill-health that vulnerable people may experience.

Care Management and Assessment (1991) – with a focus on effective use of resources and the promotion of inclusion and choice within an equal opportunities agenda. This also addressed the needs of carers and wider support networks with an emphasis on human rights and self-determination.

The Care Programme Approach (1995) – the delivery of care that involves carers and service users in an inclusive, safe and accountable way. The emphasis here is on the coordination of services within an interprofessional focus that promotes choice, independence and empowerment.

The National Service Framework for Older People (2001) – the eight policy standards identified within this policy are: opposing age discrimination; ensuring an inclusive and person-centred approach to planning and service delivery; intermediate care to ensure older people can maintain their own accommodation and avoid long-term hospitalisation or residential care; ensuring that there is an appropriate skills base within hospitals to meet the needs of older people; better diagnosis and treatment of stroke patients; prevention of falls strategy; a wider awareness of the multiplicity of physical and mental health issues that can impact on older people; and the promotion of health and well-being for older people generally. (See Single Assessment Process section later in this chapter.)

Fair Access to Care Services (2003) – the promotion of consistency in the way that older people's needs are assessed; the overarching promotion of independent living skills and support; a more systematic and consistent approach to risk assessment; and a more consistent approach to review and meet the needs of older people accessing services for the first time and, more importantly, those who have been within the care system over a longer period.

Mental Capacity Act (2005) – focuses on capacity as opposed to incapacity (see also the Adults with Incapacity Act (Scotland) (2000)) with a consideration that people may not always make decisions that are in their best interests but this has to be viewed in the context of self-determination, choice and human rights. Also that prior expressed wishes of clients are acknowledged in any focus of treatment or engagement and that any intervention is the least restrictive and in the best interests of the older person.

Mental Health Act (2007) – this amended the Mental Health Act (1983) with its powers of compulsory detention and treatment, the Domestic Violence, Crime and Victims Act (2004) and the Mental Health Act (2005). The amendments are in light of conflicts that were identified within the Human Rights Act 1998 and particularly within a perceived breach of Article 5 of the Human Rights Act 1998 that guarantees liberty and security and that stipulates that 'Everyone has the right to liberty and security of the person'.

Care management and assessment: background

As far back as the inception of the National Health Service and Community Care Act 1990 legislation there has been some confusion as to what specifically care management means or represents (Fisher, 1991). It is certainly the case that it sits within the focus of a more neoliberal aspect of market forces and political invective, and practitioners have to query and evaluate the potential conflicts with an ethical and person-centred approach to meeting the needs of older people. Essentially, where there is a focus on resources, however pragmatic, at the expense of meeting individual need there is a potential for care management to focus on controlling aspects of older people's lives. This may be in opposition to an active engagement with individual need.

Hughes (1995) further speculates that there may be confusion between the roles of the practitioner who carries out the initial assessment with an older person and the person who manages the care package itself. This is particularly the case where social care, unlike health care which is free at the point of entry, is means tested. This is something of a departure from previous social work roles where the assessment and provision of services frequently emanated from the same source. This also needs to be considered and evaluated as, under the National Health Service and Community Care Act 1990 guidelines, there is a stipulation that 75% of services accessed have to be purchased from the private or independent sector (Barrett et al., 2005).

Care management and managerialism

Again the whole ethos of the 'purchaser–provider' split has gained common currency within practice without a concurrent dialogue on the 'commodity-based' language of the marketplace in relation to meeting the needs of individual older people. Indeed, there is clear evidence to indicate that a move to this more market-based economy of care may be eroding the long-term social work skills base where practitioners struggle to make sense of a commitment to person-centred practice at the expense of meeting increasingly stringent budgetary constraints.

Postle (2002) has identified that an increasing priority of care management has been to ration scarce resources and as such has lost considerable ground from its inception and conception of a more focused and globalised emphasis on care and need. There is evidence within the social work profession that any further evolution of managerialism or increased over-professionalism, while developing the role and identity of the profession within a public forum, may increasingly undermine the confidence of older people who use the services (Fook, 2003). In effect, policy decision making and the regulation of services become increasingly devolved from the experiences of those working directly with vulnerable clients, with a potential decrease in an emphasis on social justice.

Awareness of diversity

This may also be the case where the power and control aspects of professional practice take precedence over active engagement with older people. McCaffrey (1998) speculates that this divergence of roles between care managers and frontline staff may lead to an object relations-based 'splitting' as a defensive posture against taking responsibility for unpopular or difficult decisions. He also suggests that this tension can predicate new ways of thinking and practice, although the potential for blame, stress and tensions within staff teams also has to be considered. Whatever the overall view, there needs to be a re-engagement with structural policy and the research base to ensure that there is a reinvigoration of social work skills and knowledge to meet the current and future needs of older people.

Without this there is an increasing likelihood that the focus of practice will increasingly involve those processes and procedures to evaluate risk rather than a more global and holistic approach. Indeed, an over-emphasis on generic risk and its perception may come at the expense of a true sense of the individualism of all older people. There may also be an increasing correlation in viewing risk as a first port of call when assessing any older person with a concurrent need to check and supervise older people. This has the potential to leave the way open for an infantilist approach and a negation of fundamental human rights. A significant feature here of practitioner knowledge is an understanding of difference and particularly in relation to disability, race and ethnicity. The word 'race' is based on a social construct and has no basis within a biological determination. If we do belong to a race it is the human race and part of an ethical understanding of practice is that everyone belongs to this particular club! While race may have undergone some significant changes in understanding over the years, it is as the root form of 'racism' that it tends to be invested with the most significant meaning. Ethnicity is more closely related to those aspects of culture, language and faith as well as a sense of shared common identity. If older people are disadvantaged by a lack of rights, inclusion and poverty then how more can this be exacerbated if those features of identity are also denied them (Lander, 2010)?

Concurrent with this is a more philosophical debate about the nature of knowledge itself and how this is constructed. It is generally perceived that any professional making an assessment is doing so in an objective and professional way. Nevertheless, this may also involve the practitioner sorting the perceived problems of older people into 'categories' that may effectively be no more than an extension of the labelling process. Fook (2003: 116) suggests that these assessed 'problematic' areas of older people's lives 'must somehow be constructed in categories which are non-threatening, powerless or acceptable in some ways to dominant groups'. These exemplars raise the uncomfortable fact for practitioners that one person's empowerment may lead to the disempowerment of another person. If the worker perceives older people as a homogeneous group characterised by neediness and an inability to engage effectively with their own future needs then it is easy to categorise and label older people and in the process to *ration* any sense of empowerment within this focus. Essentially this is what the nature of control and power is about – the capacity for one person to make summary suppositions about another based on personal views rather than personalised, individual practice.

Different types of assessment

There are variations in assessment that can address human growth and developmental theory and knowledge across the life course as well as the relationship older people have with their social and lived environment. The former may be mitigated by an awareness and understanding of the enduring psychopathology of the older person and particularly the stressors that may have impacted from childhood and been carried across time and space (Higham, 2006). The latter assessment approach relates to those more structural aspects of older people within society and the forces of ageism, poverty and gender construct that create stress and coping problems in older age.

The Department of Health White Paper *Our Health, Our Care, Our Say* (2006a) proposed that the Single Assessment Process would incorporate the previously existing panoply of assessments (risk, social care and specialist) under one umbrella. The rationale for this was to avoid duplication of information and services and to encourage a more collaborative approach to meeting the needs of older people and any identified vulnerable groups. At the same time the guidance identified the four main areas of assessment that would be undertaken under the new process as:

- Contact assessment: This is where the basic information regarding the older person's need would be gathered by anyone deemed competent to carry this out.
- Overview assessment: Again, this could be carried out by anyone deemed competent by the supporting agency and would cover a more comprehensive range of issues related to physical, social, environmental and emotional needs. It is clearer here that this would involve some knowledge of underpinning human development across the life course and may trigger the need for specialist services.
- Specialist assessment: This would relate to a specific area of need that the older person has identified and would be carried out by someone with specialist knowledge of benefits, developmental needs or any area that is stopping the older person moving forward and retaining a level of independence.
- Comprehensive assessment: This would be carried out where there are a range of enduring and complex needs from physical and mental health, to housing and benefits and welfare. It is likely that this would involve a multi-professional approach drawing on a wide range of agencies and skills within a collaborative and inclusive forum to meet these presenting needs.

Assessment skills

The significant feature of any professional assessment is the ability to engage with the older person to ensure that a proactive and fluent approach to need is utilised. This is not as simple as it sounds and will involve drawing on a range of communication skills and a background focus of theory and knowledge (see Chapter 3). Without entering into the ongoing debate on the nature of knowledge between the scientific and social work knowledge base, the skilled practitioner will inevitably make use of those more intuitive skills, i.e. what appears to be right, from a critically reflective perspective. The paradox is that intuitive skills are developed over time and based on personal and skills development.

Single assessment process

A critical feature of care management is the Single Assessment Process that is part of the evolution of the National Service Framework for Older People (Department of Health, 2001b) (see Single Shared Assessment in Scotland). This stipulates the person-centred and inclusive approach that practitioners need to address for any effective assessment and focuses on listening, individualism and holistic evaluation, where services are designed to meet need as opposed to a one size fits all approach (Milner and O'Byrne, 2009). The National Service Framework for Older People seeks to identify those older people who may be disadvantaged or at risk of harm and the focus is on the promotion of independent living skills and the prevention of any further deterioration in health or well-being generally. While the eight standards for the Single Assessment Process have been identified above these more generic aspects have to be considered within a person-centred and cultural framework that takes note of the multiplicity of disadvantages that can impact on older people. These may relate to ageism, ethnicity, stigma, health, housing, welfare and well-being (Martin, 2011).

The care plan for the single assessment process

The Single Assessment Process was introduced in England in 2004 and is underpinned by Department of Health policy and guidance (2001b, 2002b, 2003). However there has been a consistent level of confusion as to what the terms 'integration' or 'multidisciplinary' working and assessment really mean (Dowling et al., 2004). There is a danger, particularly in times of recession where agencies seek to protect their own philosophical and financial independence, that the assessment process will not move beyond the 'forming' stage of collaborative working (Mullender and Ward, 1991). Essentially this relates to forming bonds of trust within a group working process where individuals share information, skills and a commitment to practice and engagement to ensure that there is no unnecessary duplication of effort or spending.

Care planning related to the Single Assessment Process should consider the following areas with due consideration of the *questioning*, *procedural* and *exchange* models of assessment (Smale et al., 1993):

- Whether the older person has consented to this interaction and how and with whom any information collected will be shared. This is fundamental to inclusive, collaborative and ethical practice.
- An overview of needs with due consideration of risks to health and independent living and the potential for development or rehabilitation in the future. There needs to be a clear statement here of any risks agreed on by the older person. This could be remaining in unsafe or unsuitable accommodation when the older person does not wish to be rehoused.
- What part the older person will play within this process with due consideration of the rights and responsibilities of participants.
- The contribution of wider support agencies – carers, family and community-based organisations – and what they can be reasonably expected to provide.
- The frequency of intervention of these support agencies and a clearly defined statement as to who will do what and when.
- Clarification of any costs that may be incurred by the older person through this process, particularly where there is a potential need for nursing care.

- Contact details for a named person who will be responsible for overseeing the formulation of the care plan and contact details for another responsible person in the case of unavailability or emergency.
- A clear statement, including dates and participants, of the monitoring and review process to ensure the care plan is a living, meaningful document that meets the current and developing needs of the older person.

Exercise

- While considering the assessment process you might like to consider any recent engagement you have had with an older client where you have been attempting to assess need or risk and relate that experience to the above themes.

It is worthwhile here to stipulate that any future care needs will not necessarily be based on increasing needs but may be mitigated by increasing capacity and ability through time (Department of Health, 2002b). Research by Abendstern et al. (2011) into integration within the assessment of older people with health and social care needs indicates that there is a lack of clarity as to the type of assessment that should be carried out to meet these specific needs. At the same time there is an awareness among the respondents in their study (Single Assessment Process lead officers) of the need to consider a range of assessments to meet the developing needs and circumstances of older people in a changing political climate.

CASE STUDY

Soraya is 75 years of age and was born in Bangladesh. She has lived in this country for over 60 years and has recently come to the attention of the social work department after a fall in a local supermarket. Soraya appeared malnourished when she was taken to hospital and seemed quite confused as to what was happening. The duty social worker has met with her and stated that he must contact the immediate family as it is 'most likely' Soraya would be looked after by them. Soraya has a poor grasp of English and the social worker is struggling to understand her and to assess her immediate need. The social worker is intimating within his initial report on Soraya that she may be suffering from 'dementia' and that he will need a full medical assessment. Soraya is insisting that she wishes to go home as soon as she has finished her treatment in the hospital and has informed a nurse who also comes from Bangladesh of this.

? Reflective Questions ?

- Can you identify any cultural assumptions here that may be potentially discriminatory?
- How could the level of communication between Soraya and the social worker be improved?

- What other reasons could there be for Soraya appearing confused?
- What do you think are the key areas that the social worker would need to understand to effect a successful assessment outcome for Soraya?

The study by Powell et al. (2007) clearly identifies the wishes of older people to have a significant role in the management of their own health and well-being as well as in self-promotion of independent living skills. More importantly, the research evidences a desire by older people to engage with peer groups and younger people as a facet of intergenerational awareness and understanding. There is something paradoxical in the wisdom and maturity of age refocusing on a more 'youthful' engagement with the younger generation as part of an inclusive relationship. These relationships are central to any effective assessment that includes the more holistic aspects of older people need (Wenger and Tucker, 2002).

Human Rights Act 1998

Underpinning all of these aspects of care planning is the Human Rights Act 1998 that came into effect in the UK in October 2000. The Act comprises 16 basic rights to protect individuals from exploitation and harm. These have evolved from the European Convention on Human Rights (1950) with its defined articles related to protection. While the progenitor of this may be based on atrocity and circumvention of human rights during the war years, ironically the Human Rights Act is increasingly being used to protect citizens from the encroachment of state and political abuse. This may relate to a passivity or even an unwillingness to meet the needs of older people within the community where there is a clear statutory obligation to do so.

Some Useful Policy Documents

Department of Health (1989) *Caring for People: Community Care in the Next Decade and Beyond*. London: The Stationery Office.

Department of Health (2000) *The NHS Plan: A Plan for Investment, A Plan for Reform*. London: The Stationery Office.

Department of Health (2001) *Care Homes for Older People: National Minimum Standards*. London: Department of Health.

Department of Health (2001) *National Service Framework for Older People*. London: Department of Health.

(Continued)

(Continued)

Department of Health (2002a) *Fair Access to Care Services: Guidance on Eligibility Criteria for Adult Social Care*, LAC (2002) 13. London: Stationery Office.

Department of Health (2002b) *Guidance on the Single Assessment Process for Older People*, HSC 2002/001: LAC (2002)1. London: Department of Health.

Department of Health (2002c) *Women's Mental Health: Into the Mainstream*. London: Department of Health.

Department of Health (2003) *Guidance on the Single Assessment Process for Older People: Implementation Guidance for April 2004*. London: Department of Health.

Department of Health (2004) *The National Service Framework for Older People*. London: Department of Health.

Department of Health (2006a) *Our Health, Our Care, Our Say: Making it Happen*. London: Department of Health.

Department of Health (2007a) *Putting People First: A Shared Vision and Commitment to the Transformation of Adult Social Care*. London: Department of Health.

Department of Health (2007b) *Putting People First: Transforming Adult Social Care*. London Department of Health.

Department for Works and Pensions (2008a) *Income-related Benefits: Estimates of Take-up in 2006–2007*. London: DWP Analytical Services Division.

Department for Work and Pensions (2008b) *Households below Average Income – 1994/5 to 2006/7*. London: DWP, Information Analysis Directorate.

Department of Health (2008c) *Health and Care Services for Older People: Overview Report on Research to Support the National Service Framework for Older People*. London: Department of Health.

Department of Health (2009a) *The Common Assessment Framework for Adults: A Consultation on Proposals to Improve Information Sharing around Multi-disciplinary Assessment and Care Planning*. London: Department of Health.

Department for Work and Pensions (2009a) *Opportunity Age Indicators – 2008 Update*. London: DWP, Older People and Ageing Society Division.

Department of Health (2009b) *Shaping the Future of Care Together*. London: Stationery Office.

Department of Health (2012a) *Better Care to Prevent Falls and Fractures will Improve Lives and Save the NHS Billions*. London: Department of Health.

Department of Health (2012b) *Research and Development Work Relating to Assistive Technology 2011–2012*. London: Department of Health.

Assessment criteria for older people

CASE STUDY

Rosemary is 78 years of age and is currently occupying a council tenancy. She has fallen and broken her hip and has recently been discharged from hospital and is quite specific that she can manage at home despite the concerns of the hospital social work staff. She has stated that she has lived in the house all her married life and brought up her children there and wishes to remain there for as long as possible. While her house is on the ground floor there is narrow and restricted access to the bathroom and cooking area and Rosemary is finding using a Zimmer frame within the house impossible. You are a social worker and have been asked to visit Rosemary to carry out an assessment of need. Rosemary is willing to take part in this but is adamant that she will not relinquish her tenancy.

? Reflective Questions ?

- What areas of assessment do you think need to be addressed?
- How far reaching do you think the assessment should be in meeting her physical, environmental and emotional needs and how could these be addressed?
- Who else do you think could contribute to this assessment and in what way?
- What specific knowledge, information and personal skills should you draw on to complete this assessment?
- What value and ethical considerations do you think you would need to consider when completing this assessment?

There is a legal requirement for a local authority to carry out an assessment of need for any older person who presents as being in need of services. This may not always be an assessment focused on support within the community as these needs may be better addressed within a more intensive and therapeutic environment (Glendinning et al., 2008; Walker and Beckett, 2003). Whatever the specific needs of the older person the assessment is seen as the foundation for any professional care management engagement. Where eligibility is identified then the older person would be assessed within the following four categories of need/risk as identified under the guidance from the Fair Access to Services (2003) (FACS): *critical*, *substantial*, *moderate* and *low*. The critical assessment would consider a persistent and enduring threat to life or health from abuse or exploitation; the substantial assessment would include an inability to carry out day-to-day living tasks with a minimum of support services in evidence; the moderate focus would be on an inability to carry out some personal tasks such as work and a commensurate lack of support services; and finally the low assessment of need would include an inability to carry out some personal tasks as well as a deficiency of support services. Local authorities have a commitment under s.47 (1) (b) of the National Health Service and Community Care Act 1990 to provide services for those in need but this is predicated on the resources available to meet these needs. Some local authorities may only intervene when there is a perceived critical risk or need and may not consider meeting any needs other than this. Irrespective of the necessity to have a pragmatic approach to policy and available finance, there is a clear ethical dimension here to making an assessment that the local authority is unwilling or unable to address. The moral dimension of whether it is ethical to carry out an assessment knowing that the identified needs cannot be met should also be considered here.

The effect is that there may be an increasingly small number of older people deemed to be in need while family and any community support will be left to pick up any shortfall. This is at odds with the more inclusive aspect of care and one can only wonder how an older person with enduring difficulties in life skills and well-being generally will interpret this (Ray et al., 2009).

Within the Department of Health's *Care Management and Assessment: Manager's Guide* (1991a) and the *Care Management and Assessment: Practitioner's Guide* (1991b) there are seven core tasks identified for meeting the care of someone in need: information gathering; determining the level and scope at which assessment will be carried out; assessing the actual need; care planning; carrying out the care plan; monitoring the effectiveness of the care plan; and regular reviews of the care plan to meet the changing circumstances of older people (Sharkey, 2007). Without this continuum of evaluation it is likely that the care planning process will become static and fail to meet developments and need in the longer term. Taylor and Donnelly (2006) identified that assessment and decisions about the long-term care of older people were often prompted by a specific crisis and that this could sometimes cloud the judgement of professionals when making a decision. They speculate that professional decision making should recognise that a more holistic range of support mechanisms in place from family, friends and community as well as a close awareness of the expressed wishes, needs and fears of the older person.

Safeguarding

What is safeguarding? Safeguarding adults addresses a range of areas where there may be a need for additional measures to ensure client safety. This may be related to illness, disability, capacity or the frailty brought about by old age. Safeguarding can be at a personal or multi-agency approach where risk and vulnerability is assessed through the 'No Secrets' guidelines. The 'No Secrets' guidance was issued under s.7 of the Local Authority Services Act 1970 and places a responsibility on local authority staff to pass on any concerns regarding neglect or abuse of a vulnerable person. Michael (2008) defined the relationship between safeguarding and health care as the capacity any society has to care for its most vulnerable members.

Within any consideration of safeguarding there has to be a presumption of capacity, irrespective of the individual choices an older person may make (Milner and O'Byrne, 2009). The rationale for this is simple. Disadvantaged groups will be further stigmatised where there is a tendency for service providers or even carers to legislate on their behalf with the implicit assumption that they know better than their client. Research suggests that between 2% and 4% of older people and their carers are at risk of neglect or mistreatment. This can be by structural agencies and service providers or by family members and may include emotional, financial, physical and sexual abuse (Mowlan et al., 2007; Mullender, 1996).

Safeguarding Vulnerable Groups Act 2006

This legislation came about from the public inquiry by Sir Michael Bichard (Bichard, 2004) into the murders of Holly Wells and Jessica Chapman by Ian Huntley in 2002. The report focuses on the vetting and barring of those individuals deemed to be a risk for working with any vulnerable groups and ensuring that those individuals are prevented from having access to those groups. The Act makes it mandatory to carry out pre-employment checks on all employees who intend to work with vulnerable groups. The Act allows for carers, families and those in receipt of direct payments to check this list for any potential employees and for local authorities to refer individuals to the independent body, the Independent Safeguarding Authority, to assess risk.

The Department of Health identified the following areas that this legislation will cover:

- Increasing the protection of vulnerable adults through increasing awareness of risk and building on the Protection of Vulnerable Adults (POVA).
- Allowing decisions about risk to be related to individuals' pre-existing criminal records.
- Ensuring a more up-to-date and more easily accessible range of information on those who may be deemed a risk and that this information is disseminated more speedily and widely to those working with vulnerable groups.
- Expanding the range of agencies and workers who will be eligible for checks as to their suitability for working with vulnerable groups (DH, 2006).

Protection of vulnerable adults (POVA)

This was introduced in 2004 to protect vulnerable adults (those who are 18 and over) within care settings in England and Wales. Central to POVA is the list of potential employees deemed unsuitable to work with vulnerable adults. Workers who are deemed to be in breach of professional practice and standards will be reported to the POVA list managed by the Department of Health (DH) and will remain on this list until there is clear evidence that they no longer pose a threat. Employers are encouraged to access this list when employing new staff and anyone whose name appears there will be deemed unsuitable to work in this area. This reinforces s.81of the Care Standards Act 2000 which identifies that there will be a list of individuals who are not considered suitable to work with vulnerable adults.

The General Social Care Council (GSCC) identifies key areas that social workers should address when working with vulnerable adults:

- Promote and protect the rights of vulnerable service users and carers.
- Support and promote the independent living skills of service users while protecting them from harm and danger as far as is reasonably possible.
- Respect the rights of service users while ensuring at the same time they are not a danger to themselves or others (General Social Care Council, 2002).

Additional Legislation Addressing Safeguarding Needs

Human Rights Act 1998

Data Protection Act 1998

Care Standards Act 2000

Freedom of Information Act 2000

Care Homes Regulation 2001 (Reg. 37)

Mental Capacity Act 2005

NHS Act 2006

Equality Act 2010.

In Scotland there is a different range of legislation including the:

Adults with Incapacity (Scotland) Act 2003

Mental Health (Care and Treatment) (Scotland) Act 2003

Adult Support and Protection (Scotland) Act 2007.

Self-directed support and personalisation

Personalisation is the capacity for older people (and all adults in social care) to both make choices and influence policy and practice that impacts on a sense of independence and well-being. A significant feature of any consideration of personalisation is that the older person is no longer to be viewed as the passive recipient of services but as a sentient being with experiences and wishes and the capacity to make important decisions about both present and future needs (Gardner, 2011). Concurrent with this widely held view of personalisation is that it has the potential to shift a consideration of risk from the state to the individual. This could then actively disadvantage older people, who may increasingly be perceived as the cause of their own personal, physical or emotional misfortune. This could also be at a time when the individual is already struggling against more structural discrimination through poverty and lack of resources. One person's personalisation may be another's disadvantage and this is particularly the case if the vulnerable older person has not the skills or the physical or psychological strength to engage within this process (Ferguson, 2007).

Self-directed support is the progenitor of personalisation itself. It sets the scene for an inclusive and collaborative approach to older people's needs while firmly placing them at the centre of the decision-making process as to what these needs are. The emphasis is on 'self-assessment, person-centred planning, self-directed support and training for service users' (Parker and Bradley, 2010: 134). Thompson (1992) also refers to that ontological (the study of being) aspect with its emphasis on individuals having the capacity for change and to influence decisions that may impact on them. This is what is at the heart of both person-centred practice and the potential conflict that can exist between the older person and the practitioner where they may both seek to manifest action and control based on their own interpretation of the world.

This is not a new concept and is contingent on the premise enshrined within the National Health Service and Community Care Act 1990 that sought to provide a greater level of choice through a mixed economy of care. So how is this to be achieved, particularly within a climate where there are genuine fears about all future funding to meet the needs of vulnerable groups? There is a clear connection between the concepts of personalisation and independence both in terms of thinking and lived experience. Secker et al. (2003: 375) identify independence generally as the lack of dependence on others, but within the field of older people services there is a much more complex definition. Here it is identified as not only based on 'self-reliance but also self-esteem, self-determination, purpose in life, personal growth and continuity of the self'. This 'continuity of the self' is at the heart of the more ontological aspect I previously referred to and may include a more philosophical and spiritual dimension beyond any resource implications. Essentially, this is what it is *to be* and that meaning is just as important as resources in pursuit of a fulfilling life in older age.

Direct payments

Direct payments are legislated for under the Community Care (Direct Payments) Act 1996. This gave local authorities the powers to implement direct payments and this was extended to those over the age of 65 in 2000. Direct payments are designed to enable older people to manage their own care and to effectively manage their own health care. There has been a diverse response to these direct payments particularly in how they are managed, the impact on staff time and employment and whether there are the core skills available within the profession to manage these often complex financial dealings (Leese and Leese, 2006).

Individual budgets

These are a more flexible response to the domestic, social and educational needs of older people. While direct payments are focused more on statutory provision, individual budgets utilise a much wider range of funding streams commensurate with the areas of support it seeks to provide. As with direct payments there are no additional government funds provided so individual budgets have to draw on a range of existing resources through the Resource Allocation System (RAS) such as the Independent Living Fund (ILF) and Supporting People (SP), although some research speculates as to whether this is simply a strategy in cutting costs by devolving this budget across a range of pre-existing resources (Beresford, 2007). This is a less bureaucratic system where individual receipts are not required for all spending and so there are grounds for stating that it is a more inclusive, choice-driven and personalised approach to meeting need. The downside is that there is evidence that older people, particularly, find the process onerous when it comes to the planning and management of the whole financial process (Glendinning et al., 2008).

The Social Care Institute for Excellence (SCIE) evidences that there is a need for more information and support to encourage older people to take up more personalised forms of self-directed support through accessing personal budgets. Newbronner et al. (2011) suggest that there is a clear need for more effective partnerships between individuals and agencies to ensure there is clear and readily accessible information in the public domain regarding personal budgets. The following areas were identified as key themes in maximising access to these budgets:

- Integrated working with health and vulnerable communities.
- Clarity within the risk assessment and risk management aspects of older people's need.
- Encouraging a creative response to meeting need as well as dedicated services to support older people in accessing personal budgets.
- Ensuring the older person has the opportunity to exercise choice to ensure maximum personal control over any personal budget.
- Overall monitoring of the budgets to ensure maximum efficiency (Social Care Institute for Excellence, 2011).

Key Issues to Consider Regarding Personal Budgets

- While personal budgets give a greater degree of control, choice and independence in purchasing services there may be concern as to how these budgets are managed and how the monies can be spent.
- There will be a need for trained staff to support the budget holders to exercise maximum control when meeting their own needs.
- There should be a systematic response to any concerns through information dissemination, peer support from existing budget holders and clarity as to the relationship between older people and service providers when negotiating packages of support and care.
- Carers, whether family or other community-based support, will have to be considered as to their role in supporting individual budgets and provision will need to be considered for those older people who may not have this level of support. (Newbronner et al., 2011).

Conclusion

There is still work to do in relation to meeting the needs of older people in the longer term. There have undoubtedly been major advances in relation to independent living and self-sustaining budgets to meet these needs but therein lies the problem. Increasingly, policy decision making and the media are likely to place undue and negative attention on older people and the role they play in society in general. There is little point in having personalisation without personhood. The inevitability of age and ageing needs a much more engaged approach, where the starting point needs to be: what can we put in place to meet the needs of an ageing population that has provided the support and infrastructure for the current generation?

 Recommended Reading

Brown, K. (ed.) (2010) *Vulnerable Adults and Community Care: Post-Qualifying Social Work Practice* (2nd ed.). Exeter: Learning Matters. A very good integrated text that could be used for student study and challenging practice in the field.

Coulshed, V. and Orme, J. (2006) *Social Work Practice* (4th ed.). Basingstoke: Palgrave Macmillan. Includes a very useful chapter on adults and the process of community care.

Means, R., Richards, S. and Smith, R. (2008) *Community Care Policy and Practice* (3rd ed.). Basingstoke: Palgrave Macmillan. Very good historical perspective on community care and a real breadth of perspectives including a European focus.

Sharkey, P. (2007) *The Essentials of Community Care* (2nd ed.). Basingstoke: Palgrave Macmillan. This volume offers a good discussion of the more social work aspects of community care in practice.

5

MENTAL HEALTH AND WELL-BEING

Learning Outcomes

This chapter looks at:

- Definitions and meaning of mental health and well-being.
- Socio-medical models of understanding with an emphasis on the medicalisation of older age, ageism and discrimination.
- How policy and practice can promote mental health and well-being with a critique of the perceived 'problem' of older age across gender and perceptions of ageing.
- A refocusing of how policy can meet the more personalised issues of well-being and happiness in older age.

Introduction

Significant numbers of older people experience mental ill health for a range of differing reasons. This may relate to declining health and long-term illness or a sense that the best years may be behind them with a commensurate fear of the future. As I have explored within the context of social work skills in earlier chapters, if older people are considered exclusively within the domain of their physicality then it is likely that their individual sense of *integrity* will be diminished. The diminution of this sense of self can only have negative consequences for the older person's perception of coping, both now and in increasing old age. The focus in this chapter will therefore be a pragmatic realisation of the vagaries of older age and its consequences with an emphasis on what mental health and well-being is. In conjunction, we need to remember the rather arbitrary nature of what old age is and how this 'chronological age' is a fairly loose benchmark of when the majority of people may retire. Again there is no necessary correlation between retirement and a consideration of what old age really is (WHO, 2013). Old age may increasingly be viewed as in the 'eye of the beholder' within a more personalised focus rather than as part of a more structurally determined negative stereotyping. This chapter will also identify relevant policy and what impact this has in the promotion of older people's mental health and well-being, with a focus on inclusion, empowerment and an active collaboration with older people in meeting their own care needs.

A wider definition of mental health and well-being

Mental health is defined as a state of well-being in which every individual realises his or her own potential, can cope with the normal stresses of life, can work productively and fruitfully, and is able to make a contribution to his or her community.

The positive dimension of mental health is stressed in the World Health Organization's (WHO) definition of health as contained within its constitution: 'Health is a state of complete physical, mental and social well-being and not merely the absence of disease or infirmity' (WHO, 2011).

Manthorpe and Iliffe (2009) have gone further than the above definition. They offer a more psychosocial aspect and suggest that it is not just the absence of disease but that it is the more fundamental 'dislocation or detachment' of the older person from their lived experience and positive ongoing social attachment that is significant. If we consider this more holistic aspect then it is not enough to view the older person as a sum of infirmities but as someone who is viewed within a personal life course and experience.

A negation of this individualism allied to poor resilience over the life course may leave an older person feeling dislocated from any support mechanisms. At the same time, this may involve a diminished sense of personal integrity that can only have a negative impact on an older person's potential for coping in the longer term. This may be further reinforced when the service user and carer agenda is considered and whether that dichotomy between inclusion and paying lip service to real need has been fully addressed. Rankin (2004) suggests that there has been a lack of consideration of the views of clients in decision making about their own care and that this may be exacerbated where there is a poverty, ethnicity and a mental health dimension. There is clear evidence that where older people are included in research into their participation in policy making that this has to be properly managed. Scourfield and Burch (2010) suggest that older people may be disadvantaged and made to feel 'powerless' if they are included within research where they have no real influence on decision making and that wider personalisation agenda. Barnes (2005) supports this assertion and suggests that the process of participation itself is as important as the perceived outcomes within participatory research for older people.

The increasing focus on the personalisation agenda also raises the issue of whether social workers are best placed to act in this 'brokerage' role when they are accountable within a more statutory context. The question therefore arises as to whether any brokerage should be exclusively accountable to the client's needs as part of a more functional system of support and advocacy (Beresford, 2007; Scourfield, 2008). Sullivan (2008) postulates that this role may be a decreasing feature of the working experience and practice of social workers as there is an increasing emphasis on models of assessment, risk outcomes and managerialism. Implicit within the personalisation agenda is that professionals will engage with this through a person-centred approach.

What is person-centred planning?

This is a way for people to have choice and control over their lives and is rooted in a philosophical sense of the nature of personhood. This should include active community involvement and a sense that older people can exert control over services that impact on them. It focuses on the abilities of the older person as opposed to the disability and on 'skills rather than ills'. The obverse of person-centred planning is where there is an over-emphasis on assessment without any appreciable increase in quality delivery of service within that subtext of the nature of ethical practice (Hunter and Ritchie, 2008).

Well-being

This is again quite difficult to define in that it may relate to good mental health, relationships, a sense of connectedness with the environment (Kitwood, 1999) or that purely subjective sense of the world in the context of positive feelings of the self or community. Individual feelings may however be difficult to quantify as to their supportive powers in coping with adversity. Well-being may have a set of predictive factors but may ultimately reside within the individual lived experience across the life course of the older person (Rutter, 1987). Bond and Corner (2004) go further and state that it is this very subjectivity that is at the centre of what well-being is as it is so closely connected to the older person's individual sense of life satisfaction and how this is assessed in relation to the totality of their individual lived experience. This is rarely accomplished in isolation and families will generally have some role to play. Older people can also become more resilient and adapt readily to changes in their loss of social networks by increasing their involvement with the wider community (Waite and Das, 2010). This may result in a focus on quality rather than quantity of relationships, which may tend to be more of a feature of the young as they explore and experiment within their evolving personal and social networks.

The background

There are a plethora of theories related to well-being. Consistent themes have referred to the work of Bowlby (1969), Rutter (1975), Ainsworth (1962), Erikson (1995),

Maslow (1987) and Fairbairn (1954) in relation to how individuals have been able to negotiate through early life experiences. It goes without saying that given the unique experiences of individuals and how they assess their own coping capacity, these needs may be difficult to legislate for in a social policy context.

Resilience

Resilience can be defined as the way in which an individual has successfully adapted to adversity. Resilience traditionally resides within the focus of the psychopathology of individuals and more specifically within adaptive behaviours in childhood (Zautra et al., 2010). The surprise from research on resilience is that children have a unique capacity for being well through the life course into old age irrespective of the earlier traumatic life experiences they may have had.

Resilience across the life course

If there is not some established sense of resilience (Gilligan, 2001) across the lived experience then older people may be left with an increasing ratio of life stressors in old age. This will certainly test any capacity for being and remaining well and *sustaining* an enduring sense of mental health and well-being. This is a significant issue in Britain today and there are serious problems associated with deprivation, discrimination, poor housing, violence within relationships and a more longitudinal sense of exclusion from that which the wider public would consider a right (Butler, 2004). Within a theoretical and evidence-based approach, G. Windle et al. (2008) have proposed that psychological resilience is related to a sense of self and efficacy, personal competence and how this is developed over the life course. This is further supported by the perception on the part of older persons of being able to influence decisions that impact upon them both individually and collectively. Netuveli et al. (2008) have characterised that sense of 'bouncing back' from adversarial situations to a previous stage of coping as the most significant feature of resilience. Their research has presented some notable findings, not least of which is that women are more resilient in increasing older age and that socio-demographic variables such as education, income and class are not necessarily predictors of resilience.

Predictors of resilience and well-being

Conversely, there is evidence to suggest that high levels of social support prior to the adversity and during the event are more likely to result in a successfully resilient outcome. This raises the obvious link here between effective and successful emotional engagement with others and the capacity to bounce back from adversity in old age. This is reinforced by Gallo et al. (2005), who suggest that older persons' self-esteem and their more generally optimistic outlook may be a good determinant of their capacity for resilience in older age with an attendant impact on the capacity for being well and coping with adversity.

This is at the heart of what mental health and well-being is with its focus on the contribution to social integration and belonging rather than an over-emphasis on declining health and a more disease-orientated (medical model) approach to old age.

Old people were not always old

Implicit within this consideration is a statement which seems obvious in its simplicity and that is that 'older people are not born old'. Unlike youth, with its sense of imper-manence that will be outgrown, older age is grown into and beyond and sits as much within the existential considerations of being as opposed to that more pro-scriptive nature of decline (Thompson, 1992). This existentialism relates to that debate that exists between individual freedom and choice and those political and socio-economic aspects of the world (Thompson, 2000). This may be particularly the case in relation to the mental health and well-being of older people where their sense of engagement with personal choice, self-advocacy and influence may be at odds with their perception of how they are engaged with and treated from a societal and structural perspective.

Socio-medical models of understanding

There is a profusion of theories that explore the amorphous nature of ageing. Some of these relate to biological ageing with its emphasis on the 'decline before the fall' and is a one-dimensional attempt to explain the ageing process. This process is as diverse as the process of youth with its differing experiences, levels of maturation and engagement with friends, family and a wider society. Older people characterised in this biological sense may therefore readily feel that they are being judged on a set of values and scales by which they have little consideration or understanding and may never hope to aspire to.

It is unsurprising that older people may feel disadvantaged, excluded and confused by a configuration of ascribed attributes that they do not recognise, with a commen-surate negative effect on their mental health and well-being. In an absolute sense this is a facet of ageism and is therefore discriminatory either in practice or within a laxity of reflection on how older people may feel at being characterised in this way. This will be compounded where there is an accumulation of years and a potential for reinforcement of already ageist thinking. Research by Lapid et al. (2011) clearly evidences that within the group defined as the 'oldest old', that is those in the over 90 age group, there was a consistent disparity in the positive aspects of quality of life that the respondents identified as opposed to caregivers who consistently scored this on a lower scale. If the primary qualification for effective social work practice is listening and engaging then this raises the possibility that practitioners, as part of the wider structural consideration, may also hold these negative and ageist views and perceptions (Allen et al., 2009).

Sheila Harper has been at the centre of her local community since the late 1950s. She has been the mainstay of the local Girl Guides, church and community activities and also supports a considerable number of older people in the community with their daily needs, access to services and help in sorting out their benefits. Sheila has always maintained good health and these community-based activities have been a major support to her since her husband Richard died last year. Sheila has fallen and broken her hip and has been hospitalised. While the nursing staff is able to support Sheila's physical needs she is becoming increasingly depressed and frustrated that she cannot go home. The doctor has told Sheila that it is unlikely she will be able to return home in the near future as he has concerns about who will look after her. This has had a traumatising effect on Sheila, who has tried to tell the doctor that she has 'duties' within the community that she needs to see to. The doctor feels unable to engage with this aspect of Sheila's care as he thinks the primary concern should be to ensure that Sheila accesses a care setting to meet her 'future and continuing needs'.

? Reflective Questions ?

- What impact would a clear understanding of mental health and well-being have on an assessment of Sheila's needs?
- What understanding of life history, coping and resilience would help in an understanding of Sheila's mental health and well-being?
- How might the ageing body influence how older people are perceived by medical staff irrespective of Sheila's potential for coping?
- How would you characterise the level of communication between Sheila and the medical services here?

Westerhof and Tulle (2007) have posited that there is an inherent paradox within the medicalisation of older age. While disease may be a facet of ageing there is nothing to suggest that ageing itself is a disease. The significance here is that while disease can be addressed and potentially cured, older age cannot. If there is this association of disease with ageing then it is inevitable that older age cannot be 'cured' but still needs to be engaged with. Older persons may inevitably feel that the very fact they have lived for a long time will inevitably place them within a focus of disease that they do not recognise on an individual basis. Indeed, the focus on the medicalisation and corporeal aspects of older people may still have as their benchmark a focus on the language of youthfulness. It may become increasingly difficult for older people to grow into an accepting and accepted older age from the point of view of the older person and society when ageing itself has become associated with so many negative connotations (Williams and Bendelow, 1998). These facets of ageing and ageism can place an older person within the restrictive focus of labelling and social opprobrium where their very existence may become a focus for concern and confusion. This is particularly the case when we consider the older person across the life course with an understanding of how psychological forces can both sustain and diminish the mental health and well-being of older people. There may be even more fundamental forms of disengagement where the spiritual dimension of the older person may be not acknowledged or ignored altogether (Bano and Benbow, 2010). This can hit at the heart of what it is to be, and have a concurrent negative impact on an older person's sense of self and well-being.

Discrimination

The iniquity of discrimination in the face of declining physical health will have a deterministic effect on the sense of well-being of older people, and a commensurate effect on mental health generally. Concurrent with this, Holloway (2010) suggests that rehabilitative psychiatry has become 'unfashionable' in an age of austerity and clearly focuses his argument within the social work domain on the level of distress caused to individuals. This humanistic approach also focuses on the possibilities of maximising the potential for coping for those in distress and the impact this will have on the funding of support services in the future.

Empowering older people

Empowerment and its meaning is multifaceted. It is a critical aspect of social work practice with its emphasis on supporting, encouraging and advocating for older people to take and retain control over their own destinies. At the focus of empowerment is the ability to negotiate with older people on their own terms and within their capacity to identify their presenting needs. Any failure to do this will inevitably mean that practitioners are more likely to impose their own values and in the process disempower and oppress older people and will be at odds with value-driven and effective practice (Watson and West, 2006).

Current developments in social work have attempted to refocus the older person at the centre of interactions that impact on them. This is at odds with the more ageist and medicalised approach that formerly persisted. Nusberg (1995) identifies a complex association of factors that counter well-being such as lack of resources, poor educational achievement, declining health and widespread negative and ageist attitudes. An empowerment model of social work practice characterises the social worker in an enabling role, supporting and providing information for the older person's identified needs. Essentially this should not be an issue of power and who devolves power to whom but an awareness and understanding of what power itself is. If it is conferred, then by implication this means that the person giving this power has a potentially more powerful position. The nature of empowerment is therefore to support older people to empower themselves (Thompson and Thompson, 2001).

Policy and Practice and How it Promotes Mental Health and Well-Being in Older Age

Mental health and well-being and associated law and policy directives underpinned by ethical and value-driven social work practice do not exist in isolation. Developing practitioners need to be increasingly aware of the political nature of policy directives as well as new evidence-based practice and a developing social work skills base.

What does the future hold?

Manthorpe and Iliffe (2009) refer to the general level of 'gloom' that pertains to any thinking about mental health and well-being in later life generally and more specifically as to whether these needs can be met. The demography of older people is changing quite radically. Those baby boomers born post-war will reach middle-age and die between 2010 and 2040 but after this period the number of older people is expected to reduce due to a declining population and poorer levels of health in those born after this period. In 2005 there were just under 10 million people in the population over 65 years of age out of a total population of 60 million. This is expected to increase to 15 million by the year 2031 (Help the Aged, 2006).

Due to developing health care, housing, nutrition and a better awareness of healthy living the fastest growing group within the older population will be the over eighties. This group is expected to rise from 2.4 million in 2009 to 4.3 million in 2029. While this is a large increase it is still a small group of older people in relation to the total population. Political forces have traditionally indulged in scare tactics in relation to the 'problem' of the ageing population, warning that older people will have to be more accountable both for their own health and care needs in the future (Vincent et al., 2006). This will have the potential effect of blaming people for being old as opposed to meeting the needs of an older population.

There tends to be an ideological 'no fly zone' when it comes to addressing this issue in a pragmatic way through longer-term personal and structural investment for future needs or the potential for increased taxation to meet these needs. The stumbling block is and will be whether an increasingly pressurised workforce will want to sustain increasing demands on their finances without any immediate or longer-term perceived net benefit to themselves. What is certain is that there has been a real sea-change in the way services for older people are currently being addressed and the Department of Health has just released figures to indicate that spending on mental health (particularly for older people) has fallen for the first time in a decade (Boffey, 2012). Conversely, within the debate on the perceived 'problem' of old age there is very little debate on the future voting demographic of this older population. Future governments may seriously need to address how older people will view their lifelong contribution to society in the context of a wider political reluctance to meet their longer-term needs. So, mental health and well-being are not opposites in terms of understanding but different aspects of how older people may cope with their changing circumstances across the life course. This premise is firmly rooted in the individualistic nature of the lived experience of all older people.

CASE STUDY

Chris Staunton is 64 years of age. He is still working as a part-time lecturer at his local university where he has spent the majority of his working life. He came from a working-class background and was the first of his family to attend university and have a professional career. He has recently been diagnosed with prostate cancer and this has hit Chris hard, particularly as he is very close to retirement. His local health authority has refused to consider the use of a new drug for this form of cancer that has had proven beneficial results, because of the cost. A representative from the local authority has suggested that Chris could fund the cost of this privately although this is prohibitive. Chris has also overheard one of the practitioners suggesting that as he has had a significant income over the years that he should pay for his own health and support needs. Chris has now decided to take an action against the local authority on the grounds that his human rights have been denied him and that the local authority has a duty of care to him irrespective of his financial status.

? Reflective Questions ?

- How would you characterise the approach by the hospital staff to Chris's needs?
- What role should empowerment and inclusion play within Chris's relationship with the medical staff?
- Can you identify any areas of discrimination using the PCS model?
- How might you interpret the Human Rights Act 1998 in relation to Chris's current and ongoing needs?
- How might current financial thinking impact on the potential for Chris to receive the treatment he feels he is entitled to?

Mental health, well-being and human rights

There is an ongoing debate, at a social policy level, on the impact of poor mental health and well-being within the UK. Increasingly this is being couched within the terms of human rights and what all citizens should expect as part of the understanding of what constitutes the totality of a successfully lived life. The Human Rights Act 1998, which enshrines the Articles of the European Convention on Human Rights (1950), makes specific reference to liberty and security, family life and privacy and the right not to be discriminated against as a focus of what all persons could reasonably expect as part of an unencumbered age. These articles sit at the heart of the debate on self-determination and the right to life and happiness that are an implicit part of health and well-being.

The social work focus on the conflicts that may exist between a social versus medicalised model of care is also a feature of this policy. Beresford (2005) has suggested there may be a dominant emphasis on medical services as opposed to human rights. This is also analogous to the media's socially deterministic focus on the decline, frailty and non-contributory status of older people generally. From an empowering and inclusive aspect this will also need to be addressed by a consideration of the more proscriptive features of the Mental Health Act 2007 which extend compulsory powers of treatment beyond the hospital environment (Lewis, 2009). This focus on human rights should now help to refocus policy in general as part of that indicator of emancipatory practice and human rights, although there is little to no evidence that these tensions will be adequately addressed within these times of stringent financial cutbacks.

The legislative context

The Equality Act 2010 excludes discrimination in the 'provision of services and exercise of public functions', of which the promotion of public health and well-being is a primary factor. The National Mental Health Development Unit (NMHDU) has been designated to support the implementation of mental health policy in England by the Department of Health with a range of other stakeholders. It has identified evidence of mental health problems among the older population with 40% of those over the age of 65 presenting with mental health problems to their GP. This is further exacerbated when ageism is considered in relation to older people being excluded from services that younger clients would take as a right, low referral rates from GPs to specialist older age services and poor service provision for older people generally (Healthcare Commission, 2009).

Underpinning social and psychological awareness

Rates of depression and poor mental health are up to two times higher among women than men in the older age group and this is part of a continuum of social and psychological factors related to life experiences and sociological factors. These include poverty in old age as part of fractured working lives due to child care, abusive relationships and a concurrent sense of social isolation. Sociological understanding in relation to construction of identity and role is also a significant determinant here and has to be considered within a paternalistic, patriarchal and rights agenda to ensure that the status quo thinking is not a reinforcer of ageism. Bereavement and disability will also be determinants, particularly for older women, who will experience these losses over a longer period than men due to their longevity (Department of Health, 2002c). What is consistent within the research literature is that addressing mental health problems does not address the bigger picture of encouraging and supporting a greater sense of mental health and well-being across the wider community (Huppert et al., 2005). While resource implications, particularly within a recent world economic decline, will have a significant role to play in addressing and alleviating presenting problems of well-being for older people, this is not the full picture. Environments that create the opportunity for personal fulfilment, engagement, positive sense of self and feeling socially connected underpinned by a positive sense of psychosocial well-being are more likely to lead to a successful health outcome for older people. While social work practice and understanding may not always engage with the totality of the lived experience of older people's lives, it is true to say that there are consistent features of coping across the life course that are more likely to lead to better mental health and well-being (Department of Health, 2010). Interestingly, while most research on mental health and well-being in older people inevitably reaches something of this conclusion there is little in the way of a pragmatic response as to how this will be achieved. Government policy that refers to the quantification of life satisfaction in the here and now without a critical evaluation of those more psychosocial aspects that lead to poor health and well-being may find that there is a struggle as the cart pushes that particular horse uphill. If poverty, isolation and exclusion are predictive factors in poor mental health then it may not be possible for current legislative processes to address these issues at a time of economic decline. Whatever the outcome, there must be a discourse on what this really means for older individuals. While loneliness is frequently cited as a factor in old age, it is much less likely to be addressed in the context of its significant impact on well-being. Yang and Victor (2011) have identified marriage, health, extended family and education as significant features in avoiding loneliness and associated rates of depression. Interestingly, Victor and Yang (2012) have also identified the quality of relationships rather than the quantity as a predicator in avoiding loneliness in older age.

Key areas to address to ensure what are the key areas in addressing health and well-being

A starting point would be a system that supports older people's basic needs of nutrition, heat, financial resources and emotional engagement as opposed to a more amorphous consideration of *satisfaction*. Satisfaction may relate more to a capacity to put up with circumstances that the majority of the population would not. Without these acknowledgements there is less likelihood of a successful conclusion to the dimension of ageing as a time of discovery of new personal and social meaning as distinct from an over-focus on a social problem approach (Silverman, 1987). It is therefore likely there will be a significant impact on the mental health and well-being of older people as long as their physical and psychological energies are being utilised in survival strategies. Quality of life then can be viewed from the premise of structural need and how this is perceived by policy makers in addressing how this need will be met. It is evident that old people have a concise idea of what their needs are based on a clear sense of where they have come from and of individual identity (Bond and Corner, 2006).

The agency approach to mental health and well-being

Age Concern and the Mental Health Foundation rolled out their inquiry into Mental Health and Well-being in 2003 due to concerns that the needs of older people were not being adequately addressed in this area. This was followed by the first report from the UK government inquiry into Mental Health and Well-being in 2006. The report identified that poor quality mental health is not an inevitable consequence of the ageing process but that a failure to address this will result in significant loss of quality of life for older people and a concurrent increase in the budget to meet longer-term care needs. Lee (2006) identified within this report that apart from a focus on supporting and enhancing quality of life in a broader sense there are more practical aspects of what could be done to promote a wider societal awareness, acknowledgement and acceptance of the specific needs of older people in increasing older age.

The intergenerational focus on understanding well-being

Lee's (2006) report has a profound and philosophical focus as it not only relates to more pragmatic areas of encouraging social inclusion and acceptance through a more positive media depiction of older age but also addresses intergenerational engagement between older people and the young. This is a dual concept approach where the primary function is to share experience in the promotion of understanding and respect and to prepare younger people for the inevitability of their own older age. Research by Stuart-Hamilton and Mahoney (2003) clearly evidences that while younger people may learn the language and some awareness of ageism this may not result in any significant attitudinal shift.

The longer-term prognosis here may be that younger people themselves disengage from the ageing process with an unwitting potential for storing up anxieties for their own older age and its attendant sense of self and well-being generally. A sense of how the nature of ageing and ageism is socially constructed is reinforced within the research work of Polizzi and Millikin (2002). Their respondents reacted more favourably to characterising positive aspects of older people when they were simply given an age bracket (70–80) than when they were asked to identify characteristics of 'old' people. The very words 'old' and 'older' then hold significant meaning for all members of society. All language can be invested with significant meaning beyond the dictionary definition and this is no less true of older age where these very terms may be imbued with a range of negative connotations both within society generally and internalised across the life course.

The compression of morbidity

Wherever the discussion takes us within the medical, social and policy debate there is evidence that increasing health care will offset some of the health fears that older people experienced in the past. This may however result in what Fries (1980) referred to as the 'compression of morbidity', where older people could maintain a high level of health until advanced old age where the accumulation of health problems would then be accentuated over a shorter period of the life course. Conversely, older people's mental health and well-being could be adversely affected by more complex features of illness and disability over a longer period. Whatever the rationale, it is incumbent not to treat health or lack of health as something specific to older people but more of a continuing feature of the life of everyone. This being the case, issues of mental health and well-being are better addressed as a continuum and accumulation of life opportunities related to better health generally. Interestingly, while ageism is often identified as a feature of a lack of understanding of older age, particularly among the young, this is also an opportunity for older people to express issues related to their health and well-being (or lack of) to a younger generation.

Views of older people in service design

Manthorpe and Iliffe (2008) have brought this debate into a modern focus by seeking to address issues of understanding of mental health and well-being in older people and a consideration of how the commissioning of social care can be addressed and by whom. When older people are actively involved in the design of policy this has a transformational role both on the policy itself and on what social justice means for older people (Barnes, 2005).

Mental health is increasingly being removed from a purely medicalised approach to one of public concern. In keeping with a more expansive view of the complexity of this area of health there could be a greater awareness of the individual identities of older people and how these have developed over a lifetime. Concurrently, working with older people is often undervalued, under-resourced and under-remunerated with a lack of qualified staff to negotiate through the maelstrom of mental health issues in older age. The researchers suggest that 'in no other sector of social care is the private sector so dominant and diverse, or partnership working so complicated by combined physical and mental health conditions, and frequent changes in both' (Manthorpe and Iliffe, 2008: 5). Whatever the eventual outcome, there has to be a pivotal role for primary care services in maintaining good mental health and well-being. This should be considered as part of a continuum of community-based support and an acknowledgement of the specific problems of isolation and bereavement that can impact on the health of older people (Murray Parkes, 1987; Thompson, 2012; Weinstein, 2008).

The Partnership for Older People Projects (POPP)

This is further supported by the national evaluation of the Partnership for Older People Projects (POPP), an initiative to increase awareness of how to:

- Promote independent living skills in older people.
- Reduce an over-reliance on institutional care and acute hospital admission.
- Address issues of delayed discharge.

This identifies the key areas of prevention of deterioration, risk and crises assessment and the harm associated with them and a focus on skills building that is less institutional and more appropriate for their needs. The evaluation identified clear advantages and savings across a range of issues from institutional care to increased health benefits and more developed independence skills. Most tellingly, accident and emergency attendance reduced by 29% and overnight hospital stays reduced by 47% (K. Windle et al., 2008).

Clarkson et al. (2010) refer to the increased need for self-assessment by older people in relation to preventative services in meeting their needs. These will include the understanding that older people's self-identified needs remain the focus of any intervention that attempts to meet these needs and are ultimately only definable by the older person's sense of self and wishes. This will involve a more targeted approach on the current and continuing needs of older people. There will be an emphasis on low level needs that help to promote older people's engagement with the wider community. These lower level needs may be more readily addressed in terms of access to information and the range of services and potential interventions available than higher level needs which may still need to be addressed by a more complex assessment and resource implications.

Permeating all of this will be a consideration of the dichotomy that may exist within these defined needs and resource limitations in an uncertain world. While the POPP initiative has undoubtedly presented a series of beneficial aspects in relation to coping and inclusion, it is less clear if the intervention itself is the key feature of change here or whether external forces related to changing personal and wider support networks should be considered. In its totality the research does indicate that when older people are engaged with in a way they assess as meaningful and related to their individual circumstances and wishes then there is more likely to be a successful outcome in relation to their mental health and well-being.

The values and ethics of understanding

This human flourishing is inextricably caught up in the complexity of ethics, values and dignity. Sulmasy (2008) postulates that to understand human rights we have to understand human dignity and how this may be 'attributed' or 'intrinsic'. The former is in relation to the value conferred on others by one's accomplishments, while the latter is more focused on the ethical dimension of worth purely because one is a person. While these may extend the more traditional social work emphasis on ethics and values in practice they concur with that wider agenda of rights, needs and, in the realms of mental health and well-being, a sense that to be old is not legitimate grounds for judgementalism from any quarter.

Bringing the policy up to date

A Sure Start to Later Life: Ending Inequalities for Older People (Social Exclusion Unit, 2006) suggests that services for older people should be formulated in the same way as those for children, with the services being brought together for older people as opposed to the more fractured and disparate delivery of services at present. The focus here is on addressing exclusion within a personalisation context. Older people will be the leaders in impacting services as opposed to searching for limited resources at times of personal stress. These resources can be related to community inclusion, activities and inadequate support services. From a more psychosocial perspective it is unlikely that those who have been socially excluded in middle age will become included in old age. On the contrary, older people are more likely to become increasingly isolated in older age.

Given that older people may be reluctant to engage with or define their mental health and well-being then the targeting of these resources is a key to any success in meeting these needs. The report addresses key issues of poverty and deprivation at an individual level and raises the fundamental question of the ethical and moral dimension of older people living in poverty in the twenty-first century. This potential focus on what Galbraith (1999) refers to as the 'indecency' of old age and its attendant impact on self-esteem and resilience is one of the key factors in how older people may view their own coping and well-being generally.

Our Health, Our Care, Our Say: Making it Happen (Department of Health, 2006a) reinforces this theme with an emphasis on community-based approaches to meeting the needs of older people. This clearly identifies how the future care needs of older people will be different from any previous age and may be less about moving from a sense of absolute deprivation and more about achieving well-being into an increasing older age. The report is unequivocal in its assessment that meeting these wider needs is the way forward to promote a secure sense of self and more independence and quality of life.

This commonality of integrated services is further reinforced within *Putting People First: Transforming Adult Social Care* (Department of Health, 2007b). The report

emphasises universal services, including transport, community security, leisure, education and health. Issues of transport may become more fundamental in older age
where access to support services may be more difficult. Access to free travel for those
over 60 is a laudable aspect of more recent government awareness but this will only
be as effective as the quality of the transport services provided. Within an increasingly
deregulated service more isolated communities may be put increasingly at risk. There
is likely to be a correlation between this sense of physical isolation and that associated
with exclusion from physical and emotional support systems. The report identifies
personalisation of services as critical rather than any sense of 'one size fits all' and
that this inclusive focus should also extend to how an older person will feel valued
and respected within their community of choice.

   Opportunity Age was published in 2005 with update in 2008 by the Department for
Work and Pensions to ensure that the tendency to characterise older people as overly
dependent is challenged within society (Department for Work and Pensions, 2009a).
The research addresses key areas of health and fulfilment and the full participation of
older people within society. While the inclusive aspect is an increasing feature of policy
related to health and well-being for older people, fulfilment tends to be somewhat
amorphous in that it is entirely specific to the individual experience of older people
which will be more difficult to legislate for. What is clear is that there is a correlation
between a sense of fulfillment and a sense of well-being.

   Age UK (2011c) has assessed the new Health and Social Care Bill, whose second
reading took place in January 2011. This was followed by the King's Fund (Timmins,
2012) overview of the Health and Social Care Act 2012. This legislation had something of a protracted journey through the House of Commons and the House of
Lords with accusations that it is less a grassroots overhaul of the National Health
Service (NHS) and more a back-door privatisation of health care. Strategic health
authorities and primary care trusts will be abolished in 2012 and 2013 respectively
and general practitioners (GPs) will now be involved in the commissioning of
health care services. There is a strong emphasis on competition within health care provision, with the inclusion of 'any willing provider' of care. GPs and the British Medical
Association have been explicitly opposed to any 'market economy' approach in the
past. Significantly this now means that local stakeholders will have NHS monies
disbursed and may have to make those ethical decisions about need and how health
care resources will be managed and rationed.

   Age UK (2011c) and the King's Fund (2012) have identified the importance of the
totality of all patient care and not just in those areas where it is possible to treat
patients quickly and show results. This is particularly the case in respect of older people, where there may be a range of illness presenting at any one time. Again this raises
the potential impact (or lack of) in relation to the personalisation agenda and whether
older people are adequately canvassed or included in the dialogue between health and
social care services. Age UK (2011c) makes specific reference here to the ageist attitudes that still apply to treatment of older people within the NHS and how the UK lags
behind other EU countries in the treatment of cancer, strokes and heart disease (Clark,
2009). There tends to be a 'year zero' mentality where the totality of an older person's
lived experience may not be assessed or addressed and results in those living in care

homes particularly having difficulty in accessing more community-based services. A key feature of this is to ensure that not only the mental health of older people is addressed but also that wider continuum of well-being that permeates all of the older lived experience. There are several documents that readers might like to address here.

Department of Health (2013) *Making Mental Health Services More Effective and Accessible*. London: DH.

Office for National Statistics (2013) *Measuring National Well-Being – Older People's Neighbourhoods*. London: HMSO.

CASE STUDY

Clare Poole lives in the Peak District and runs a smallholding where she is largely self-sustaining. She is 79 years of age, the years and climate and hard physical work have taken their toll. Clare is finding it increasingly difficult to get about. She is in receipt of a basic state pension and is experiencing real difficulty in paying for food and fuel that she would formerly have provided for herself. She does not have any close neighbours and those she has often find it difficult to negotiate the track to her isolated house. The bus service is very irregular and Clare does not know how she is going to manage. She is becoming increasingly isolated both on an individual and community basis and this is having a negative effect on her sense of self and well-being generally. Her physical health is still relatively good. To compound this she has a range of animals she looks after on her land and is very worried that she may become unable to sustain them in the longer term.

? Reflective Questions ?

- What are the immediate issues that need to be considered here in meeting Clare's needs?
- What role should Clare play in defining and meeting these needs?
- How might issues of benefits, nutrition, heating and transport be addressed and what other agencies might you involve to support these needs?
- What specific areas of practice do you need to address to ensure that Clare's general well-being is addressed.

Conclusion

It is important that any dialogue in relation to health and well-being is not overly focused on illness, disease and decline. These are features of the experience of some older people but cannot be used to characterise a homogeneous group as this will inevitably make it more likely to miss the individualism of older people. Neither can health and well-being be characterised as the absence of illness but more in the context of the lived totality of experience and what this means to individual older people.

Older age and the whole conceptual view of health and well-being may increasingly become difficult to define as life expectancy increases and developing health care pushes forward the boundaries of longevity. Within this paradigm older people should increasingly be viewed in terms of their potential contributory status, both for previous and current generations, and for their role in shaping the future world.

 Recommended Reading

Bond, J., Peace, S., Dittmann-Kohli, F. and Westerhof, G. (eds) (2007) *Ageing in Society*. London: Sage. This text addresses gerontology (the science of ageing) from a European perspective. It has highly informative chapters on the nature of ageing with a focus on psychological ageing and retirement and coping in later life.

Cattan, M. (ed.) (2009) *Mental Health and Well-being in Later Life*. Maidenhead: McGraw-Hill/Open University Press. This is an extremely good read and covers areas of empowerment and isolation in later life with a sound policy and person-centred focus.

Galpin, D. and Bates, N. (2009) *Social Work Practice with Adults*. Exeter: Learning Matters. This publication has a strong emphasis on personalisation and the promotion of independent living skills with a particular focus on inclusive practice.

6

DEMENTIA

Learning Outcomes

This chapter looks at:

- Promoting a wider understanding of what dementia is and how the different range of conditions can lead to loss of functioning and coping generally.
- This chapter will also address a range of interactions between those diagnosed with dementia, professionals and extended support mechanisms through family, friends and the wider community.
- A consideration of how practice will address a more global perspective of need in relation to dementia and how narrative approaches can help to support and sustain those with dementia in terms of coping in the present and decision making for the future.

What is dementia?

Dementia is the deterioration of intellectual and cognitive capacity due to loss of cells in the brain and there is an increased likelihood of the development of dementia in advanced old age (Stuart-Hamilton, 2006). It is an inevitable consequence of ageing that there will be some loss of brain function but within the range of symptoms characterised by dementia, this can in some instances be catastrophic. Only 20% of those over the age of 80 develop dementia although there is a small and significant percentage of working age people (2.2%) among those with dementia who develop what is known as 'early onset dementia' (Knapp et al., 2007). This may result in a range of deficits of cognition and self-care where there is a negative impact on social functioning (Whalley, 1997). The symptoms can impact on memory (particularly short-term memory) and the capacity to communicate may also be severely affected.

Coping and awareness

While it is true to say that there is now an increasing awareness of dementia and its impact on functioning, this is often unwittingly associated with ageing itself. If we consider the nature of the ageing demographic of the UK then it is all too easy to fall into the trap of assuming the inevitability of an increasing rise in dementia sufferers. Dementia, in its many and varied forms, can affect even the young and by only acknowledging the link between age and dementia, practitioners and the wider public may engage less with an awareness of the illness and more within a structural and ageist attitude (Cook, 2008).

So while dementia will inevitably have an adverse impact on an individual's coping capacity this has to be tempered by an awareness of the individual's earlier life experiences as well as their skills and strengths viewed through the prism of individual psychological coping across the life course. Indeed, recent research (Wang et al., 2012) has suggested that there is a potential causal link between stress across the working life and increased rates of dementia. Given the acknowledged physiological damage emanating from stress itself, this suggests there may be some substance to the perceived increase in vascular dementia particularly.

Sociological understanding

There may also be a range of sociological issues to consider. Gender and poverty may impact adversely on individual coping and need to be viewed within a wider understanding of dementia and a person-centred approach to practice (Kitwood, 1999). The labelling of 'dementia' is rife with a range of negative stereotypes, particularly within the area of individual competence. If the starting point for any assessment or engagement with a person diagnosed with dementia is that he or she will be unable to have an opinion or contribute to any future planning then any intervention may be one of a controlling nature. This control may also refer more to a consideration of disability rather than ability (Marshall and Tibbs, 2006). Essentially those themes of stigma and deviance may become reinforced rather than challenged within an ethical practice focus.

The biomedical approach

While there is a wide variety of illnesses that come under the umbrella of dementia it is important to note the differing approaches to treating and engaging with this condition. There is a certain paradox in the willingness of the more biomedical agencies to offer definitions of dementia with their emphasis on decline and need and the fact that there is no clear, definitive diagnostic test for Alzheimer's due to the lack of scientific knowledge in this area. What is likely though is that any diagnosis defined solely in terms of this biomedical awareness and decline will inevitably focus on the more negative aspects of ageing and ageism and a depersonalisation of the individual (Jonas-Simpson, 2001). It is clear that an over-focus on the biomedical approach in defining dementia may view the dementia sufferer as a non-sentient being who has little or no role to play in decision making about their own future or capacity for contributing to a wider society. This may also not acknowledge the more psychological functioning across the life course which may have contributed to illness and decline in old age. Kitwood (1989) suggests that individuals who are well grounded within their feelings and emotions may preserve something more of a sense of self and relationships with others in older age even in the face of a diagnosis of dementia. In effect, any appreciation and understanding of the lived experience of individuals and the inner world they may inhabit can only support an understanding of all those with dementia. A limited awareness of the totality of the individual lived experience (physical, emotional and spiritual) by professionals and carers is the structural environment within which physical and emotional abuse can flourish (Adams and Manthorpe, 2003). Practitioners should also be aware of the possibility that an older person who is experiencing depression because of loss, grief or unresolved life experiences may inadvertently be diagnosed with dementia (Maynard, 2003). This is particularly the case where older people buy into the 'understandability phenomenon' (Blanchard, 1996) of depression where significant numbers of older people believe depression is an inevitable consequence of ageing itself. Research indicates that it is not in fact the nature of depression but older people's beliefs about their own ageing that is significant here. This indicates that it is a self-fulfilling negative stereotype of the nature of ageing in a modern world that may potentially be driving this thinking (Law et al., 2010).

CASE STUDY

You are working as a trainee social worker attached to a closed ward in a hospital for patients suffering from dementia. You have been asked to interview Joan Fletcher, who has been recently admitted after being found wandering and confused in the grounds of the local hospital where she had been admitted after a fall. Joan is extremely lucid with clear memories of her experiences from the past. She is always extremely well presented and takes particular attention over her makeup and manicured nails. You have a sense of real engagement with Joan and are somewhat confused as to the diagnosis given her apparent capabilities. Joan then offers to drive you home in her car which is parked outside. She fails to recognise you on subsequent meetings and always asks to drive you home at the end of every meeting.

?   Reflective Questions   ?

- Why do you think it would be a benefit to know something of the personal narrative of someone diagnosed with dementia?
- How might you respond to Joan's offer of being driven home?
- Do you think there is anything symbolic and important about how Joan presents and expresses herself?
- What are the potentially negative consequences of a lack of resolution of the life stages for those diagnosed with dementia?

Demography of dementia

The demography of an ageing population can bring these themes of the medical and the metaphysical (the nature of being) into conflict in an age of austerity where cost is defined as a predeterminant of how need will be met. This is increasingly a feature where the focus of the research into the causes of dementia has traditionally resided within the biomedical aspect. In an increasingly client and older person focused approach to social work it is incumbent upon practitioners to understand the different forms of dementia. This is to ensure that a person-centred and equitable approach is delivered to older people, particularly if they are unable to negotiate more traditional forms of communication.

Within the demographic context of ageing and planning for the future of an ageing population and a potential increase in those with dementia there is little distinction made of the different forms of dementia in policy planning (Gordon and Spicker, 1997). The over 65-year-old population is projected to rise by over 60% over the next 25 years (up until 2031)to 15.8 million. It is projected that by the year 2071 over 65s will comprise 26% of the population (ONS, 2008). The projected demographic of this ageing population is approximately 15.2 million by the year 2038. The reason for this significant increase in longevity of the population is due to improvements in healthy lifestyles, improved medical interventions and nutrition. There may however be a concomitant increase in dementia diagnoses in the future due to the age demographic and this may have a disproportionate impact on older women with their increased lifespan (Fraser, 1999).

On a global scale there were 600 million people over the age of 60 worldwide in 2000 and this is projected to increase to two billion by 2050 (a threefold increase), comprising over 22% of the total world population (United Nations, 2009). Interestingly the incidence of dementia is not consistent across the world. There is a speculative 100% increase in dementia diagnosis in developed countries between 2001 and 2040 but a disproportionally higher figure of 300% in underdeveloped countries over the same period (Ferri et al., 2005).

Ethical understanding

From a social work ethical perspective this suggests that we need to be well informed not just on the whole subject of dementia but on the varying illnesses that are considered under the dementia umbrella. This is to ensure that individuals diagnosed can be assessed and engaged with in a way that meets both their individual and human rights. A failure to do so will inevitably result in a less person-centred approach, a lack of a wider understanding of dementia and a more generic 'off the shelf' approach to engaging with this vulnerable group. This is particularly the case when there is clear evidence of the diversity of individual experience through narrative approaches and, more importantly, a sense of individual awareness of the prognosis of the dementia itself (Clare, 2003).

Types of dementia

There has been a wide spectrum of dementias identified in recent years but for the sake of brevity I propose to address the four main types that practitioners in the field are more likely to encounter.

Alzheimer's disease

One of the most common forms of dementia is Alzheimer's disease, which accounts for over 50% of all cases identified. This causes a loss of brain cells and a destruction of neurotransmitters that result in memory loss. In physical terms there is a shrinkage of the temporal lobes and hippocampus sections of the brain. These areas are responsible for the storage and retrieval of information and hence have a negative impact on the individual's ability to remember detail and make decisions. In more advanced cases this can result in an inability to speak with a propensity for confused and anxious behaviour (Alzheimer's Society, 2012). This is a degenerative illness that can have an imperceptible beginning and is frequently masked by a perceived general decline in old age. Sufferers are frequently aware of their declining faculties and may seek to mask these symptoms from their family and other support networks. The stigma of dementia has undoubtedly had an impact on how freely people may discuss this with others and in the meantime valuable interventions involving information, support and medication may be missed out, with a concurrent impact on the course of the illness itself.

Vascular dementia

This is the next most common form of dementia and is responsible for approximately 20% of diagnoses. Vascular dementia can be characterised by damage to the brain from a succession of small strokes and the most common form of this dementia is known as multi-infarct dementia (MID). The progenitor of these strokes may be hypertension or any organic illness that causes damage to the arteries in the brain. The impact of MID can be characterised by loss of skills and when these are related to daily living tasks such as cleaning and cooking this can have a very dramatic impact on the individual's coping and social engagement with others. The illness can also be characterised by periods of lucidity followed by periods of deterioration.

Dementia with lewy bodies

This is a relatively rare form of dementia. It has similarities to Alzheimer's but with the significant difference that damaged cells and their attendant deposits, known as Lewy bodies, are only really detectable post-mortem. The main effects are similar to Parkinson's where spasm and shakiness in hands are common. It also affects the spatial awareness of sufferers and may result in falls and significant injury. Because this form of dementia leaves those diagnosed with a propensity to hallucinations it is best to avoid any form of anti-psychotic medication.

Korsakoff's syndrome

This is a unique form of dementia in that there may be a partial or even a full recovery and it is associated with heavy and persistent alcohol consumption. Unlike Lewy's where there may be a single cause, Korsakoff's may be the result of a multiplicity of factors, from the toxicity of alcohol itself on brain cells, poor vitamin and nutritional intake to damage as a result of falls. The irony here is that if the falls are caused by excessive alcohol consumption then this is something of a double whammy! There is a particular correlation between Korsakoff's and thiamine (B12 vitamin) uptake and research has shown that treatment with thiamine can stop or even diminish the effects of alcohol. Even though this form of dementia is treatable the stigma of alcohol addiction may make it difficult for those diagnosed to seek help and may also make them feel stigmatised within any support services where the perception may be that this illness is somehow self-inflicted. The accumulation of life experiences and negative stressors across the life course may be as important a consideration here as the effects of the alcohol, as one may be inexorably driving the other.

Alec is 57 years of age and is a retired fisherman. He has worked on fishing boats since he left school at 14 and the hard physical work in severe weather conditions has left him with severe arthritis resulting in poor mobility. Alec has been a frequent and heavy consumer of alcohol over the course of his working life. He has recently come to the attention of the social work department when his neighbours contacted them to express their concerns about Alec. He had been 'wandering' to the shop in his pyjamas and his appearance was very dishevelled. Alec's flat is very chaotic with discarded bottles and newspapers everywhere and there is a noticeable lack of food in the house. A social worker had visited Alec and persuaded him to visit his local GP to assess his general well-being. The doctor commented on Alec's poor personal hygiene to the social worker and the fact that he smelt of alcohol, although Alec had not been drinking that day. Alec was unable to answer the questions related to the names of politicians in the current government that the doctor posed to him and the GP suggested that Alec could have Alzheimer's disease. Alec was very shocked by this diagnosis, left the surgery and immediately visited the alcohol section of the local supermarket.

CASE STUDY

? Reflective Questions ?

- What impact do you think this diagnosis may have had on Alec and why?
- What is the evidence here for this diagnosis?

(Continued)

(Continued)

- What other illness could Alec be suffering from?
- What impact could Alec's physical and living conditions play in his appearance and diagnosis?
- Do you think an awareness of Alec's life story and psychological coping throughout his life would be beneficial here?
- From an ethical perspective how could the needs of Alec be better addressed?

Social work skills and practice with dementia

Tanna (2004) states clearly that there is no cure for Alzheimer's disease but that a consideration of the benefits of routines and a reduction in a range of stressors impacting on the person affected will have beneficial effects. While there is still an over-emphasis on the more medicalised approach to dementia there is an increasing awareness of the positive role that psychosocial interventions, education and respite for clients and caregivers can have. Innes (2009) characterises the care a person with dementia will receive as largely dependent on how the disease is 'conceptualised' by carers, medical practitioners and extended support agencies. Post (2000) speculates that if the person with dementia is defined exclusively within their contributory aspect to society then it is inevitable that they may not meet these taxing benchmarks and are therefore more likely to be discriminated against. In a more global sense organisations such as Age UK and Alzheimer's UK have raised the awareness of dementia as part of a continuum of living as opposed to a definitive ending. It is in the neutral territory between these two interactions that the conceptualisation and practice of effective social work resides (Iliffe et al., 2005). What is clear from the stigmatising consideration is that this is more likely to create a climate of fear around any diagnosis and may adversely impact on any early therapeutic interventions. It is the labelling of behaviours (including dementia) that alienate individuals within a focus on ageing, illness, gender and ethnicity (Thompson, 1992). So stigma will both deny individual rights and reinforce the more adverse aspects within a structural and societal view.

Needs and interventions in dementia care

There are developing methodologies for assessing the needs and engaging with those with dementia. Scott and Clare (2003) identify a range of psychological interventions offered on a group basis that seek to support the individual experience within a collective and supportive environment. These range from the more traditional aspects of reminiscence working and validation therapy to a more cognition related aspect in more recent times. Woods (1996) identifies reminiscence working as the capacity to retrieve past memories and utilise these in current and future coping through enhancing self-worth. The validation aspect (Feil, 2002) is that past events influence current thinking and behaviour however inconsistent the presenting behaviour may be. Research into both these interventions indicates that there is limited longer-term positive impact (Neal and Briggs, 1999; Spector et al., 1999). Research by Sandman (1993) indicates that a cognitive approach to dementia that includes carers and an evaluation of a specific life event shows that older people may have a more positive sense of self and what the future holds. It is the case that if older people are aware of their declining powers of memory and cognition there is a greater likelihood of depression but also the attendant consequences of resilience and coping (Hughes, 1995). One of the most challenging aspects of dementia is where one partner within a relationship develops dementia and the other partner becomes the primary carer. Research by Davies and Gregory (2007) indicates that a more incremental approach to changing roles within the relationship, where the non-demented spouse will gradually take over some of the roles and coping of the demented person, is more advisable. This will ensure that the demented partner experiences less shock at the reality of the situation. The research also indicates that more engaged and previously secure relationships will have a positive bearing on coping through developing dementia for the affected and non-affected partner.

Social work role

The role of any social work intervention in the case of dementia is to gain as much information as possible about the past and current coping of the older person to be able to engage effectively with her or him. This will be particularly important where there has been an underlying additional problem such as a learning disability and where the individual's social and cultural background will have a significant role to play in cognition, awareness and resilience (Prasher, 2005). Within any consideration of these assessments are the needs of carers and how they can be supported, particularly as they may be playing a significant role in this long-term care. Wilkinson et al. (2005) reiterate the importance of knowledge and training for staff and carers as a critical determinant in effecting positive outcomes for dementia within learning disabilities. While support groups are frequently held up as a pragmatic response to meeting the needs of carers for those with dementia there is not a solid body of evidence to support how actual findings from dementia research will follow through into practice (Pillemer et al., 2003).

The emerging person in dementia care and Kitwood's 'malignant social psychology'

Previous cultures of care for those with dementia, based on biomedical approaches to disease and care, have been dehumanising. 'Personhood' is the term Kitwood (1987) identified, meaning that a person still feels connected to both an internal sense of self and a more engaged relationship with the wider community. Previously poor interactions with those identified with dementia were largely based on the assumption of poor communication capacity. O'Connor et al. (2007) have noted the importance of having a research focus on personhood in dementia as a means of broadening the locus of attention. This has therefore focused on personal narratives as a means of shifting the focus from the biomedical disease model to that of a more person-centred and personalised approach. Indeed, the personal conception of reality leads those with dementia on an inexorable journey towards those memories that are invested with powerful emotions and memories as the focus of who and what that person is and as a repository of past coping (Westius et al., 2009). This past coping, when acknowledged by practitioners, is a powerful source of information and skills that can be utilised by practitioners when engaging with the demented client.

Kitwood (1997) identified that the low status within society of older people with dementia and the poor level of care they were afforded was a more significant factor. He suggested that 'personhood' did not exist as an entity in its own right but was rendered by the way relationships function and where a positive attitude of trust and respect was conferred by the wider society (Bowers, 2009). This is a fluid process that ebbs and flows with the degree and quality of support and empathy for the circumstances of those with dementia.

Kitwood (1995) coined the phrase 'malignant social psychology' to identify the very negative impact of these environments on those with dementia and also suggested that these environments exacerbated the problem rather than alleviated the stressors of confusion and fear. This malignant psychology was specifically identified as a result of poor interventions by carers, irrespective of any malicious intent, that negated the individual sense of self. Research indicates that where personhood is undermined through an over-focus on the medicalisation of dementia this may result in a negative spiral of 'depersonalisation' and further reinforce psychological decline (Kelly, 2010). Kitwood (1997) identified 17 areas of what he defined as 'personal detractors', where interactions could reinforce negative stereotypes of older age and a lack of awareness and empathy for the 'wholeness' of the person with dementia.

Exercise

- Students and practitioners might like to consider the following list of 'personal detractors' and attempt to define what they mean and how they might adversely impact on older people with dementia.

- Treachery
- Disempowerment
- Infantilisation

- Intimidation
- Labelling
- Stigmatisation

- Outpacing
- Invalidation
- Banishment
- Objectification
- Ignoring
- Imposition

- Withholding
- Accusation
- Disruption
- Mockery
- Disparagement.

These features of malignant social psychology can be accessed more fully in Kitwood (1999).

Structural oppression

Gwilliam and Gilliard (1996) have also identified that rather than people with dementia being defined as 'disabled' it is societal structures and their inability to engage with the 'difference' of others that creates this disabilism. Increasingly, the focus of dementia is on an awareness and appreciation of the life forces that have impacted on individuals with dementia and attempting to view them from the perspective of psychosocial understanding. There also has to be an awareness of the structural opprobrium that consistently prevails within this particular diagnosis.

In effect, Kitwood (1997, 1999) challenged the ethos of the medical model of care as one that has the potential for reinforcing stigma rather than highlighting individuality and person-centred approaches to practice. He identifies an understanding of the personal narrative and empathy as core skills here. This identification of a 'social model of dementia' no longer focuses exclusively on the pathology of the illness but addresses wider issues of social, institutional and more interpersonal aspects to come to an understanding of dementia (Cook, 2008).

Exercise

- You are a social worker attached to a care home setting where there are a large number of clients diagnosed with dementia. There is a poor level of staffing and training within the care home and it can prove difficult to monitor the movements of the more able clients when meal times or personal care issues take staff away from the main seating areas. You have heard a rumour that a staff member has tied a client with dementia into her bed on occasions to stop her 'wandering'. You have also heard staff describe residents as 'crumblies' and use other derogatory and negative terms and some staff members have expressed the view that most of the clients are a 'waste of space' as they have no awareness of what is going on around them.

> **?**   Reflective Questions   **?**
>
> - How do you think you could engage with these members of staff?
> - What do you think may be driving these very negative stereotypes?
> - What role could training and supervision play in helping to resolve this situation?
> - What could be done to actively promote the rights and well-being of these clients?

Social work skills working with dementia

Person-centred

What do we mean by person-centred here? This is a developmental aspect of that more humanistic focus exemplified by Carl Rogers (1959, 1961) where he identified areas of 'genuineness' and 'empathy' as critical for any person-centred approach. He characterised these attributes as important for any positive engagement with clients, where they could grow in a constructive manner through this interaction. Rogers (1961) clearly identified the development of the person as the ultimate goal for this form of intervention. He also suggested that the individual's self-image is one of the most important areas when addressing the individual's capacity for coping in the future and refers to a 'perception of external reality' (Rogers, 2002: 209) to make sense of that situation that an older person may find him/herself in. In essence this is Rogers' primary imperative of 'positive regard' becoming internalised as the individual's sense of 'positive self-regard' as a means of internal awareness and protection (resilience).

Personhood

If this level of cognition is impaired through dementia or a lack of engagement or awareness by workers or carers then it is likely that the capacity for well-being and life fulfilment will be seriously impaired. It is therefore critical that the person and the personhood of the individual is central to any interaction to ensure that core needs of empathy, dignity and inclusion are not just met but advocated for. This is particularly the case in relation to the impact of a diagnosis of dementia on the older person. There may be feelings of anger and frustration, fear of losing friends and a sense that it may be meaningless to explore the pathology of the illness because of the inevitability of the outcome (Rimmer et al., 2005).

Specific features of person-centred practice that should be acknowledged include a respect for the more subjective aspects of an older person's lived experience. This is what is at the centre of an empathic focus and carries a sense of the 'wholeness' of the person, irrespective of whether these needs, wishes and interpretations of the world are at odds with the perception of the practitioner (Morton, 1999). There may also be a more focused approach on what a person feels as opposed to what a person thinks. The former is at the heart of inclusive and considered practice whereas the latter may become the focus of a debate on interpretation of need that an older person with dementia may never hope to win. What identifies person-centred practice within the realms of dementia is the facilitative role that the social worker plays within the engagement and where the power and control has to lie within the domain of the older person's wishes. Essentially, if the individual personhood is maintained, particularly within the earlier stages of diagnosis, then it is much more unlikely that the person will develop those 'secondary' characteristics of dementia that may further exclude the person from their relationships and environment. This will have the inevitable effect of further stigmatising the older person with an attendant focus on ageist attitudes rather than an appreciation of the human history of the individual (Adams and Manthorpe, 2003).

Despite the rhetoric on person-centred approaches to dementia there is evidence that within the UK such services are often inadequate. Recent media examples of what could realistically be described as torture within care settings tends to support this premise.

CASE STUDY

Frank is 66 years of age and works as a machinist at the local factory. His wife has recently died and Frank is finding it increasingly difficult to manage at home with shopping and cleaning. He has been neglecting to cook meals on a regular basis and he has been appearing increasingly distracted at work. In the past week Frank has caused an accident that injured a workmate. His neighbour has accompanied Frank to visit his GP, who has informed Frank that in his opinion he has the early stages of dementia and that he should return the following week for further tests. Frank is in a total state of shock at this diagnosis and the perfunctory manner with which he has been treated. He is now unable to return to work as he is fearful of causing further accidents and has said to his neighbour that his 'life is now over'.

? Reflective Questions ?

- What is your understanding of 'personhood' within this engagement between Frank and the doctor?
- How would you characterise this meeting within a person-centred focus?
- Can you evaluate the interaction within the context of malignant social psychology and a social model of dementia?

Cultural and ethnic awareness

The UK is becoming an increasingly culturally diverse society. Implicit within this assertion is the premise that theories of ageing and illness that are purely western in thinking may not meet all the diverse needs of this changing population (Giddens, 2009). While it will always be problematic in considering a theory of ageing that fits all groups, at the very least there should be an expectation that the culturally diverse aspects that go to make up a consideration of the age and illness of older people should be considered (Tilford, 2009). This is particularly the case within the fourth age (people over the age of 80) where there may be a greater predisposition to developing dementia (Phillipson and Baars, 2007).

Where there is a lack of understanding among care providers of ethnicity and cultural beliefs this can only compound the difficulties of diagnosis both for the person and the wider family and support networks. It is also important to acknowledge how minority ethnic groups with a shared value and belief system may develop a collective knowledge of dementia (Boise, 2009). This shared belief system may have a positive aspect of seeking out information and knowledge related to dementia or may reinforce feelings of stigma or a culturally deterministic need to protect vulnerable adults within their own milieu (Dilworth-Anderson and Gibson, 2002).

While policy makers need to preserve a sense of ethnic and cultural awareness when addressing dementia within these groups to ensure a recognition of diversity, there may also be wider considerations related to intra-group variation that practitioners in the field may not be aware of. In a climate where the whole subject of cultural diversity and awareness is being questioned from a western ideological perspective there needs to be a refocusing on information, training and awareness generally of the needs of potentially excluded ethnic and cultural groups. As long as policy makers and practitioners subscribe to that sense of the 'otherness' of people from a wider ethnic and cultural diversity, it is more likely that these groups will be further marginalised. This is particularly the case where part of this cultural discrimination is an understanding that individuals with dementia within these particular groupings will have their needs met exclusively within that cultural domain.

How to develop more engaged services

Beattie et al. (2005) have suggested a range of options that could be offered to these disadvantaged groups that would support their engagement with dementia support services: that services be offered within the person's own home to avoid the stress and potential stigma of attending a more formal office-based venue; that services with specialist knowledge be used irrespective of whether they are based within the area the client lives in; and that there is an enhanced level of flexibility within individual areas to meet the needs of this population.

If a professional level of assessment is to be achieved then this engagement with clients within their own supportive environment is a critical feature. The older person and carers are better able to make an informed choice as to their current and future needs (Victor et al., 2009). A lack of consideration of the often faith-based aspects of an individual's culture has the potential for levels of misunderstanding of what cultural diversity represents and a propensity to view a prevailing white, western, ethnocentric aspect as the norm. Like the process of assessment itself, there is a direct correlation within working with cultural and ethnic diversity where the process should be ongoing, imaginative, reflective and with a mutuality of learning that is at the heart of social work engagement. The ultimate function of the provision of culturally sensitive services is to promote a sense of well-being among those with dementia and their carers, with a particular emphasis on an understanding of the conceptual framework that the family utilises to make sense of the older person's needs, behaviour and prognosis (Mackenzie et al., 2005).

? Reflective Questions ?

- What do you think are the important questions to consider when working with clients with dementia and their families from differing cultural and ethnic backgrounds?
- How important is it to define the knowledge base of those with dementia and their families in relation to dementia?
- As part of a wider consideration of dementia, what aspects of language, gender, understanding and support would you need to consider within a social work engagement with cultural groups?
- What could you as a practitioner do to ensure you could effect the best possible outcomes when working with diverse cultural and ethnic groups?

Communication

Our capacity to communicate with others is the testing ground for defining who we are, our self-perception as well as how our uniqueness is formed through the multiplicity of relationships we negotiate. Paradoxically, there is an inverse proportion of truth within the maxim that 'familiarity breeds contempt' when working with older people with dementia in an empathic and person-centred way. The opposite should be the case where policy makers and practitioners with an understanding of individual lived experience utilise a more respectful approach to those with dementia the more they engage with their inner and external worlds. It is generally accepted within society that proximity engenders a sense of understanding and closeness, whereas distance is more likely to result in an increased lack of understanding and prejudice (Neuberger, 2009).

This is a significant feature in the care of those with dementia where they may be denied access to, or a choice of, services, that more able-bodied people would demand as a right. The reality is that without this focus on interpersonal and communication skills with those with dementia, older people may be denied those more fundamental aspects of daily living such as what time they get up, who they meet and what level of privacy and dignity they will achieve (Help the Aged, 2006). This will be particularly the case within care home settings where rules, regulations and regimes may take precedence over that more personalised approach of meeting need.

Interpersonal skills

In more general terms, Thompson (2002) characterised what he refers to as 'communicative sensitivity' by an awareness of two facets of skill. One is the ability to read the situation by effective use and consideration of interpersonal skills so as to determine an appropriate response, and the other is in relation to making time for communication in a busy working life. Thompson (2011) further reiterates that practitioner failure to engage with those with communication problems due to dementia are indulging in a 'defeatist' stance that further reinforces discrimination.

Goldsmith's (1996) work in relation to communicating with those with dementia develops a more profound locus of attention. He couches the capacity for communication within a social disablement focus where it is the responsibility of the professional to find meaningful ways to engage with those with dementia. He goes further and speaks of a capacity for entering into the individual worlds of the older person with dementia through an appreciation of the individual pace of the person and an awareness of the multiplicity of communication styles that exist. This is particularly important within the assessment process, and especially at the diagnosis stage of dementia. It is clear both from an inclusive and person-centred approach that a less interrogatory approach is more beneficial to someone who may be in a state of shock at the diagnosis itself. The simple expedient of sitting beside the person diagnosed and moving at a comfortable pace through the documentation with a commensurate clarification of what is being said and what is meant will prove more effective (Marshall and Tibbs, 2006).

Communication skills

Within the busy lives of carers and professionals it is too easy to miss opportunities for successful communication with those with dementia. As those diagnosed may find it difficult to read signals and interpret meaning it is important that there is clarity of understanding from the point of view of the carer. This should include clear body language directed at the older person with appropriate non-verbal communication and use of a more tactile focus. Statements should be expressed in clear, uncomplicated language that is not subsumed with subordinate clauses (Higham, 2006; Lishman, 2009). The pace, tone and expression of interest in the older person can only have a positive effect and further reinforce an empathic engagement which the older person will respond to.

At the same time, non-verbal communication may take on a much more significant role where the person's more formal modes of expression have been diminished or are difficult to interpret. Significant features of non-verbal communication are eye contact, an open facial expression, appropriate touch, the tone, pitch and speed that we communicate at and the ergonomics of the space the intervention takes place in. The surroundings should be appropriate for this interaction with a concentration on lighting, furniture and the orientation of where the person with dementia sits and even whether they are able to choose this space (Killick and Allan, 2002).

Presentation

A feature of non-verbal communication that also needs to be considered within communication is the style of dress of the practitioner. While no one would wish to undermine the individual's right to self-determination and self-expression, which is at the heart of our interpretation of individual experience and need, this may have a more complex focus when it comes to modes of dress. Older people with dementia may become confused or frightened by practitioners who appear with exposed tattoos, an eccentric dress style and a surfeit of metalwork in the face as these may have a significant interpretation and meaning to the older person that have been largely lost as part of a more modern experience. Kitwood (1993) specifically refers to 'body language' and suggests that when more traditional forms of communication fade people with dementia retain a heightened awareness of this and refers to it as the 'vehicle' that supports those more diminished verbal communications.

Additional skills

We often assume that skills are intrinsic to our personality whereas in fact they are often learned over the life course. So what are the core skills that practitioners should have and develop when working with those with dementia?

Listening

This may seem like the most obvious of skills but has to be approached in a sensitive and informed way. Language that appears confused and disjointed may pose as many problems for the client as the practitioner. Starting with an assumption of meaning is a useful starting point as opposed to dismissing statements that do not appear to make 'sense'. Biographical detail will support this and sometimes a constant reference to 'the world through a lens' may not relate to the philosophical dimension of the world but the fact that the older person was a photographer during a working life! So while listening is clearly a key social work skill this should also be focused within that more ethical dimension of 'hearing'.

Patience

Again, this is a skill that can be learned through listening, confidence and an ability to remain in control and stay calm when circumstances appear to be spiralling out of control. This can also involve an awareness of and an ability to engage with and handle strongly held emotions. This is particularly the case if specific feelings, memories and fears of difficult personal experiences are aroused (Thompson, 2009). This 'emotional intelligence' is fundamental to self-knowledge and an ability to engage effectively within challenging communication situations in dementia services (Thompson, 2011).

Warmth

Personal warmth and creativity go hand in hand and are the benchmarks of an anti-ageist and engaged form of communication with those experiencing dementia. While De Hennezel (2008) refers to individual warmth encouraging creativity and a sense of meaning, the practitioner has to take pleasure in the striving and achievement of those with dementia to achieve a sense of connectedness and unity with their surroundings.

Different forms of communication and engagement

Narrative identity

This refers to where the past, present and future of those with dementia can be engaged with thorough knowledge of individual lived experience (Crichton and Koch, 2007; Williams and Keady, 2006).

Personhood

Any appreciation of the nature of personalisation within dementia has to encourage an evidence-based practice (research) approach. This will include a consideration of human rights and an engaged and inclusive approach to meeting the needs of those with dementia (O'Connor et al., 2007). At the same time, individuals with dementia involved in research may be highly resistant to this diagnosis as they struggle to come to terms with this new identity. Pearce et al. (2002) goes further and advocates not referring to dementia at all during research unless it is first referred to by the respondents.

Quality of life

A key feature of maximising quality of life is where the person with dementia is encouraged to be as independent and as autonomous as possible, for as long as possible. This is an ethical approach to inclusive and engaged practice where both carers and clients are supported (Bamford and Bruce, 2000).

Recognition of a spiritual dimension

The spiritual dimension of older people's lives has traditionally been the preserve of the nursing profession. It has often been closely associated with palliative care and end of life nursing (Powers and Watson, 2011). Increasingly, however, this is being perceived as a natural (although with some suspicion within the pragmatic world of social work) focus of attention of the social work profession. It encapsulates that intrinsically unique aspect of all persons and is key to who and what they are. It is also being given increasing emphasis within social work training and care standards generally.

Other social work knowledge skills

Telecare

Putting People First (Department of Health, 2007a, 2007b) specifically refers to Telecare as a feature of promoting personalisation. This can involve a range of devices and sensors installed in the home of a person with dementia to ensure they are able to maintain independent living for as long as possible. An alternative view is that practitioners have to be very careful to pay 'attention to concerns held by all stakeholders, particularly in regard to individual choice, surveillance, risk-taking and quality of service' (Percival and Hanson, 2006: 888).

Complementary therapies

Where practitioners become overwhelmed by the potential degenerative aspect of dementia then focusing on the senses of the client can be beneficial. This may mean the person is treated more holistically and may potentially have a calming and supporting role (Moyle, 2008). Examples of these are reflexology, aromatherapy and massage.

Participation and deliberation

There should be an emphasis on storytelling and other narrative therapies as a means of recognition for those working with people with dementia (Barnes, 2005; Powell, 2008; Scourfield and Burch, 2010). Exploration of internal worlds will have a positive impact on the social work understanding of those with dementia. It may even provide the key of coping in the past to effect coping in the present and future.

Understanding loneliness

Practitioners should recognise the very significant impact loneliness plays within the lives of older people and how this may potentially be exacerbated by additional feelings of isolation in early stage dementia. This should be considered with the more community-based focus of community care legislation and how independent living may be at the expense of isolation.

Carers and families

Impact of personal narratives

The great philosophical question that has not yet been resolved is what is the nature of the person with dementia? This question is at the heart of the personhood debate and whether this aspect diminishes with the progression of dementia or whether this is an irreversible process. If this is the case then how do we explain those aspects of someone with dementia who may suddenly present within a locus of attention with recall of the current situation (Goldsmith, 1996)? The debate therefore may be more related not to a loss of functioning but an inability to access those memories and cognitions that are more a functional aspect of organic brain injury. In essence, the personhood and humanity of the older person persists but the external world may lack the capacity and resolve to access this sense of the person with dementia. The personal narrative defines the person's sense of self with an individual understanding that cannot only be a predicator of future awareness but also act as a starting point for a wider care and structural awareness and engagement with that person, particularly by carers and practitioners (McAdams and Janis, 2004). When those with dementia lose this facility to construct personal narratives as the illness progresses then the individual sense of personhood can be maintained by narratives that relate to the person and are recounted by others as a repository of knowledge and care (Bowers, 2009). A focus on the ballroom dancing skills of a person when young may be more meaningful to someone with dementia than a more psychologically based focus on the nature and meaning of existence itself.

Support skills in dementia care

The role of the worker here is not one of leader or organiser but more one of a conduit through which is filtered the information identified by the client. In the same way as assessment, this is a fluid and dynamic process where individuals may construct a multiplicity of identities. The process for professionals here is to be aware of and acknowledge that this range of identities is no different from the range of identities constructed by the wider population without the stigmatising label of dementia to contend with. This should leave practitioners open and able to consider the interpretation of the subjective experience of those with dementia within their own locus of experience and to view this as part of an emancipatory process (Keady et al., 2005). While it is true that certain aspects of identity in relation to age and gender are more fixed, issues of personal identity and particularly personal qualities are more fluid and dynamic and therefore subject to a more creative and negotiated engagement. If a challenge exists it resides not within the domain of labelling and more structural aspects of oppression, but within the creativity practitioners are prepared to expend to interpret these identities. The paradox is that where a sense of confusion and lack of engagement exists the identities of those with dementia may be characterised in a very singular way (homogeneous) and, more importantly, by the practitioner him-/herself (Small et al., 1998). The focus then is to view the narrative approach as a means of configuring both ourselves and others in time and space that weaves a sense of connectedness with both internal and external worlds.

Capacity for reflection

There has often been an assumption that those with dementia are unable to reflect on their experience. Within the UK the National Health Framework for Older People supports research into narrative approaches with those diagnosed with mild to moderate dementia. Those diagnosed are aware of the challenges they face as well as being able to evidence a profound sense of loss of role and wider engagement with friends and the community. The evidence for this awareness is identified within the research on the preservation of self where those affected seek to preserve as much of their old identities as they can, which of itself presupposes a sense of awareness. This can take the form of writing notes as reminders of activities and seeking the support and advice of others (Clare et al., 2005).

Bereavement

Bereavement is defined as a sense of loss that is a characteristic of all cultures and is a core human experience. Grief is the intra-personal aspect of bereavement and mourning is related to that social expression characterised by the attitudes and values of the culture within which the person resides (Weinstein, 2008). While there is both a pragmatic and philosophical aspect to how practitioners engage with clients with dementia who are approaching end of life, there is also another dimension in how we engage with those with dementia who experience the bereavement of another person's death (Oyebode, 2009). This can have a much more complex dimension where the person with dementia may not have resolved earlier issues of psychological development and where there is an attendant lack of resolution of important relationships and a lack of resilience across the life course (Bowlby, 1969). Research evidence suggests that there is a correlation between these early secure attachments and a capacity for coping more effectively with bereavement.

Disenfranchised grief

The effect of this grief cannot be underestimated as the person with dementia strives to make sense of the person who is lost or missing. The older person may use the more traditional range of strategies to cope with bereavement but with the added dimension of an increased cognitive impairment. The result can mean strategies of denial that the person is really dead or an inner persuasion of the unavailability of the missing person as a rationalisation of this loss (Grief and Myran, 2006). This is where the skilled practitioner must use all the skills of evaluation and analysis in attempting to recognise those more abstract metaphors for loss utilised as a means of coping for the older person. If the person is not informed of any bereavement then the likelihood is that the older person will not be able to engage with the mourning process. The ethical issue here cannot be underestimated, particularly if the person is unable to remember that there has been a bereavement and where the reiteration of this news will result in a continuum of grief and distress. The big ethical question is whether to tell or not. Rentz et al. (2005) have suggested that it may be more ethical not to tell rather than cause a recurring sense of loss and emotional pain that may never become resolved. Just as importantly is that sense of disenfranchised grief (Doka, 2002) where the person with dementia is deemed not to understand the grief of loss as part of that wider negation of the personhood of the older person.

Conclusion

The study of dementia and social work practice is a constantly evolving area where dementia is no longer viewed as an end in itself but part of a continuum of endings. Whatever form the dementia takes there is a sense that those diagnosed may attempt to engage with their sense of loss and communicate this to others. This means that this evolved social work role will increasingly become more fluid, where an acceptance of the personhood of the individual will have to take precedence over the more biomedical approaches that currently exist. There is no room within an ethical approach to social work for the abandonment of this vulnerable group within a wider discourse on fiscal prudence.

  Recommended Reading

Downs, M. and Bowers, B. (eds) (2009) *Excellence in Dementia Care: Research into Practice*. Maidenhead: McGraw-Hill/Open University Press. An extremely useful text on the subjective experience of dementia as well as family coping and the skills needed to support those with dementia and their carers.

Innes, A. (2009) *Dementia Studies: A Social Science Perspective*. London: Sage. This text addresses dementia from a social-psychological and a social-gerontological perspective. There is a strong focus throughout on the nature of personhood for those with dementia and an emphasis on the research base.

Killick, J. and Allan, K. (2002) *Communication and the Care of People with Dementia*. Maidenhead: Open University Press. This is a very person-centred text based on the lived experience of those with dementia. It has a very helpful range of personal views and experiences of dementia with a particular focus on ethical practice when working with this group.

7

ASSESSMENT AND INTERVENTION

Learning Outcomes

This chapter looks at:

- A range of models of assessment to underpin both understanding and engagement with older people using models of ethical practice and practitioner knowledge base.
- Person-centred practice and new models of coping.
- Psychosocial intervention with an overview of Erikson's life stages and making sense of the past.
- Cognitive behavioural therapy and early life modelling.
- Task-centred working and the process of inclusion to effect positive change.
- Crisis intervention and the psychodynamic awareness of equilibrium.
- Narrative approaches and an engagement with the lived experience.
- Object relations and the intergenerational aspect of unresolved engagement and emotional pain.

Assessment

We live in changing times. While it may be relatively easy to negotiate through areas of ethics and values in relation to assessment and intervention with older people, we also need to ask what drives these differing perspectives? In Chinese Confucian philosophy, respect for elders is advocated not through obedience but through respect for lived experience and knowledge. Dogberry, in Shakespeare's *Much Ado About Nothing*, refers to 'when the age is in, the wit is out', which may relate more to a modern perspective on older age generally. It is also true that in post-Industrial Revolution times those skills, possessed by older people, that may have been valued within a rural setting, may have become obsolete or devalued within an urban setting. There is certainly some evidence to suggest that those belonging to a lower socio-economic group may invest more energy into relationships with older people who may still be contributing to the net worth of that family unit(y). Interestingly, one of the most positive images of older age and wisdom appears in the character Gandalf, from *The Lord of the Rings*. Sadly, there does not seem to be a female equivalent for wisdom and age! In a modern context it is left to legislators to address issues of dignity and respect and perhaps it is this that defines the nature of how this dignity is defined in a modern world.

Assessment is at the heart of all practice and intervention within professional social work. It is the bedrock of understanding on which rests a clear focus of professional knowledge, practice and reflection. It is all too easy to miss out the impact of assessment where there is an emphasis on outcome-driven practice. Practitioners have to retain a clear focus on the expressed wishes and needs of the older person, however challenging this may be.

Without this person-centred focus on the needs of older people the practitioner is more likely to become disengaged from the client's need and an empathic response to inclusion, risk assessment and emotional pain. This may further disadvantage an older person who is already struggling with complex physical, emotional and mental health issues coupled with an individual reflection on the meaning of existence and what the future may hold. Assessment is also critical for ensuring that there is adequate information available for care planning based on needs as distinct from planning based on resources.

Approaches to assessment

It is important that the social worker is focused on the specific and presenting needs of the older person to ensure that there is an appropriate level of assessment and that the proper tools for the job are utilised. Smale et al. (1993) have identified the three key approaches to assessment as follows.

Questioning approach

The assessor is expected to have a repository of knowledge of agencies and resources available and to ask the appropriate questions to interpret need and to take responsibility for an appropriate course of action. In effect the practitioner will be seen as 'expert' here.

Procedural approach

This assessment is led by the function of the agency and what it can provide and whether the older person meets the criteria for accessing those services. In areas of scant resources this can encourage practitioners to *negatively* assess the needs of older people to ensure they have an opportunity to access services (i.e. make the needs of the older person seem worse than they really are). The longer-term effect of this is to buy into a negative stereotyping of older age and to place increasing demands on already under-resourced services. Paradoxically, this feeds into an ageist agenda while at the same time potentially increasing access to service provision.

Exchange approach

The exchange model starts from the premise that the older person will be expert in the assessment of their own needs and that the role of the assessor will be one of collaborator where a mutuality of sharing and support will be the main focus. The person-centred approach also ensures that the older person will be able to iden-tify the key areas of progress that need to be made. The worker will still take respon-sibility for the overall resolution of the identified problem areas in relation to resources and the ability and willingness of the older person to participate within this process. A key skill here will be communication, both verbal and non-verbal.

Within inclusive and ethical social work practice every effort should be made to ensure that the older person is able to make informed decisions about their cur-rent and future welfare. This needs to incorporate an understanding of the power imbalance that can apply within these interactions and the negative impact this can have on the coping of the older person. While the exchange model is clearly defined as a collaborative process, the questioning model is only as effective as the ability of the assessor to ask the right questions and have a wide enough com-munication and knowledge base to be able to interpret the information received (Walker and Beckett, 2003). If the assessor does not have a wider understanding of the psychological and sociological forces that can impact on older people then it is likely that he/she will miss key events, inferences and areas that the older person may wish to avoid (Coulshed and Orme, 2006). The reflective practitioner will also review the progress of any assessment style by frequent review to ensure that it is still appropriate particularly within the context of increasing or diminishing coping capacity.

Theory of assessment

It is evident that there is a widely held functional aspect to assessment in that it seeks to achieve an outcome. The question practitioners have to ask is, who is the instigator and real assessor of the needs of the older person and what is the under-lying policy and knowledge base that leads this process? It is incumbent, within an ethical perspective, that social workers are aware of and are able to reconcile their personal values with those of their clients (Levy, 1976). Walker and Beckett (2003) give an overview of guidelines for social workers to lessen the likelihood of personal bias within any assessment undertaken with older people. These include seeking out effective supervision so as not to become over-awed by power differentials within formal social work settings, increasing self-awareness and the potential for critical self-evaluation. This is particularly in relation to personal values and professional practice and recognising that assessments are purely subjective unless substantiated by a secure theoretical and knowledge base.

This is evident within the work of Howe (2002, 2009) where he identifies a wide range of theoretical and underpinning knowledge that supports effective working with older people. This can include:

- An understanding of underpinning theory from cognitive behavioural to the more psy-chosocial aspects of older people's coping and what has led to this. Essentially this is about attempting to understand and evaluate past life events in the context of current presenting behaviour and how this understanding can help realise a sense of self for the older person. The reconciliation of these life events is likely to lead to a greater capacity for coping.
- An awareness of the sociological and structural forces that can impact on older people in the form of poverty, labelling, ageism and stigma. This will also include how political ideology and material resources impact on coping and the nature of discriminatory and oppressive practice generally.
- A consideration of how older people construct their own subjective experience within society and how this is evaluated by social work practitioners.

CASE STUDY

Robert Costello is a social worker in training. He has come from a very challenging back-ground where his parents experienced long periods of substance misuse and mental health problems. Robert has struggled to make sense of his early life experiences and is inclined to try and rationalise these experiences and keep his head down within the working environment. He has recently been delegated a 75-year-old male client to work with as part of his developmental training and has been asked to complete an assess-ment of needs with the client. This client, Hugo, has come from a similar background to Robert's and it is evident from their first meeting that Hugo's early life experiences have adversely impacted on his life. Hugo has experienced poor mental health, recurring prob-lems with substances misuse and an inability to sustain any long-term relationships. Robert has found himself becoming increasingly anxious when working with this client and has been experiencing feelings of helplessness and panic when attempting the assessment.

- Why do you think Robert is experiencing these feelings?
- What method of assessment do you think is appropriate here?
- How important is an understanding of developmental psychology here?
- What could Robert do to help alleviate this situation and where could he seek support?

What is an effective assessment?

Milner and O'Byrne (2009) identify five key stages of assessment that should be addressed and they state that these should be subject to the same methodological rigour that a practitioner would undertake within primary research. The evidence gained should be valid and any other professional practitioner in similar circumstances would gather similar results in terms of replication and authenticity. These foci should be supported by a sound knowledge and theory base, excellent communication skills and the capacity for reflection, evaluation and analysis on the evidence gathered from the older person. Effective assessment should liberate clients from the trauma and dysfunction of previous experience and thinking as well as promoting human dignity and a wider sense of social justice that is implicit within ethical practice (British Association of Social Workers, 2002).

Preparation

Who needs to be involved here? If the assessment with the older person is interview-focused then prepare the questions and ensure the client has a copy of these. Discuss with the older person the purpose, scope and limits of the interview and what both parties are hoping to achieve by this process.

Information gathering

Ensure that information gathered is clearly accessible to those with the permission and right to access this information and in a form that the older person can view. Make use of communication skills and a range of open and closed questions to ensure the content and veracity of what the older person is saying is properly recorded. A significant feature here will be the ability of the assessor to make sense of these data and to ensure that personal opinion is clearly differentiated from fact.

Assessing and analysing the information collected

There is a clear duty here to attempt a hypothesis of the information gathered and again this has to be checked with any key participants (family, GP, support services) but more specifically the older person (see Exchange Approach). This is where the theoretical and knowledge base of the assessor is most important. The older person may have a range of problems ranging from physical and mental health, to problems of resources and psychological well-being. This latter area may need an incisive knowledge and application of developmental psychology based on early life experiences, issues of resilience and the capacity to emotionally engage with others. Given the power imbalance that can exist between practitioner and the older person, the assessor may also be viewed as part of the structural oppression that the older person has experienced over the life course. The assessor therefore has to prepare for the range of defensive mechanisms that the older person may resort to as a means of protecting an already fragile central ego that may present as resistant to the intervention of the assessor. The role of the assessor here is to test and speculate on the information gathered and, where possible, to review this information with the support of concerned others.

Forming a plan of action

An action plan can never be securely formulated without a specific working through of these previous stages. To do so would be at odds with a personalised, inclusive and ethical approach to the assessment process. Any plan for the future has to be agreed with the older person and should include how progress will be measured for effectiveness, meeting need and a continuum of evaluation. A plan that does not meet these criteria is at odds with the personhood of older people who may already struggle with making sense of their lived reality in the face of cultural and structural oppression (Milner and O'Byrne, 2009).

Person-centred practice and partnership

Partnership is essential to any interaction within social work practice although this will not be absolute when working with older people. The power differential that exists between practitioner and client, particularly within any statutory focus, may mean that it is less likely to be an equal relationship. However, the essence of partnership working is the understanding that the client is worthy of respect purely because he/she is a person and that the views of the older person will be acknowledged, recorded and acted upon (Walker and Beckett, 2003). The wider focus on partnership working extends to the interprofessional context where the participating agencies (medical, psychologists, mental health services, education) are working collaboratively and to a common goal (Martin, 2011).

Any consideration of effective practice also has to accommodate the needs of partnership with other agencies that may be substantially governed by their own concerns about resources, objectives and statutory obligations. The more person-focused approach will consider the totality of the older person's life experiences, particularly relating to their emotional development and coping. The practitioner who has an awareness of the older person's psychological journey will be better able to support and nurture the older person to make informed decisions about his or her own futures. As Howe (2002: 85) so succinctly observes, 'Altering the meaning of experience brings about a change in behaviour'; and this will be particularly important where there has been a level of dysfunction or trauma in the older person's life. There may need to be a reinvestigation of former thinking and a reinvestment in new ways of coping. The locus of attention within person-centred practice then is defined by the boundaries of the client's reasoning and understanding (Mearns, 2003).

Lifespan development and psychosocial intervention

Given the crucial differences between all older people and their differing life experiences it is not a radical shift in thinking to recognise the equally diverse interpretation of these life events for older people. This challenge can relate to the more practical areas of coping with the inevitable frailty of older age as well as that more philosophical dilemma of meaning and existence. Perspectives related to social policy and biological ageing may have significance for the developers of these themes that are largely lost or even irrelevant to how older people experience the world (Thompson, 1998). The role of the practitioner is therefore to have a comprehensive understanding of those areas of psychological development allied within a sociological context that provides the background subtext to understanding older people across their individual lives. Sugarman (1986) proposes that a significant way to understand older people is to have a view of the totality of their lives through a narrative or biological approach. This entering into the lived experience not only satisfies a significant aspect of ethical practice (value and respect) but also emphasises the application of underpinning theory to support this. Again this relates to the sense of assessment where outcomes may be exclusively related to the personal opinion of the assessor unless reinforced by appropriate theoretical understanding.

Erikson's life stages

Erik Erikson (1995) developed one of the most significant psychosocial developmental theories based on individuals negotiating stages of psychological development across the life course. He suggested that as each stage of development was negotiated to a 'favourable ratio' it would help to build on and sustain the psychopathology of the individual, resulting in a better capacity for coping and emotional engagement with others and the maintenance of a clear sense of identity. Erikson postulated within his final stage of 'integrity versus despair' that a mostly favourable balance of the preceding stages would lead to an individual who was secure in his/her sense of self in older age; a person who could look back and to some extent look forward with a sense of achievement and pride in past life events and without an overarching fear of death. In effect, this is a resolution built on achievements, relationships and the capacity to engage with a wider society over the life course. There is a clear correlation between the satisfactory resolution of these life stages and crises and satisfaction in later life.

Interestingly, Erikson came to recognise late in life as his own achievements in older age continued to develop that this final stage may not necessarily have as its conclusion a consideration of death but more a focus on development. These themes were developed by his wife Joan after Erikson's death. Erikson came to view the stage of integrity versus despair as not the conclusion of the life cycle and not necessarily dependent on previous life stages. This new ninth stage could be a period of development and transition where previously unresolved stages might be revisited within a focus of 'gero-transcendence' (Brown and Lowis, 2003). This also, however, relates closely to that individual sense of nature of existence and of movement beyond a more rational and materialistic view of the world to a more reflective and even spiritual aspect of being and belonging.

Psychodynamic intervention

Psychodynamic intervention is characterised by a focus on the unconscious and this can cause difficulties within the power balance of engagements between social worker and the older person where the repository of power may be seen to reside with the practitioner (Trevithick, 2005).

A significant feature of social work exploration of older life experience is the use of reminiscence working. Reminiscence is considered a healthy and natural process that both helps to make sense of the past and supports an engagement with a younger cohort of people in the present. Interestingly, the work of Muthesius (1997) suggests that this primary focus of reminiscence places the older person in the present while utilising past experience to both inform and engage with a new generation. Those older people who are unable to consider this engagement with the present are less likely to reminisce than those who are and practitioners would need to recognise this as a potential for an ongoing inability to engage with others. Therefore, conducting a life review will be considered a positive feature of older age as opposed to the wider consideration that this may reinforce thoughts of regret and of opportunities missed.

The world will have changed in significant ways for older people, not least with regard to the moral and ethical codes of their youth. This of itself may be cause for a sense of despair in older people where traumatic events from the past, with extreme feelings of guilt, may now seem everyday to an outside observer. The role of the practitioner here is to support and contextualise these emotions while at the same time focusing on a more cognitively aware aspect to reduce these longstanding feelings of self-blame and guilt.

Psychodynamic intervention can raise extremely strong emotions, within both the practitioner and the client. Unresolved issues of early life experiences may come to the fore and impact on the presenting behaviour of the older person in the form of resistance or defence mechanisms (Walker and Beckett, 2003). Denial, projection, transference, sublimation, and somatisation may be manifested by the older person. It is therefore incumbent upon the practitioner to become both skilled in an understanding of the underlying theoretical knowledge while also recognising how dysfunction in early life can be carried through into older age. This is particularly important within the spheres of attachment and emotional development across the life course. At the same time only those skilled, trained practitioners should engage in this intervention. The majority of students will relate the psychodynamic process to a critically evaluative aspect of their own knowledge and understanding and the relationship of theory to practice.

Cognitive behavioural therapy

The substance of this theory is that all behaviours are learned but that some behaviour may lead to high levels of dysfunction within both thoughts and behaviours. While the presenting behaviour of the older person may appear as chaotic or depressive as a result of ageing, ageism and labelling across the life course, any intervention will have at its core the understanding that both behaviour and cognition will have their beginnings within earlier and recurring life experiences. The behaviourist aspect is built up over the course of social and physical interactions where we learn how to behave based on the responses we get from these presenting behaviours (Wilson et al., 2008). In the context of older people, behaviours of aggression or withdrawal may be related to early life experiences or 'modelling' the behaviour of others within dysfunctional settings and is at the core of social learning theory. At the same time an older person may have internalised through earlier life experiences that 'being seen and not heard' is a useful survival strategy. This may then become a feature of individual behaviour that may result in an inability and fear of engagement and emotional entanglements in old age. An additional response may be where an older person seeks a form of invisibility which may disengage them from support agencies and even benefits agencies to their personal financial detriment. With regard to the cognitive aspect the focus is on individual perception and how individuals interpret their own social context and reality (Beck and Beck, 2005). This involves a new 'cognitive restructuring' where the older person is encouraged to view life events through a more positive filter and where the practitioner supports and encourages the older person to seek new ways of disengaging from faulty and damaging thinking. This can be by dialogue, questioning, reasoning and a focus by the practitioner on reformulating and reviewing thinking that is not based on an objective and rational overview.

If this cognition is adversely affected by early life experiences then the older person may not be able to 'read' the signs of engagement with others and may be suspicious of attempts at engagement. Unconscious drives are awakened at times of stress and the urge to *regress* may overpower the individual's capacity to make sense of the real nature of any communication or intervention. This is particularly the case where there is a high propensity for self-blaming where this has become internalised as the main locus of attention within thinking and self-perception.

Angela is 80 years of age and is a tenant in a local authority care home. Her early years were characterised by parents who drank to excess and frequently left Angela alone or with neighbours for long periods. Angela left home at 16 and met Terry, a local plumber, soon after. Their relationship was very passionate and Angela soon became pregnant. Terry married Angela as it was the 'right thing to do'. Terry's drinking was soon out of control and he became increasingly violent towards Angela and the children. Angela's lack of money often meant that there was little for food, heating and clothing for the children and Terry frequently accused Angela of being a 'bad mother' and 'useless' around the house. He also encouraged the children to join him in attacking Angela's capacity for housekeeping and coping generally. Angela has now presented as someone who appears very low in mood most of the time and tends to be very isolated from staff and other older people within the home. You have been asked to intervene with Angela to support her needs within the home.

? Reflective Questions ?

- Why do you think Angela presents with such a poor sense of self and why do you think she is so self-critical and self-blaming?
- What aspects of sociological thinking could you bring to bear within this intervention within a consideration of gender construct, poverty, role and labelling?
- What aspects of your understanding of cognitive behavioural therapy could you make use of to support Angela and effect a positive change?
- Why might Angela be resistant to your interventions and what strategies might she make use of?

Task-centred working

Task-centred working is an approach developed out of a dissatisfaction with a longer-term and occasionally unfocused psychosocial approach to interventions. At the same time practitioners have to be wary of an exclusively behaviourist approach where presenting behaviour rather than underlying psychopathology may be addressed. Reid (1978) developed a range of areas within the lives of clients that could benefit from this more structured approach. I will refer here to the main British theorists Doel and Marsh (1992, 2005), who developed this theory in Britain and where this intervention has become a commonly used but often misunderstood model.

This is a short-term intervention where the older person and the social worker agree on a process of exploring the breadth of presenting problems; negotiate a well-defined and mutually understood goal to be achieved (preferably using written agreements to support this); define the individual roles of the participants with a clear statement as to what this is and to negotiate an ending. The focus here is on ensuring that the older person can be supported in new levels of independent living and decision making.

The intervention focuses on key areas of problem classifications as identified by Reid (1978) and here I place these within the context of potential older person needs and engagement.

- Interpersonal conflict: This can be with family, friends, carers or neighbours.
- Dissatisfaction with social relationships: This can be reflected in low mood and a general sense that older people may not feel they have a role to play in a society that tends to value youthfulness rather than experience. Youthfulness may be a negotiable asset while experience may only be viewed through an ageist lens.
- Problems with formal organisations: Many older people, through a sense of independence developed over many years, may not develop the skills or confidence to engage with formal organisations. This can relate to housing, continuing education and particularly the benefits agency. It is not surprising that there are frequent surpluses of monies left unclaimed by older people who find it a traumatic experience to admit they may need social and financial support but lack those formal skills of engagement to pursue these legitimate claims.
- Difficulties in role performance: The social worker will have to be particularly aware here where personal prejudice and poor communication may miss the real emotional distress an older person is feeling at the loss of a valued role. This may be of husband, wife or provider where the older person may have taken pride in personal skills which are not as valued in a modern world and who may have invested a large part of their identity within those skills.
- Reactive emotional distress: This will involve a real sense of awareness of the losses an older person may have experienced over the life course and how depression and anxiety may be a feature of older age, particularly if there is a decline in physical and mental health and a sense of well-being generally.
- Inadequate resources: This is increasingly a feature of older age for those who have been in poorly paid or part-time work, who are living in poor standard housing and are disengaged from the support of the wider community. This will be compounded when coupled with factors of nutrition, access to health services and loneliness. More recently this will have focused on real fears over the means to pay for food, heating and transport costs (Reid, 1978).

Characteristics of task-centred intervention with older people

Task-centred working is unusual in that it is characterised more by the coping capacity of the individual as opposed to any wider pathological dysfunction (Doel and Marsh, 1992). It starts from the premise that older people have within themselves the attributes and skills, built up over the course of a lifetime, to engage with the processes of effective change. The critical aspect of this method needs to be considered more in the context of engagement as opposed to an intervention where the older person may be perceived in the role of passive recipient. The focus here is on a continuum of evaluation and, more importantly, the process of negotiation with the older person in the identification of the problem to be addressed (Walker and Beckett, 2003). It is the older person who will be supported and encouraged to identify the main area of concern he/she may have and the role of the practitioner is to encourage, question and focus the client's concerns into a manageable goal. The process of engagement here may prove to be as effective as the achievement of any goal as this will involve a high degree of communication skills from the social worker in supporting, defining and interpreting what the problem really is. This needs to be assessed within the experience of some older people where a lack of resources across the lifecycle may have resulted in a practice of 'make do and mend' (Lynch, 2010), not complaining about personal circumstances and, to a large extent, not drawing attention to oneself. This is at odds with the work of Bury and Holme (1991) who characterise dependency as a natural feature of societal engagement. Conversely, older people, rather than being perceived in the context of neediness, should be considered within the focus of reciprocity and how individuals with differing needs can support each other at both a personal and societal level. Again the practitioner has to be careful here that the need of the older person is not missed within an environment where the older person seeks to minimise his/her problems. There is evidence to suggest that older people have a much more personalised view of their coping capacity based on how they may be feeling at any one time rather than a consideration of any range of problems across older age (Slater, 1995).

Crisis intervention

What is a crisis? This is a commonly used phrase which has lost something of its meaning through common usage. Within the realms of social work practice it is clearly defined within the context of a transitional state where the usual patterns of coping that an older person has developed over a life course are no longer adequate to meet the presenting difficulties (Wilson et al., 2008). There is a clear focus here on a psychodynamic understanding of development and the level of resilience an older person will have built up to deal with presenting problems. A sudden shock to this coping system through changing circumstances in terms of environment, health or bereavement may leave an older person unable to draw on that repository of intellectual and emotional skills that have formerly supported them. This imbalance of the usual individual equilibrium or 'homeostasis' will have a deeply unsettling effect on the older person and may result in a complete incapacity to cope at a specific time in life (O'Hagan, 2000). Social workers will also need to be aware of a consideration of systems theory where the older person may need to be assessed within the family or wider social network to effect any change.

It is important that the practitioner intervenes as soon as possible when a crisis occurs. I have been asked many times over my working life how I know when someone is in crisis? The simple answer is that 'you'll know'! An older person presenting in crisis may exhibit a range of characteristics from chaotic thinking, complete numbness, to anger, depression or in extreme cases a feeling and threat of self-annihilation where the person becomes overpowered by a lack of coping (Higham, 2006). This is an opportunity for the professional practitioner to use all the skills of communication, theoretical knowledge and advocacy to ensure that an empathic approach is manifested and to support the older person to a new sense of coping. Initially, this will almost certainly involve an advocacy role to allow for the older person to regain something of that equilibrium that has been lost during this crisis. Effective crisis intervention with older people should focus on their coping across the life course as a means of revisiting previous coping as well as an acknowledgement that a presenting crisis may also be the result of an erosion of the personality across this period. There also needs to be an understanding that an older person in crisis will be able to regain that former level of coping both now and in the future. As Payne (2005: 98) observes, crisis intervention 'focuses on emotional responses to external events' and the role of the social worker in supporting the older person to view these distressing events within rational thinking is critical here. Essentially, the role of the social worker will be to ensure that the older person is encouraged and supported to change levels of dysfunctional thinking that may be complicit in bringing about this crisis.

Narrative approaches

Personal narratives help us to make sense of our lived experience. They create a sense of meaning within a developing discourse where the personal narrative is revised and reviewed to create new meaning.

The role of the practitioner is to support the older person in reviewing and analysing previous experiences within the context of meaning and experience to support new levels of coping with adversity (Payne, 2006a; Thompson, 2011). It is also the case that individual narratives may be heavily influenced by the social history and context of the older person and how these are managed and interpreted. Narrative approaches can liberate older people from disturbing and unsettling life events as well as validating individual experience within a personalisation agenda. They have the capacity for individuals to create a new and more life affirming narrative about themselves where resilience will be acknowledged and valued over a more narrow medicalised model (White, 2002).

A focus for the practitioner will be on how the personal narrative is delivered and the emphasis the older person gives to certain life events. This is likely not just to indicate the importance placed by the older person on a specific event but offer guidance to the practitioner as to how the older person may be interpreting life events and their social context. McAdams (1997) speculates that the personal narrative is similar to psychological stages of development where the main themes are laid down in childhood and come to fruition in adulthood and where older age is a time for reflection and evaluation. Practitioners within this understanding should be better able to support and evaluate an older person's personal narrative, particularly if this illustrates early life dysfunction that is adversely affecting coping in older age. It is likely that a person who presents with a positive outlook on life and views older age as a time of development and growth is more likely to have successfully negotiated earlier life stages and to have a positive personal narrative. Essentially, within the narrative approach lies the individual's sense of identity (Plummer, 1995) and this will include theories of adult development and how an older person's quality of life can be improved.

The practitioner engagement is person-centred and needs to be well focused since this intervention may be longer term as the older person is encouraged and supported to make sense of earlier developmental experiences and his/her role within them. Communication skills and a sense of genuineness are important here if the older person is to manage traumatising and bewildering feelings and particularly if these feelings and fears have become subsumed within the unconscious (Trevithick, 2005).

The role of the practitioner here is to deconstruct the problem by separating it from the person and encouraging the older person to view the problem in a more abstract way. The purpose of this is to draw on the older person's repository of previous coping skills to encourage a more focused approach to problem solving. One of the key areas to be addressed here is how the older person may have become 'enslaved' by the problem and what has led to this lack of resilience and powers of resistance (Milner and O'Byrne, 2009). There may be particular challenges when engaging with those with dementia which Kitwood (1999) previously characterised as a form of interventionist 'nihilism' without a secure foundation in process, outcome and hope for the future. The narrative approach here may act more as a means of speculating what an older person would have liked to happen based on prior knowledge. The challenge is for the practitioner to assess this information in a climate where there may be increasing pressure to make decisions based on political and financial expediency rather than identified and expressed older person choice and need.

Barnett's (2000) use of 'memory stories' to promote communication with those with dementia is a case in point and is central to an ethical approach to the philosophical question of what it is to be. There is also evidence to support an increase in life satisfaction through reminiscence working where the emphasis is moved from a more materialistic aspect of coping to something of a more transcendental (beyond existence) nature (Wadensten and Hagglund, 2006). This is that area that lies within a spiritual domain.

Object relations and internalised pain

When we refer to object relations here what do we really mean? It is true that the word 'object' has an impersonal meaning that may be at odds with the more engaged personalised approach of professional practice. Within the context of this theory the 'object' is always a person. Unlike the more Freudian emphasis on pleasure seeking, object relations is much more focused on emotional engagement with others. While

Freud's analysis has the *ego* mediating the pleasure seeking *id* and the conscious aspect of the *superego*, Fairbairn (1954) suggested that the ego is fully formed at birth and that the ultimate goal of the person is to achieve a meaningful relationship with another person (the object). He characterised the three stages that an individual would progress through to achieve this mutuality as: *infantile dependency*, a *transitional period* and *mature dependence*. Infantile dependency is defined by the subsuming of the child within the focus of the primary carer while attempting to manage these relationships. The transitional phase relates to the ongoing work of the person in breaking away from this early dependence to form more mature relationships based on a realistic acceptance of what the relationship and interdependence between one person and another is (Cashdan, 1988). This theory has as a central theme the sense that the child will unconsciously 'split' off aspects of the caring figure that are unsatisfactory and do not meet the presenting needs of the child. This splitting can view the other person (the object) as having good and bad characteristics. If the intolerable aspects of another's behaviour are acknowledged then the child will have to either deny and render into the unconscious these unmet needs or alternatively idealise the aspects of the carer's behaviour that the child can relate to. This 'splitting' can render the carer as all 'good' (exciting) or all 'bad' (rejecting), with a commensurate relationship with the 'needy' and 'punitive' split from the central ego. The needy child may view the object as exciting but when the child's needs are not fully realised this may trigger that more maladapted, unconscious, punitive drive. A person seen as all good may suddenly be perceived as all bad. Not only that but the repression of these feelings may lead a split off *punitive* person not only to punish those (in a psychological sense) who have not met these needs but also to punish the neediness of others where this neediness has elicited an unfavourable response in the earlier development of this person (Teyber and McClure, 2006).

If these splits and repression of earlier life experiences are not resolved through the transitional period into mature dependence it is likely that these feelings of need and the punitive aspect will be carried through into adulthood. A needy split off central ego may result in a person who is prepared to remain within a relationship because of the extreme feelings of needing to be emotionally engaged with another person, irrespective of how the person is treated within this relationship.

This mental representation that an older person holds may not be a true representation of the other person but an idealisation of the person based on the desperation to be in a relationship (Ryckman, 2008). The problem is that this may only relate to part of the other person as opposed to the totality which is at the heart of all successful emotional engagements. Conversely, a split off punitive person may be unable to engage at any meaningful level with others and may even punish those who express need across the life course because the younger self was punished for expressing need and therefore internalised the notion that need itself is bad.

From the perspective of object relations and older people the practitioner has to be able to consider the real impact of earlier life experiences and what defensive postures the older person may use in coping. The net result may be an older person who has never been able to engage at an emotional level throughout his/her life and the impact this will have on a general sense of resilience, coping and well-being. The split off needy child may become the needy older person and the same may be true of the split off punitive child who becomes the punitive adult who manifests as a disengaged, unemotional and fatalistic person masking that inner frightened lost child.

Conclusion

The level and process of engagement with older people may be as important as the potential outcome achieved. If older people are not the focus of a more personalised and person-centred approach it is likely that the ongoing debate as to how we meet the needs of older people will be futile. This is particularly important at a time when these needs may become subsumed within a wider debate of how we maintain current services at a time of economic decline. The range of assessment tools and methods of engagement with older people provide a fulcrum on which hang the needs and rights of all older people. The balance is achieved by sound professional judgement and an awareness of the overarching ethical principles of practice.

 Recommended Reading

Beckett, C. and Taylor, H. (2010) *Human Growth and Development* (2nd ed.). London: Sage. A very good overview of the range of psychological developments and how these may relate to social work practice.

Lishman, J. (ed.) (2007) *Handbook for Practice Learning in Social Work and Social Care, Knowledge and Theory* (2nd ed.). London: Jessica Kingsley. A really thorough text that addresses the finer detail of interventions and the development of the reflective practitioner.

Martin, R. (2011) *Social Work Assessment: Transforming Social Work Practice.* Exeter: Learning Matters. A thorough text that works through the assessment process in clear detail.

Milner, J. and O'Byrne, P. (2009) *Assessment in Social Work* (3rd ed.). Basingstoke: Palgrave Macmillan. A seminal text for any developing practitioner.

8

GERONTOLOGY

Learning Outcomes

This chapter looks at:

- The wider dimension of gerontology and ageing.
- Sociological perspectives on the construction of old age and the cohort effect as well as theories of ageing.
- Definitions of the third and fourth age of ageing and the relationship to class and income.
- Psychological ageing and coping and resilience in old age. The chapter will also address the more existential aspects of the fourth age, the ninth stage and gero-transcendence.

Introduction

The scientific study of ageing is known as gerontology. By scientific here we mean those factors that go to make up the totality of understanding of what old age is and how it impacts on a specific group of people. This is not a simple task. There is an understanding among the general public of the nature of physical decline that may occur in old age and this is frequently related more to those biological and clinical considerations of meeting physical and potential care needs.

Biological ageing is identified as the decline that occurs across the life course in relation to physiological ageing and is characterised by a range of factors from lifestyle and nutrition to the potential for genetic predisposition to a range of illnesses. Social gerontology, on the other hand, seeks to address those other dimensions of the role that the state and society play within this continuum and is a science based on the individual scope for coping and functioning, rather than a metaphor for universal decline (Weaver, 1999). It focuses on the study of the economic and social aspects of older people and ageing populations generally. Increasingly there has been a focus on older people across the life stages as opposed to a more specific study of old age itself, with its emphasis on potential need and decline (Johnson, 2005). The former acknowledges how the older person has developed over a lifetime whereas the latter may be much more inclined to view the older person in terms of an inevitable decline.

Ageing and its study has been something of an evolutionary process over the past 50 years. While older people may have been characterised formerly in terms of their frailty and deterioration there is an increasing awareness of the need to re-evaluate the role and function of older people in a modern society. As Brearley (1976: 433) so succinctly states, 'Growing old is no longer a simple process'. This chapter will address these complex issues of understanding in relation to social gerontology and its emphasis on the social and demographic aspects of ageing. This will include a more modern approach to issues of health and well-being and the capacity to function as an effective and valued member of society for as long as possible (Phillips et al., 2010).

Cultural determinism

Implicit here is the need for a more radical and existential view of the older person in relation to cultural gerontology and the meaning of age, both from a personal development aspect and a social policy perspective.

This cultural aspect has as its determinant the consideration that humanistic, feminist and ethical awareness need to be considered as well as those more formal structures of pensions, retirement and the impact ageing has on the individual (Andersson, 2003). While cultural awareness is a factor in a wider context of gerontological understanding, practitioners have to ensure that any rigid adherence to a cultural norm or stereotype of ageing may also adversely impact on the variety of life experiences of older people generally (Constable, 2009). Essentially this is not just a consideration of living and the road travelled but what the meaning and understanding of this journey is.

The policy aspect

The importance of the policy dimension is not a new concept and cannot be underestimated at a time when there is a constant debate on how the care of older people will be provided in the future. This has tended to scapegoat older people in terms of their financial burden on society (Walker, 1996). There is no doubt that there should be an ongoing research base defined by the ageing demographic that places older people at the centre of how services are developed and controlled. The current subtext in relation to the 'problem' of the ageing population has within it the implication that age itself is a determinant of decline and therefore older people generally. Any focus on the vagaries of biological ageing at the expense of a consideration of the social context of older age in a time of economic decline will inevitably refocus blame on older people and reinforce the nature of their perceived dependence. Social gerontology therefore increasingly concentrates on life course aspects of ageing as opposed to a discourse on any sudden arrival at old age and what this means for the individual (Johnson, 2005). Without the life course view the totality of the individual older person's lived experience may be rendered invisible within a more functional aspect of decline and dependence. Increasingly, there has been an emphasis on a developing awareness of the social and economic forces that can come to bear on older people. These aspects are more likely to be determinants in a successful negotiation of older age as opposed to that more biological approach to functioning (Phillipson, 1998).

Robert McLean is 90 years of age. Until recently he has been able to care for himself and his neighbours have reported that they have not seen him for a few weeks and he is not answering his door. The police have gained access and reported that Robert is in a poor physical state and appears quite confused. A social worker has been allocated to assess his needs. Robert states that he feels 'hopeless' and 'useless' and that he cannot stop thinking of his friends that were killed during the last war when Robert served in mainland Europe. He wonders why he has survived to live so long when his friends died so young and is trying to make sense of this. He has clearly had very poor fluid and nutritional intake over the past week which may be a contributory factor in this level of confusion and he states that he doesn't 'really care what happens to me now'.

CASE STUDY

? Reflective Questions ?

- Why do practitioners need to consider the wider cultural, philosophical, ethical and spiritual aspects of older age?
- Why might a focus on a purely biological aspect of old age itself deny the basic rights of older people?
- What areas of Robert's assessment would you need to consider to ensure that those more holistic needs of Robert are met?
- Can you place Robert within a critical understanding of how structural (societal) forces may disadvantage him?

Sociological perspectives on age and ageing

While sociology is the study of human society it also focuses within gerontology on how old age is socially constructed in a modern society and how this is likely to mitigate against older people leading fulfilling lives (Tulle and Lynch, 2011). This may be particularly the case in respect of women whose demographic profile indicates that they live longer on average than men and consequently may remain in ill health and poverty over a longer period. The reality of the social construction of old age may be related to a series of life events and experiences that appear normal or everyday to the people experiencing them. A closer analysis may show a very different picture. The lived reality of older age may be as much related to social and culturally defined events across the life course such as class, housing, health and education, and the poverty of resources and opportunity that may adversely impact on these aspects (Macionis and Plummer, 2008). When the total life experience of the older person is considered then it is likely that there will be clear sociological themes that will support an understanding of this. These could include a consideration of class, opportunity, construct of gender, poverty and the construct of ageing itself.

The intergenerational aspect

As a general rule of thumb those born within a class structure that supports a sense of expectation through consistent and dependable resources, education and good health and nutrition are likely to preserve this across their individual and family lived experience. The reverse is also true, although not absolute, in that intergenerational aspects of poverty of resources and opportunity will have negative consequences in older age. Individuals may play out the dance of time to a predetermined tune and the price they pay may be increased ill health and poverty into an increasing old age (Markson, 2003). The gerontological underpinning of this is that lack of resources in older age may be more related to life opportunities and a lack of resolution of those life events that lead to coping and resilience in older age. This is particularly the case within neo-liberal (conservative) social policy. The welfare state may be under a consistent attack as public monies are devolved from the public to the private sector in the generation of profit. When this is cloaked in the language of more effective use of resources and consumer choice then it may become increasingly easy to see the individual trees without an overview of the wood (Gilleard and Higgs, 2000). This potential dismantling of the welfare state as a means of reducing the stigmatising aspects of ageing and ageism may allow for greater personalisation of services. It may also apply more readily to those more affluent older people but is unlikely to protect the more vulnerable in society. The focus of gerontology therefore has to include a discourse on how the links between the older person and the state are being potentially eroded and the concurrent sense that the state may feel it does not have a responsibility to support the current and continuing care of older people generally. There is something of an inevitability where the rights of older people may become increasingly eroded and where they are perceived to be the cause of their own misfortune in not providing for a secure future. The paradox here is clear. While older people may never have had the resources to provide for this older age, the state, which has denied older people these resources, may then blame older people for this lack of financial acumen across the life course.

The debate needs to recognise the disparity that exists between the working young and the older retired person. Also between well-off older people and those who have been unable to prepare for retirement and may increasingly be categorised as needy and dependent in old age.

Whatever the outcome it is inevitable that for the foreseeable future older people will move from a consumer status to objects of consumption where their net contribution will become increasingly diminished as their structural reliance increases (Foucault, 1988). The resolution to this problem is a more clearly focused approach to longevity and the demographics of older age within a more inclusive policy-making process.

I will consider the following three theories that address gerontology within a sociological context.

Activity theory

This theory addresses the nature of ageing and how older people who are actively engaged within their communities may have a greater predisposition not just to a satisfactory but also a successful old age. Research by Havinghurst et al. (1963) suggests that this activity is a necessary component of successfully negotiating the later life stages and has a particular benefit for psychological health. Underpinning this thinking is that older people may have invested a substantial sense of who they are as individuals within their working lives. At retirement they may reinvest these energies into other pursuits such as volunteering, kinship care or a reinvestigation of unfulfilled interests from earlier life stages.

What does this mean for the older person?

The theory is not specific in relation to how older people who are not engaged at this level will cope or whether this chosen inactivity will have a negative impact on successful ageing. There are several issues I wish to draw attention to here. Firstly old people preserve a unique identity and even issues of poverty will impact on different individuals in different ways. Too often there is a homogeneous view of older people having similar characteristics, while the opposite is the case. The heterogeneity of older people suggests that individual differences in older age are as unique and specific as they are within any age group, including the young.

Older people may choose to withdraw from the vagaries of life as a means of approaching and accepting the inevitability of death or to pursue a more existential and philosophical aspect of what the future may hold. Nevertheless, there is clear evidence that being involved in activities of choice, with others and at a level that gives satisfaction has proven beneficial life outcomes for older people (Harlow and Cantor, 1996).

A significant aspect of sociological thinking is that it may be less a case of older people withdrawing from society but rather society disengaging from the older person.

This shrinkage of the experienced world may reinforce those ascribed roles of vulnerability, frailty and need and may become exacerbated within the context of the 'problem' of old age and how it will ultimately be engaged with (Thorson, 2000). From a gerontological point of view this raises significant issues of how current and developing policy in meeting the needs of older people is negotiated. Also what, if any, role does personalisation play within an agenda that focuses on the 'needy' older person? The reality is that due to increased awareness of healthy lifestyles and to developing health services there has to be a reinvigoration of the assessed role of older people in the developing world. This dialogue has to take place outwith an associative debate between old age and ill health.

Disengagement theory

Cumming and Henry (1961) postulated the theory that old age would inevitably include a process of disengagement from the cares and ills of the world. This functionalist approach suggested that it is a natural progression for older people to withdraw from society through retirement and bereavement (Phillipson and Baars, 2007). This may also be related to a wider disengagement from society and relationships as older people refocused their energies on a more reflective approach to their future. This sense of inevitability is problematic on several levels. Not all people may be influenced in the same way by their socio-economic position, particularly in terms of resources, and may be forced into a *disengagement* where they would otherwise wish to *engage* (Mauk, 2006). An institutional acceptance of disengagement in this form may preclude professionals from acknowledging the real fears and emotional pain of older people. This may be at a time when they do not have the physical or emotional resources to engage with their wider community or relationships generally. This would also appear to be at odds with a more activity-focused perspective where life satisfaction *appears* to be enhanced by a new and developing sense of self through the promulgation of new interests and relationships (Neumann, 2000). As a sociological theory of ageing, disengagement theory may have that air of absolutism that is in conflict with an empirically evidenced approach to understanding. The question that has to be asked is whether this disengagement is true of all older people in all cultures irrespective of those wider sociological forces of poverty and gender. If it is not then the theory cannot exist as a truism but part of the panoply of understanding that is at the heart of gerontological studies. From a more developmental and psychological perspective it may be that disengaged older people have always been disengaged and their presenting behaviour in old age may be an indicator of a succession of unresolved life stages. Not to acknowledge this leaves practitioners unable to consider or recognise the emotional pain of old people. This may also be at a time where the older person lacks the emotional strength to express this need and when the inevitability of death may be a prevailing concern.

Continuity theory

Continuity theory evolved as part of an attempt to answer the dichotomy that appeared to exist between activity theory and the wider context of disengagement. Atchley (1989, 1999) suggests that older people in fact maintain that sense of self, value and self-worth even after they have retired from paid employment. The theory suggests that there are internal and external forces that can come to bear in pursuit of these personal ideals. The internal forces are influenced by the capacity for self-reflection, emotional engagement with others and the ability to make decisions based on these skills. The external forces that older people can draw on refer more to attributes such as previous roles, skills built up over a lifetime and the capacity to renegotiate personal relationships to meet a new older age.

The premise therefore is that there is no reason why there should not be a successful retirement and, more importantly, a successfully lived later life where those social bonds and sense of self are explored and reinforced. It is also worth considering the role that leisure may have where not every older person may be imbued with a strong ethic to work. Increasingly, older people are appreciating that leisure time also allows for continuity in that it can be a time to explore new ideas and ways of living as well as allowing time for that more reflective aspect of the lived older experience. The problem with continuity theory is that it is difficult to research given the very variable aspects and uniqueness of all older people. In the same way that we acknowledge ageism as a destructive force within society, with its limiting and ascribed roles of vulnerability, we also acknowledge this diversity of ageing and how there is not a single theory that fits older people in any absolute sense. Blau (1981) suggests that, contrary to the widely held belief that the lives of older people constrict with age in terms of life opportunity, an increase in leisure time may allow older people to take on new roles and explore new opportunities in training, development and identity (Gilleard and Higgs, 2000).

Essentially older people do not exist in a microcosm. They increasingly inhabit the intergenerational world where the skills and knowledge developed over the life course will act as a conduit for links with the past, present and the future of their wider social network. Interestingly, continuity theory views disengagement as more related to a disruption in the physical or mental health of the older person than any natural consequence of the ageing process itself. Consequently, those older people with a solid repertoire of life skills built up over the life course are more likely to have better coping strategies across this life course. At the same time, we need to be able to critically evaluate the life course as 'normal ageing' in the context of the very different life experiences and global impact that there is on the lives of older people from a variety of ethnic and cultural backgrounds. These life experiences may be intrinsically tied up within a web of poverty, ageism and lack of opportunity for older people as opposed to a more holistic and global approach to understanding older people and an ageing society within a modern world (Phillipson and Baars, 2007).

The third age

Within any conceptual framework of the nature of ageing there should be a consideration of the differing ages that older people may experience. Townsend (1981) identified older people who do not have a social identity role as being reduced to the role of 'pensioner' where this dependent status will leave pensioners potentially without a voice and with increased likelihood of poverty in older age.

While the ageing process may be a part of the continuum of living, old age may be experienced very differently by different older people. This can relate to early life experiences, the capacity for resilience and coping in the face of life stressors and adversity and the ability to engage at an emotional level with friends, family and the wider community.

> You may wish to consider attachment theory here and particularly the work of Ainsworth et al. (1978), Bowlby (1969) and Howe (1995, 2011). Can you see how early childhood attachments can have a significant impact on adults and older people particularly? What are the significant areas of childhood attachment that you think could adversely impact on older age? What is your understanding of resilience built up over the life course and how this will support older people?

While there can be no sense of absolutism in relation to how ageing is perceived by older people generally, there are certain characteristics of engagement with the community, active involvement in the lives of others and a sense of contributory status that can be defined as the 'third age'.

The third age may be something of an amorphous term. When, for instance, does an older person access this stage? It may be interpreted as the stage at which older people retire (Young and Schuller, 1991). It may also be part of an evolutionary process in view of the changing policy on when retirement should take place within an increasingly ageing demographic. Whatever the stage (age) this takes place at, there is a positive assumption that this is a time when life can be reinvigorated through a redefinition of a future with potentially less stress and more leisure time; a time to pursue new interests and the possibility of a more reflective lifestyle no longer characterised by the conflicts of paid work and those more competitive aspects of life (Laslett, 1996).

Even more taxing is the stage at which older people engage with the fourth age (see below), which is generally perceived to be over the age of 85 years. These older people may be increasingly at risk of declining physical and psychological powers with a commensurate increase in dependency and perceived negative social functioning (Baltes and Smith, 2003).

Personalisation and the third age

This third age group will be active within society and, more importantly, engage in the political agenda, particularly with regard to personalisation (Perry, 2009). This personalisation involves older people who are no longer to be seen as passive recipients of services that impact on them but as active citizens and consumers. They are much more likely to have a direct say as to the nature and quality of service provision and a direct role in the inception and development of these services.

Structural aspects of ageing

This dialogue has, as its starting point, a consideration of the nature of age and particularly ageism and the power imbalance that may be implicit within this relationship. Social workers, and care managers particularly, wield a significant amount of power and this has to be consistently reviewed and renegotiated with older people as structural, political, social and community-based engagements change and coalesce. This structural aspect may particularly form a part of the work of established organisations who struggle to weave a path through a changing political and economic landscape (Carr, 2007). It is all too easy to negotiate the values and ethical aspects of social work practice in a way that meets the needs of agencies as opposed to service users. The likelihood then is that the critical challenge of meeting individual need (as far as possible) becomes diluted within the sense of *'value* for money' as distinct from *values* for older people.

Implicit within this personalisation agenda is the sense of the inclusion and empowerment of older people that is itself fraught with interpretation (Banks, 2006). While no one would doubt that older people having more power in relation to decision making about their own needs is a positive step, this can be evaluated in two ways. The first is where the social worker (implicitly or explicitly) takes on the power role and through a process of devolution attempts to empower the older person (traditional). The other is where the practitioner acknowledges the more global forces of structural oppression, policy and resources that negatively impact on older people where the empowerment focus has to be one of both acknowledgement of these forces and the capacity to challenge them (emancipatory).

The work of Gilleard and Higgs (2000) helps to refocus this third age in relation to class, cohort and the generational basis. The *class* basis suggests that there has been an increasing divide in wealth inequalities among third age older people. This is evident particularly in relation to the levels of disposable income that they may possess to meet presenting needs in older age. This contrast is accentuated when the wider dimension of the demographics of an ageing population are considered. The 'have nots' may become even more visible because of their lack of resources, support systems and the capacity to consider a 'decent' older age (Galbraith, 1999).

The *cohort* aspect may define groups of older people as ageing in different ways according to life experience, resources, health and a sense of expectation of what can be achieved irrespective of an accumulation of years. This cohort effect is most clearly identified within the baby boomer generation, born after the Second World War with experiences radically different from previous generations (Haber, 2009). These older people have experienced a prolonged period of economic growth and played a significant role in the post-war cultural revolution where civil liberties, individual rights and access to services and resources denied to a previous generation would now be acknowledged as a right. An emphasis on education, increased income and leisure time has afforded this generation significant improvements in quality of life. This has been supported in the longer term by pension resources that are unlikely to be matched for future generations within the current economic climate and thinking.

More importantly, and from a policy focus, this generation is unlikely to view itself as older, needy or to accept any ideology of support or care within which they are not fully engaged. These circumstances are not the same for all older people from this cohort however. For at the same time, and related to developing technology, there was an continuing increase in part-time working practices, particularly attractive to women engaged in child-rearing. The knock-on effect of this has been that women have become increasingly trapped and impoverished in older age as they were unable to accumulate those resources and pension rights that their contemporaries may have (Oppenheim and Harker, 1996). The concurrent impact of this is that there is evidence to suggest that the price of fertility for successive generations of women in Britain today is poverty in older age (Morgan, 1992).

Social connectedness

Conversely, women are perceived to have a greater stock of social connectedness that is so important in relation to a sense of engagement with family and friends and the community, and is associated with life satisfaction more generally (Arber and Cooper, 2000). Arber (2004) suggests that men are more likely to depend on their marital partner for those areas of support and engagement generally and may have a concurrent difficulty in forming new and lasting relationships across the life course. In effect, an over-focus on employment and other areas of engagement for men, which sustains them during their working lives, may not build up enough social capital to sustain them through older age and more specifically, widowhood.

The third age sits as an extrapolation of class and cohort considerations where current generations are unlikely (and unwilling) to give up those benefits accrued across individual life courses. In effect this means that subsequent generations will be less likely to take on the role of 'pensioner' with the same alacrity of former older groups. This will have a significant impact on the role of policy and particularly the role of social work in meeting future needs and more importantly, expectations (Park, 2000).

Just as significantly, while a consideration of a third age may indeed define a specific cohort as being advantaged in relation to their sense of achievement and even the assets they may have accrued across the life course (both financial and social capital), this cannot be defined as the nature of all older people within a third age. The focus on the baby boomer generation as having been net 'takers' from society is disingenuous in that it now defines older people as a group who may be expected to contribute more to their future care needs. Jones et al. (2008) define this more in the context of cultural and societal conditions that allow for a creation of new identities in older age rather than any specific reference to individual fiscal planning, policy or pensions.

In effect, this generation of older people may wish for a society where future generations are afforded the same respect and resources, but which a younger generation,
sadly, can no longer expect.

Exercise

- Why might practitioners need to have an awareness of the cohorts within generations to effectively engage in social work with older people?
- What might the expectations of a third age baby boomer generation be and what
  impact might this have on a personalisation agenda?
- How might older people from a third age view attempts to characterise them as
  needy and dependent?
- What can we learn from a third age cohort about rights and expectations of a future
  generation?

Policy Initiatives

- *Personalisation through Participation: A New Script for Public Services* (Leadbetter, 2004).
- *Independence, Well-Being and Choice* (Department of Health, 2005).
- *Our Health, Our Care, Our Say* (Department of Health, 2006).
- *Putting People First* (Department of Health, 2007a).
- There are also a range of documents that can be accessed on the Centre for Policy
  on Aging (CPA) website (publications@cpa.org.uk) which relate to discrimination in
  health care, residential care, long-term care and social exclusion.
- The Social Care Institute for Excellence (SCIE) website (www.scie.org.uk) has a range
  of up-to-date publications on dementia, end of life care, home care, mental health
  and capacity, nutrition, personalisation and participation.

Psychological ageing

Psychological ageing encompasses a diversity of developmental themes, from the older
person's sense of self and worth as well as more specific issues of individual personality
change and mental functioning (Atchley, 1989). There are some general points that
need to be explored here, not least of which is the fallacy that individual personality
changes with ageing. Sociological research and psychological developmental theory evidences that there are no significant changes in the personality of people in older age from
their previous stages of development. If, as a child, someone is at the receiving end
of parenting and care that is below a reasonable standard then it is likely that any

emotional trauma related to these experiences may be carried through into older age. The unhappy child may grow into the unhappy adult and conversely, the securely attached, happy and socially engaged child is likely to develop into an adult with sound reasoning, well-developed resilience and an ability to engage at an emotional level with others and a wider society (see Disengagement Theory).

It is certainly the case that where older people become labelled in terms of their needs through a lens of ageist attitudes then it is likely that they will accept these negative stereotypes as true, with an attendant negative impact on their potential for self-image and growth in older age. This is particularly the case where older people take on a dependent status within a welfare system that identifies *neediness* as opposed to *needs* (Townsend, 2007). Congruent with this assertion is that there should to be a greater emphasis on individual lived experience through life narrative and a humanistic, personalised focus on understanding the fears of older people. These narratives may lie at the core of what an older person's functioning is and an understanding of previous coping and also potential for coping in the future. Within the power structures of social policy, political economy and the role of social work itself there may be little room for the vulnerable older person to negotiate a way through an ageist world with a diminishing set of social attributes and coping assets.

Theoretical understanding of psychological ageing: object relations and old age

In his development of object relations theory, Fairbairn (1954) suggested that the primary motivation for all persons is to seek an emotional engagement with other people. While the language of object relations is challenging, where the 'object' is always another person, the theory does help significantly to illustrate potential problems of coping in old age. It moves the theoretical knowledge from Freudian aspects of drives compelling actions, to an understanding that the individual will be driven to form emotional engagements with others (see Chapter 7).

Fairbairn (1954) suggested that the child would 'split' off from its conscious reality those deeply distressing feeling of not having its needs met. These 'splits' in the form of 'needs' and a propensity for punishing oneself and others for unmet needs can be significant drivers of behaviour in older age. The split off, needy child may become the split off needy older person, while there is the potential for the split off punitive child failing to engage emotionally with others in adulthood (Brearley, 2007). If the whole premise of this theory is to engage emotionally with others then I hope you can see how important it is that early childhood experiences are safely negotiated into a contented and engaged older age. The same is true of Erikson (1995) with his eight stages of psychological development (see Chapter 7). This more linear approach, each stage building on the previous, also relates to childhood issues of care and trust where feelings of security and independence are developed through to old age. A poor negotiation of these stages or an 'unfavourable ratio', as Erikson called it, may lead to an unhappy, unfulfilled and disengaged older person.

Dermot is 82 and is staying in a care home. He has no immediate family. The staff have noticed that his mood has become very low recently. This formerly outgoing and gregarious man now seems to be retreating into himself and no longer engages in activities with other residents. A fellow resident, Rose, who has had a very close relationship with Dermot over the years, has informed the staff that he has been increasingly referring back to his childhood. This was characterised by very abusive parenting where Dermot was effectively abandoned and left with neighbours at a very early age. Rose has informed staff that Dermot has said his life has been 'wasted' and that he doesn't even have a family to come and visit him.

? Reflective Questions ?

- How do you think the theories of developmental psychology (Erikson's life stages and object relations) could help your understanding of Dermot's situation?
- What are the significant issues in Dermot's childhood and how are you able to interpret these?
- What interventions do you think could support Dermot to move on with his life?

Defensive postures in old age

It may also be that the more generalised negative attitudes that older people have towards themselves are a *projection* or *transference* of more widely assimilated attitudes towards older people generally. The paradox is that these more negative stereotypes of older age may be attitudes that older people subsumed within their own personalities when they themselves were young (Ward, 1984). These may now resurface as attitudes that older people find difficulties with in their attitudes to themselves and consequently attribute to other older people as a defensive psychological strategy. Erikson's (1995) theory suggests that someone with these internalised and negative depictions of older age will struggle to reach that sense of 'ego integrity' in older age. This is the point where a more secure and engaged older person might expect to look back on a life well lived with little sense of regret. The alternative is potentially for a frightened, angry and regretful older age with a real fear of what the future holds.

Significant research has been carried out not just in relation to more policy-based issues of how the needs of older people will be met in the future but also to more profound areas of the meaning of age itself. Garstka et al. (2004) identify that while younger people may be denigrated in relation to a labelling of youth, this is a state that they will inevitably grow out of. Subsequent studies (Robins et al., 2002) evidence that self-esteem is generally high in childhood and declines somewhat during the adolescent years as individuals struggle to create a sense of identity. This rises again in adulthood as boundaries of emotional attachment and engagement with others are worked through in that sense of generativity (Erikson, 1995) and decline again in older age. The question here is why should this be? If self-esteem and the resilience that comes from an accumulation of life forces and experiences naturally dip in older age then what is the driving force for this? It would appear to be as much related to the construct of age and ageing itself, where there is a sublimation of the meaning of older age and an over-focus on the negative implications. At the same time, resilience through a focus on previous coping strategies across the life course should impart a greater sense of self and self-esteem in older age. As Stuart-Hamilton (1998) so succinctly suggests, when older people are queried about the effects of ageing, outwith any comparative analysis of youth, the results tend to show ageing in a much more positive light. The implications are that older people may subsume negative stereotypes of ageing at an earlier age themselves. They may perceive this as a stage that is distressing to grow into. On the other hand, on an individual basis, older people are likely to have a more positive aspect of their own potential for coping across the life course. This dichotomy is at the heart of future discourse in meeting the needs of older people and a wider understanding of gerontological social work.

Successful psychopathology

Implicit within the notion of successful psychological functioning in older age is some sense that earlier life stages, experiences and emotional engagement with others have been reasonably successfully negotiated. Erikson (1995) refers to that 'favourable ratio' of meeting needs across the eight stages of psychological development. The *integrity* aspect here is a reflection on a life well lived where there has been engagement and emotional attachment to individuals and the wider society, and something of an acceptance of the inevitability of death. The focus on previous life experience has a duality of purpose in both easing the path to an inevitable demise while at the same time providing a coping capacity into a future ninth stage or fourth age. Older people evidence positive engagement with reminiscence working (Muthesius, 1997) to support and reinforce individual identity. This also acts as a repository of knowledge and skills which can be passed on, in an intergenerational context, to a younger generation. The work of Atkinson et al. (1999) shows that older people are happy to engage with reminiscence working and that this in itself may support an increased sense of communication and self-esteem. Again this needs to be addressed in relation to the potential conflict that disengagement theory may present and what this says about the uniqueness of the human experience and condition and the wish to move forward and develop into an advanced older age.

The fourth age, the ninth stage and gero-transcendence

The work of Laslett (1996) developed the idea of life 'stages' through socialisation in childhood, working and family life in the second age and a post-working life characterised as the third age. The fourth age has been designated as that stage where older people may become dependent through infirmity and illness and is acknowledged as a shorter stage than previous ages of development (see Compression of Morbidity in Chapter 5). This is not however an absolute stage in that people of any age can become incapacitated. Professionals have to be careful that in any consideration of the fourth age they do not buy into a position that has more to do with ageism than a consideration of the individual needs of older people (Midwinter, 2005). Bytheway (1995) goes further and suggests that defining older people as 'fourth agers', with all its connotations of frailty, is, of itself, an ageist act. The same can be said of the fundamentals of discrimination: any attempt to define the need of a specific individual or group in a less equitable way than others at a similar stage is at the heart of what discrimination is (Baltes and Smith, 2003). While the fourth age may be an inevitable consequence of the ageing process, with its focus on care and need, this also raises significant questions regarding the personhood and citizenship of all older people. How as a society we are able to engage with vulnerable clients *in extremis* (Bond and Corner, 2001)? This is also an age where there needs to be a more rounded theoretical underpinning of ageing and coping. If the third age is deemed to be a stage where older people re-evaluate their lives, with a new sense of engagement with family, friends and the wider community, then the fourth age has to be defined in the context of individual psychopathology to make sense of both presenting circumstances and previous lived experience (Marcoen et al., 2007).

Psychological understanding

Erik Erikson (1995) viewed personality as a lifelong process of learning based on the 'favourable ratio' of negotiation through the eight stages of development he identified. He suggested the final stage of ego integrity versus despair as that stage where an older person would look back on a life (hopefully) well negotiated with an attendant sense of the inevitability of death and a sense of consolidation of the self. The work of Bartlett and Burnip (1998) identified a lack of awareness among nursing staff in relation to psychosocial understanding. This is a consistent theme throughout the literature. There is a sense that the inevitability of death may induce a concurrent lack of engagement with and understanding of the older person. Tornstam (1996) suggested that older people move into a more spiritual dimension of their lives and away from the more materialistic aspects that may have been a part of the third age. This gero-transcendence would be less related to the negotiation of the stages that Erikson suggested and a more focused attention beyond the self, to a more reflective sense of being and becoming. In effect, gero-transcendence should make it possible for individuals to answer some of those more fundamental existential questions of who and what am I and where am I going (Lewin, 2001). This is the spiritual realm (Mathews, 2009) where older people may seek some form of affirmation of who they are. This may have become enmeshed at an earlier life stage in a concentration and investment in work, whereas in old age people may seek visibility and a sense that they still count and have skills to offer (Jewell, 2004).

> **Reflective Questions**
>
> - Why do you think it is important as a practitioner to acknowledge aspects of gero-transcendence and the spiritual dimension of the older lived experience?
> - What do you think an understanding of this would lend to social work practice with older people?
> - How might you consider these issues in relation to an older person approaching death?

Conclusion

There is an increasing need among both policy-based and psychosocial understandings of older age to ensure that the specific and individual needs of older people are met both now and in the future. The gerontological approach gives practitioners the capacity to address older age and ageism in a more global context, as part of a wider understanding of the forces that can adversely impact on all older people, irrespective of their personal circumstances. This knowledge of gerontology acts as a repository of understanding and skills-based working that supports the individuality of each client. It makes it less likely that practitioners will engage, either knowingly or unknowingly, in practice that is ageist or discriminatory.

> 📖 **Recommended Reading** 📖
>
> Bond, J. and Corner, L. (2004) *Quality of Life and Older People*. Maidenhead: Open University Press. This is a very good text on the subjective experience of later life and gerontological development. There are also excellent accounts of the older person's perception of their quality of life; multi-culturalism and the nature of institutionalised ageism.
>
> Mathews, I. (2009) *Social Work and Spirituality*. Exeter: Learning Matters. This text engages with a topic that is becoming an increasing focus within social work understanding and intervention. The focus here is on that sense of "connectedness" with the wider world with a particular emphasis on disadvantaged groups such as those with disabilities and older people.
>
> Phillips, J., Ajrouch, K. and Hillcoat-Nalletamby, S. (2010) *Key Concepts in Social Gerontology*. London: Sage. This is a very helpful text where the key themes of gerontology are laid out in alphabetical order and in a very accessible text.
>
> Thorson, J.A. (2000) *Aging in a Changing Society* (2nd ed.). New York: Brunner/Mazel. This is a very comprehensive text. It addresses the social and family lives of older people as well as psychological development and physical health. There is a strong focus on ethnic diversity and end of life considerations.

9

CARE SETTINGS FOR OLDER PEOPLE

Learning Outcomes

This chapter looks at:

- What is a care setting and what defines a successful care environment?
- Citizenship and inclusion and how older people may be perceived irrespective of their individual coping capacity.
- Legislation, policy and person-centred practice and how these may both legislate for and mitigate against the needs of older people.
- Assessment and planning for care home settings and the areas of importance that should be addressed.
- Moving into a home and the process of engagement with carers and environment.
- Privacy, personhood and bereavement and how an understanding of these themes can support working with older people.

Introduction

Any transition to a care or a group care setting will inevitably involve a potential conflict of who and what may be involved. The very term 'care setting' may not have that formal societal understanding that something like 'social work' has. The former may be imbued with a sense of loss and even fear while the latter will be considered as the agency that supports older people into these institutions. Whatever the understanding, it is clear that the personalisation agenda is not a new philosophy (Biestek, 1961) and that social structures and political systems frequently struggle, to this day, to meet the care needs of older people. Why is this? Partly it is due to a paternalistic and ageist focus on the 'cost' of care for older people. Second, there is an attitude of the 'sameness' (homogeneity) of all older people that fails to address the individualism and lived experience of older people generally. Ironically, the sense of community living that is characterised by a shared group of services and resources may also be the repository of a 'one size fits all' approach that further mitigates against the individual choices, freedoms and humanity of the individual older person (Keenan, 2007). This may hit at the very heart of what it is to be and how societal and structural practices deny the individual identity of older people in an attempt to meet 'need'. This potential loss of identity has the effect of cutting an older person off from a wider support structure where the older person is characterised as 'a discredited person facing an unaccepting world' (Goffman, 1990: 31). It is no coincidence that the subtext in Goffman's writing refers to issues of 'spoiled identity' for it is that sense of individual identity couched within the whole life experience that is at the centre of how older people assess who and what they are. The same is also true of external agencies, who may struggle with this individual identity as they seek to manage increasingly restricted resources and budgets.

Older people and citizenship

Historically there has been less emphasis on the specific needs of older people and more of a focus on the labour market, independent living and community-based resources. An inevitable consequence of this is that older people may be viewed more in the context of political, structural and medical understanding rather than in the more person-centred approach that is at the heart of effective value and ethically driven practice (Johnson, 1998). Implicit within any understanding of the nature of care settings is that they are viewed and addressed within the context of citizenship and the active promotion of that citizenship. Given the real trauma that older people may experience either through the need for support within the home or, more importantly, within a care setting, it is vital that there is support and an active advocacy to ensure that citizenship is maintained (Scourfield, 2007).

What do we mean by citizenship?

Citizenship is where there is an emphasis on social inclusion rather than the more generic approach to meeting need which may deny individuals such rights (Thompson, 2009). Citizenship therefore has to be viewed from an emancipatory perspective, where issues of poverty, disability and gender are addressed as part of the uniqueness of individuals. This also has to acknowledge the collective discrimination that can apply to any disadvantaged group (Lister, 1997). A consideration of this wider 'citizen' view removes the older person from the limitations of the field of social work where the emphasis may be on a narrow field of needs, risks and resources rather than the wider socio-political field that all citizens inhabit (Parrott, 2002). The agenda then moves from one of *needs* to one of *rights* and this is a significant sea change in the perception for all disadvantaged groups. Whereas formerly individual citizens and groups may have been perceived as disabled now society itself may be perceived as disabled or disabling.

Evaluation of citizenship

A perceived problem in relation to citizenship is how it is assessed and evaluated in the light of a lack of personal power, resources and visibility in a postmodern society. There should be a concern as to whether this can be truly negotiated through a personalisation agenda when the foundations of citizenship may be missing. Irrespective of this, there should be a consideration that the sense of self and identity built up across the life course reflects a synthesis of experience, personal values and emotional attachment (Sands, 1996). This is the starting point for any practice with older people when assessing citizenship and needs in relation to care settings and support.

Exercise

- What ethical and value-driven aspects of working with older people would you consider when accessing a care setting?
- Can you define the range of social work skills and collaborative practice you would consider?
- How would you evaluate the needs and wishes of the older person?
- How would you engage with empathic social work practice and what does this mean to you?

Legislation and policy context

The legislative and policy context addresses both care and the protective aspects of supporting older people. While Scottish legislation has evolved to address abuse of adults (Adult Support and Protection (Scotland) Act 2007) there is no equivalent specific legislation in England and Wales. The issue is currently addressed through the National Health Service and Community Care Act 1990 s.47, where the local authority carries out an assessment of need where there may be a perceived risk. The problem of this rather non-specific legislation is that the older person may become disadvantaged through the process of protection. This can occur where an individual is deemed to be at risk and may be removed to a place of safety, while the perpetrator of any abuse may still reside within the home. This protection by exclusion may satisfy contemporary assessment of risk but whether this meets the human rights of an older person is another matter.

'No Secrets'

No Secrets: Guidance on Developing and Implementing Multi-agency Policies and Procedures to Protect Vulnerable Adults from Abuse (Department of Health, 2000a) is a significant document and is referred to as *statutory guidance*. As such it should be treated as if it were a piece of legislation. The document defines what the nature of abuse is and how an interprofessional and multi-agency approach should be used to address these issues.

There will be additional structural risks where an older person, having accessed a care setting, may then find themselves at the receiving end of conflict between the local authority and the care provider, particularly where there is any deficiency within funding structures. The recent withdrawal of Southern Cross homes from the marketplace of care, leaving service users feeling abandoned, is a case in point (Snell, 2011). The way that any such enforced closure is handled, particularly by care management, may be instrumental in both the coping capacity of the older people involved and more importantly, survival itself (Williams et al., 2007).

The impact of enforced moves on older people

It is important that service providers, funders and, I would suggest, the wider public are aware of the traumatic impact that the closure of a care setting can have on an older person. It is less a characterisation of the end of a specific habitation but more related to a fundamental act of survival. Even within this more traumatising aspect there are certain characteristics that may exacerbate any enforced or poorly planned move, such as gender (men tend to cope less well), age of the older person, level of anxiety, lack of communication of the procedures that are about to take place and where there is confusion brought on by physical or mental disability (Jolley et al., 2011). At a time when there are ongoing political attempts to erode the substance of the Human Rights Act 1998, practitioners need to consider whether the vagaries of the marketplace and assessment focused on risk really do meet the needs of vulnerable older people. This is particularly the case when this focus should reside as much within a human rights emphasis as social work practice. A case in point is where the role of the Best Interest Assessor under the Mental Capacity Act (2005) Deprivation of Liberty Safeguards seeks to address any potential breaches of Article 5 of the Human Rights Act 1998 with its emphasis on 'liberty and [the] security of the person'.

Underpinning this policy and legislation is the consideration of choice, inclusion and capacity and practitioners need to ensure that there is the least invasive and least restrictive intervention when assessing the needs of older people. This is particularly the case where there may be conflicting demands of care, risk, inclusion and the active promotion of choice based on resources.

Needs and wishes of older people

Domiciliary care is generally accepted to be the most effective way to meet the needs of older people and specifically where this is their chosen option. It is certainly the case that domiciliary care is imbued with a sense of individualism, coping and choice, which is less likely to be a consideration with regard to the more institutional aspects of care settings (Clark and Lynch, 2010; Peace et al., 1997). Indeed, as far back as 1962 Townsend identified the institutional and the de-individualisation aspects of care homes for older people. He clarified these views into broader sociological themes of 'structured dependency' where retirement and a focus on inadequate state support created a dependent culture among older people (Townsend, 1981). His development of these issues finds its apotheosis within the fundamentals of human rights as opposed to social policy, which he considered a potential reinforcer of this 'structured dependency' (Townsend, 2007). Concurrent with this is a consideration of the 'compression of morbidity' as identified by Fries (1980) which identifies the real medical strides made to support increased well-being and longevity at the expense of living with disabling illness over a longer period of time.

Related Legislation and Policy

Care Standards Act 2000.

Department of Health (2000) *No Secrets: Guidance on Developing and Implementing Multi-agency Protection of Vulnerable Adults* (POVA), s.80.

Department of Health (2001) *National Service Framework for Older People*.

Department of Health (2001) *Valuing People* The Care Homes Regulation 2001, Reg. 37.

Department of Health (2002) *Fair Access to Care Services*: Guidance for Eligibility Criteria for *Adult Social Care*. London: Stationery Office.

Department of Health (2005) *Independence, Well-being and Choice*.

Safeguarding Adults Act 2005.

Department of Health (2006) *Our Health, Our Care, Our Say: Making it Happen*. Safeguarding Vulnerable Groups Act 2006.

Department of Health (2007) *Modernising Adult Social Care: What's Working?*

(Continued)

(Continued)

Centre for Policy on Ageing, (2007) *Action on Elder Abuse.*

Department of Health (2007) *Putting People First: A Shared Vision and Commitment to the Transformation of Adult Social Care.*

Department of Health (2008) *Transforming Social Care.*

HM Government (2008) *The Case for Change: Why England Needs a New Care and Support System.*

Department of Health (2009) *The National Dementia Strategy*

Department for Work and Pensions (2009) *Building a Society for All Ages.*

Department of Health (2010) *Building the National Care Service.*

The Centre for Policy and Ageing has a very useful website that should be of interest to students and practitioners (www.cpa.org.uk)

Single assessment process

The assessment *process* has already been addressed in Chapter 7, 'Assessment and Intervention', and this section covers the four main *areas* of assessment (see Chapter 4):

- Contact assessment
- Overview assessment
- Specialist assessment
- Comprehensive assessment (www.doh.gov.uk/scg/sap).

Assessment can increasingly be viewed as a means of defining resources rather than a broader depiction of individual need at a time of financial constraint. Intrinsic to any professional assessment is the focus on care planning and this will only ever be as good as the breadth and depth of the assessment carried out. Irrespective of the nature of the assessment, any service user in receipt of continuing care should have a care plan that clearly defines the range and purpose of the services that are to be provided. This might be a simple care plan to address a specific issue of care or support, or a more complex plan that will involve a range of skills, resources and agencies (Pritchard, 2003).

At any level of assessment the skills, wishes and knowledge of the older person should be the focus of any meaningful interaction. At a more profound level the nature of social work intervention is related to some dysfunction within an older person's social relationships where 'the support needs of a person are inseparable from the dependability of others' (Smale et al., 2000: 147). This 'dependability' is at the heart of professional standards, training and knowledge couched within an ethical consideration of the integrity of all individuals within their wider relationships. As John Donne wrote, 'No man is an island, entire of itself …'

A useful guide for remembering the elements involved in planning is the mnemonic 'SMART'. The key elements are laid out below. It is worth remembering here that the dynamics of group living/working can make real demands on the individuals taking part. The older person may become swamped within the language and logistics of what I refer to as 'acronym alley'. This is where professionals who are unsure of their own power position within the group may seek refuge in professional language that may disarm both the older person and other professionals and ultimately leads to a dead end in communication. Alternatively, individuals within the group may collude with each other as a means of preserving personal or agency kudos and autonomy (Preston-Shoot, 2007). Anything that negates the older person as the centre of the inter-agency intervention is unlikely to have a successful outcome for that individual, although it may reinforce accepted norms of what is considered professional practice.

Specific – where the objectives are clearly identified by the older person and the supporting agency as well as the specifics of what each party will undertake.

Measurable – where the outcomes from any intervention are measurable in terms of what was initially agreed as part of the assessment and planning.

Achievable – this is where aspirational goals are set that are not achievable and further disempower the older person both in terms of the support that can be offered and the individual's sense that they can progress in the future

Realistic – where individuals and support agencies keep focused on what was initially decided rather than becoming sidetracked and the energies of the group become diffused and dissipated.

Timely – to ensure that interventions, as far as possible, are time framed to ensure that agencies maintain an agenda and that older people are not unnecessarily forced into a process of dependency (Lindsay and Orton, 2008).

CASE STUDY

Rose Monaghan has recently been admitted to hospital after a fall in her home. She has sustained a hairline fracture of her hip and is expected to be in hospital for another month. She has expressed concerns that she is not coping well with everyday activities and is becoming fearful that she will fall again and hurt herself. While Rose has a good relationship with her neighbours she does not want to become a 'nuisance' to them as they all lead busy professional lives. As a social worker you have been asked to arrange a meeting with Rose where she has evidenced a high level of distress and real concerns about her capacity to return to her own home without some level of support. She has stated that she would be very happy to take part in any assessment of her needs that might support her in the future. Rose has never married and while she has some distant relatives in Scotland and New Zealand, has led a relatively independent life. She owns her own property and has accrued considerable savings from a well-paid job as a legal secretary and a lifetime of wise investment.

? **Reflective Questions** ?

- Who might you contact to take part in any inter-agency work here?
- What policy and legislation might you have to consider during this process in terms of adjustment, care and financial planning?
- How could you support Rose through this process?
- What are the range of potential outcomes you think you would discuss with Rose to meet her current and future needs?

The care plan and 2002 guidance

There has been an increasing emphasis within care planning to ensure that health and social care agencies work as collaboratively as possible. This reflects the intent of the National Health Service and Community Care 1990 legislation and ensures that there is less duplication and a better use of resources when meeting the needs of older people. Professional recording of any decisions made as well as any potential risks are important to ensure that the various agencies involved are aware of the stage and progress of any interaction and also to ensure that there is no uncertainty within this process (Thompson, 2002). Paradoxically, while the absence of adequate written information can make for an unsuccessful interaction, too much recording may make the older person feel under increased scrutiny as opposed to an integral part of the decision-making process (Thompson, 2003b). The guiding principles are that individuals should have the right to be supported and encouraged to make decisions that do not necessarily have to present as being in their best interests as long as these do not impinge on the rights of others. Essentially, older people in the fullness of their lived experience and sentient rationalisation should be afforded the opportunity to choose 'unwisely' if that is their wish (Milner and O'Byrne, 2009).

According to the Single Assessment Process the following areas should be included within any care planning with due consideration of the legislative, policy and human rights aspect. The 12 associated guidelines can be found in the document from 28 January 2002 (DH, 2002b) on the Department of Health website. The requirement for April 2004 was that local authorities should have met these 12 guidelines as well as the following areas of knowledge and development.

By April 2004 the original 12 steps of implementation will have been met. The focus of these 12 guidelines are that older people will be at the heart of the decision-making process with a commensurate increase in social work skills and knowledge to meet these needs.

The four assessment types [see above] will be used as a framework to ensure that assessments are timely and proportionate to need.

Care plans are produced according to Annexe E of the January 2002 guidance and clients have a copy of these care plans.

Information should be collected, stored and shared as effectively as possible.

There should be adequate training for workers to ensure they are able to undertake effective person-centred assessment and needs-led planning.

Where a minimal interaction is required with an older person then this should be assessed in terms of the resources needed and the potential impact on outcomes.

Any authority that is still negotiating an assessment tool by April 2004 should consider the use of an alternative accredited assessment tool.

Care homes

What do we mean by home? A home can be characterised as a place of refuge or support where familial roles are played out within what Heywood et al. (2002) refer to as 'the emotions of home'. It can be a repository of human emotion and affection across the life stage imbued with symbolic objects and feelings and where loving relationships prevail. The loss of this supportive environment may be akin to a bereavement with all the process of managing the transitions, endings and loss that this entails (Peace et al., 2005). Conversely, while older people may retain an emotional attachment to a home, redolent of memory and place, it can also be the locus of the abuse of older people free from the scrutiny of an enquiring public (Biggs et al., 1993). This may be abuse carried out by members of the family or by external agencies such as landlords within the private sector. Indeed, Challis (1999) argues that the regulation of care is less to do with meeting higher standards of need but more a response to identified abuses within care settings.

While the benefits of home occupancy can be defined within the context of individual choice within the boundaries of legality and impact on others, the same cannot be said for care settings. Indeed, Webb (2006: 69) defines 'Standardisation [as] a key tool in the regulation of residential homes for older people'. So if as practitioners we reflect on these issues of meaning, loss, transitions and the capacity to preserve a current and future sense of self then the transition from home to a care setting may be both challenging and fraught with emotional pain and fear of the future. Conversely, this can also be a time of change and growth where the fears of becoming unwell, an inability to manage daily living and a potential for progressive isolation and loneliness will be mitigated by this new experience.

The demographics of care settings

Proportionally, there are a relatively small number of older people who live in care home accommodation. This currently comprises 4% of the total older population and is very much related to increasing age (75–84) as well as physical illness that impacts on mobility such as arthritis. Approximately a third of all older people accessing care settings do so because of a diagnosis of dementia (Bebbington et al., 2001; Froggatt, 2004).

Because of the nature of developing need in older age and the fact that changes can come about through rapidly changing circumstances there may not always be that length of time available to ensure that all stages of the transition to a care setting are adequately met (Reed et al., 2004). These changes can result in a multiplicity of losses, possibly within a very short time frame. There are real fears about the move to a strange and unknown environment with the added dimension of getting to know a new group of people (Phillips et al., 2002). Assuming that the assessment has been carried out in an inclusive and collaborative way and the care plan has been agreed by the older person and the support agencies, the next probable step is to access a care setting for the older person.

CASE STUDY

Frank Murphy emigrated from Ireland before the Second World War and has worked in the building trade all his life. He served in the army during the war and was mentioned in dispatches for his bravery, something he is still proud of to this day. He owns his own first floor flat where he has lived alone since his wife died five years ago. He has two daughters who live locally but they have their own family commitments and are increasingly worried that Frank is not managing on his own. He has a few hours home help per week but this is not enough to meet his wider needs of nutrition, cleaning and managing household bills. Frank is an outgoing, gregarious man who feels increasingly limited by the restrictions of living on the first floor now that he has increasing problems with mobility.

As a social worker you have been asked to meet with Frank to assess his current and future needs. Frank is open about his lack of capacity to cope although he exhibits a high degree of independent thinking as to how his future needs could be met. Frank has asked you about care homes for older people and what this would entail.

? Reflective Questions ?

- What financial information do you need to progress this request? This should relate to personal finances and local policy in relation to meeting needs within care homes.
- What wider psychological and sociological themes might you consider when assessing Frank for a care home?
- How would you address the fact that it is unlikely that Frank will be able to take all his belongings with him to a care home?
- How would you allay any fears that Frank might have about a potential loss of independence rights?

Moving into a care home

The Care Quality Commission (CQC) registers and inspects all care homes and sets the standards for provision of care and services under the National Minimum Standards for Care Homes for Older People (www.cqc.org.uk). Admission to a care home and moving into a care home are not necessarily the same thing. The former may be more related to the last option rather than choice for the older person, whereas the latter will involve a significant range of transitions for the individual, and professional skills on the part of the social worker. This will involve not only a consideration of policy and legislation but ethical practice, human rights understanding as well as a panoply of underpinning theoretical knowledge that will support both the older person and the worker in negotiating through these often dangerous and traumatic waters.

As far as possible this should be a seamless process, with an emphasis on the sharing of information and an inclusive process of interprofessional and inter-agency practice (Phillips and Waterson, 2002). In relation to the older person the focus will be on supporting, encouraging and advocating for as much independence as possible. The emphasis will be on capacity as opposed to incapacity.

Categories within care settings or 'outcome groups'

There are seven categories or 'outcome groups' based on the National Minimum Standards:

- Choice of home
- Health and personal care
- Daily life and social activities
- Complaints and protection
- Environment
- Staffing and management
- Administration.

The Care Quality Commission (www.cqc.org.uk) can provide a list of appropriate care settings in an older person's area and, more importantly, allow access to copies of inspection reports on their website.

Areas to consider when choosing a care setting

- Try to ensure you are able to visit the care home and speak to the residents/tenants about the services available.
- What is the mission statement of the home in terms of the services it provides and how it engages with residents in decision making about the services provided?
- If you have a care assessment that identifies specific needs, how will these be met within the care environment?
- What personal possessions can be brought to the care setting and how will choices regarding food, communication, visitors, privacy, choice and religious or spiritual beliefs be addressed?

A full account of pertinent questions to ask can be found on the Age UK Factsheet 29. This gives a very comprehensive overview of the areas that may concern an older person, especially where an older person may be experiencing high levels of stress and lacks a reasonable level of physical and psychological strength. Further information regarding payment of fees in homes providing nursing care can be found in Age UK Factsheets 20 and 10.

Supporting an understanding of moving to a care setting

Research within care settings evidence that residents valued 'social participation' as a means of feeling engaged with others and being less prone to depression and loneliness. At the same time residents recognised that cultures within care settings reflected the wider world in terms of individuals' capacity to support challenging behaviours from others and that tolerance is a key feature of group living (Abbott et al., 2000). It is also the case that there is a higher likelihood of an older person having to access care settings if there is a diminished level of social contact and engagement with others, be this immediate family or the wider community. Even where there is sporadic contact with neighbours, this can have the effect of ensuring older people are able to maintain independent living within their own homes (Charles and Sevak, 2005).

The focus is still increasingly on the provision of a 'homely' atmosphere within care settings. However, there is a significant difference in how these services may be provided between domiciliary owner-occupied care and a more regulated care setting. Peace (1998) identifies something of a canyon between the principles of 'caring about' and 'caring for' older people. The former is a universal theme imbued with an understanding of ethical and value-driven practice, while the latter may be more related to meeting complex individual needs. The home is therefore more than just a habitation but an environment imbued with a sense of self-identity, independence of action and thought, and choice (Peace and Holland, 2001).

CASE STUDY

David Parkes has arrived at a stage in his life where he is unable to look after himself properly. He has had a long and successful life and a marriage which lasted 62 years. Unfortunately his wife Ivy has recently died and this has had a very significant impact on David's coping. He has been assessed for a care setting and is willing to consider this as long as he has some choice in where he ends up. David is clearly competent to make this choice and remains lucid and independent of spirit. You are asked to support David in this choice of care setting.

? Reflective Questions ?

- What would you do to ensure David had as wide a choice of care setting as possible?
- How would you make sure that David was informed of the routines and rules of any care setting?

- How would you support an understanding of how current tenants cope with the care environment?
- How would you evaluate the role of residents in decision making and the quality of staffing support?

Privacy and identity

Private care settings may have high occupancy rates where mortgage repayment by private sector providers and profit may be significant predicators of the level of care provided. There may also be a conflict between the use of facilities and resources within the home that older people would take for granted in their own homes, such as the use of kitchens and the capacity to make choices related to leisure time, timing of meals and the capacity to engage with the wider community outwith the care setting. Older people will be increasingly marginalised by a lack of attention to these details and an over-focus on control and the attendant loss of privacy.

There is clear evidence that older people value issues of security, personal space and a sense of individualism (Phillips, 1992) and they would also prefer a higher level of independent living opportunities, even if this means there is more risk taking involved. But where older people are under constant surveillance in the care home within the guise of 'health and safety' there is an impact on their privacy, intimacy and the right to self-determination. Within any overly structured and regimented care setting there may be a consensus that it is positively dangerous to allow these fundamental freedoms of action because of the inherent risk. Morris (1993) identifies the gap within the rhetoric of care and the imposition of strictures and barriers on older people within care settings generally. While there may be an identifiable loss of the material aspect in terms of home, belongings and environment, there are also identifiable, although more abstract, losses of personal autonomy, freedom and privacy. These are highly valued by older people and are likely to become lost within the structural aspects of over-protection and control (Lee et al., 2002).

Risk assessment

Stevenson (2001) has characterised social work with older people as the poor cousin of service delivery with an inevitability that there will always be a struggle to finance this care properly. She refers to that 'reconceptualisation' of the needs of older people that is at the heart of the conflict that exists between care and individual autonomy. Indeed, social work with older people has often been relegated to the realms of the least resources with a commensurate lack of skills among the practitioners in this field (Walker and Beckett, 2003). For effective risk assessment there needs to be a promotion of creative thinking among older people to address their own perceived risks in relation to their identified needs. It is in the coming together of these two facets that an effective strategy for intervention lies (Phillips et al., 2006). What is clear is that there needs to be an integrated assessment process across all the relevant supporting agencies to effect a workable solution to the needs of older people in the longer term. Donald and Bown (2003) also suggest that a quality clinical assessment may give an early identification of treatable conditions and obviate the need for any prolonged care settings where these needs can be met within domiciliary care. A quality assessment of risk and needs is more likely to lead to a successful outcome for the older person. However, an over-emphasis on risk and need, particularly by external agencies, may lead to a negation of the individuality and personhood of the older person. These themes are picked up within the policy document *Putting People First* (Department of Health, 2007a) that recommends risk enablement panels who work collaboratively to ensure risk sharing and support for staff who may struggle with difficult decisions related to welfare, and seek to promote as high a level of independence as possible for the older person (Duffy and Gillespie, 2009). Ultimately however, and intrinsic to this whole process, is the ability and quality of the individual judgement, skills and knowledge that a social work practitioner can bring to bear on this process.

Cultures of blame

Attitudes to working with older people develop from a range of sources and for a number of different reasons. Individuals or practitioners do not suddenly start to view older people in a negative light; these are attitudes that may be built up over a lifetime. So where might these attitudes come from? The psychological focus can be defined within the three areas of cognition, the affective component and the behavioural component. The *cognitive* aspect may be based on experiences of older people we have had across our lives that we have now subsumed within our personal psychology and thinking. The *affective* component will refer to the actual feelings we have towards older people. The *behavioural* component is the way in which we engage (or otherwise) with older people. Essentially if we have positive feelings towards older people we will try to gain proximity, whereas if these feelings are negative then it is more likely we will distance ourselves from older people (Oliver, 1993). Students of attachment theory will recognise the similarities here between ambivalent and avoidant attachment, where the child may seek to maximise attention-seeking behaviour in the former and minimise attention-seeking behaviour in the latter (Bowlby, 1969; Murray Parkes et al., 1991).

Where do cultures of blame develop from?

There may be a range of reasons for this. The practitioner or worker may have had negative experiences of older people, such as long-term illness that was, or is, frightening. There may have been incidences of abuse where workers and practitioners engage in the defensive strategies of projection or transference to cope with these traumatising feelings.

There may also be a gender construct aspect where carers themselves may actively discriminate against older people whom they deem as coping less well than themselves. Even skilled practitioners may become sucked into an environment of blame where their knowledge base and theoretical skills appear to be at odds with the culture of the care setting. This can have the effect of destabilising a worker's confidence in challenging the powerful norms that may exist (Audit Commission, 2002).

There is an excellent publication in relation to Promoting Excellence in All Care Homes (2011) (PEACH). While this research focuses primarily on staff issues it also addresses a wider range of challenging topics including issues of depersonalisation, staff skills, use of language in communication, training and the promotion of dignity. This document can be accessed on www.panicoa.org.uk

What do older people value?

Older people themselves identify lack of engagement, a focus on rules and regimes and poor provision of care as the most distressing aspects of what Preston-Shoot (2003) refers to as the 'deindividuation'. This is where the needs of the client may threaten what practitioners know to be a moral and ethical practice but where they are unable to deliver the appropriate service. Preston-Shoot further identifies the following areas of defensive practice within care provision, where practitioners engage in a culture of secrets and a lack of engagement with supervision as a means of self-exclusion from the roles they know they should be carrying out. This can also extend to feelings of hopelessness and passivity in the face of the expressed needs of older people that is mutually destructive and oppressive. Smale (1996) clearly identifies that collaborative practice with older people, a capacity for engaging with the internal lived experience of older people's lives, values of dignity and respect and the capacity for problem resolution are at the heart of effective working with older people. This is particularly the case within a care setting.

The institution – a modern paradigm

Goffman (1961) characterised the bureaucratisation of care as an indicator of the institution. He referred to the dispossession of those accessing institutions. Social roles may be denied in the face of meeting the needs of the institution and the staff. The older person may therefore be shaped by the agency to fit the consensus managerial opinion with a commensurate loss of place and identity. Residential care in Britain has been viewed as something of a last resort for older people. While there has been significant review and planning to ensure something of a more 'homely' focus within care settings, particularly where the private sector charges significant sums for this service, Peace et al. (1997) suggest that there are still significant losses incurred by older people within care settings. There is not just a loss of individuality but at a more profound level, a loss of 'self'. This loss of self hits at the very heart of what it is to be and is the philosophical and psychological touchstone of existence.

The work of Goffman has been brought into the twenty-first century with something of a crash through the writings of Simon Duffy. He characterises the nature of the institutional care setting as akin to that of the concentration camp where the purpose of the presiding regime is that of 'destroying humanity' (Gould, 2008). He reiterates the belief that institutions of themselves can create a sense of powerlessness among residents where rules, regulations and regimes based on staff power and staff timetables hold sway.

It may also be the case that the ergonomics (the study of people within their environment) of the living space can have a significant impact on the coping capacity of older people. Older, more traditional nursing homes may not currently meet the current space requirements of the National Minimum Standards (Department of Health, 2001a) and accordingly there is an increasing emphasis on creating care settings that meet the needs of residents as opposed to more structural or financial demands. Lawton et al. (2000) have developed the Professional Environmental Assessment Protocol (PEAP), which addresses the more holistic needs of clients within living spaces: safety, privacy, inclusion and the opportunity for personal growth and identity. These are themes that students and practitioners will readily recognise as being at the heart of professional social work practice. There is clear evidence that where the care setting exceeds 50 bed spaces the sheer scale of the setting can lead to anonymity for residents and less likelihood that they will be able to actively engage with the care staff (Kellaher, 1986). It is certainly the case that environments designed with the support and inclusion of older clients in mind are more likely to meet their individual needs and quest for personal autonomy and happiness. Bland (1999) characterises the specific areas valued by older persons within the care setting as privacy, choice and independence and particularly the capacity for decision making. There are other more extraneous situations that increase the nature of institutionalism, such as arranging residents' seating in a waiting room style as opposed to more devolved and intimate surroundings, that can easily be addressed (Secker et al., 2003).

Put simply, there is a direct correlation between the design of care environments and the quality of life of older people (Barnes, 2002).

Loss, transition and bereavement

At the end of life is the inevitability of death. To a large degree it is not necessarily death itself that causes distress and grief but the process of dying. The 'good death' is identified as a salient feature of care within the policy document *Care Homes for Older People: National Minimum Standards* (Department of Health, 2001a). In modern western society the emphasis tends to be on individual autonomy and control where the inevitability of endings is not shirked, but where older people have time to settle affairs and have confidence that suffering will be curtailed (McNamara, 2004). From a biological perspective the ending can be defined in absolute terms but the *process* of dying cannot.

All people, older or otherwise, want to feel a sense of reconciliation with the world at the end of life. Dylan Thomas (1998) characterised this in his poem 'And Death Shall Have No Dominion' as the transcendence from the world into something uniquely individual: that sense of self within the totality of the world (Thomas, 1998). Interestingly, Erikson (1995) characterised his stage of ego integrity versus despair as that stage of hoped for reconciliation with self at the end of a life well lived or that sense of despair as the time ahead is too short to resolve painful and distressing feelings and memories (see also Chapter 7). Subsequent to this he recognised the evolution of a ninth stage where the older person would transcend the cares and ills of work to a more spiritual dimension and a gradual disengagement from life events that no longer seem or feel as meaningful as before (Brown and Lowis, 2003). Death can therefore be seen as part of and a continuum of life that may hold no fear. The sense of loss will become subsumed within the contentment of what is being left behind. The old environment has to be given up with an acceptance of the new role and place (Murray Parkes, 1987). A significant feature of this process is that there should be a spirit of openness when communicating with the older dying person. A failure to communicate or a negation or dismissal of the queries and concerns of the older person may centre the entirety of the person's experience on illness itself. This will further distance the older person from a sense of engaging with and belonging to the wider community of support. While the work of Seymour et al. (2002) does not give specific answers to what it is that older people need at the end of life, it does indicate that older people are prepared to discuss these issues and that there are positive outcomes to be had from answering specific questions about personal control and palliative care. While this may not be within the realms of the more philosophical aspect of ageing, it answers questions that are fundamental to individual personhood and dignity. Lloyd (2004) identifies the nature of 'independence, autonomy and citizenship' when assessing modern gerontological thinking in relation to older people. Nevertheless, she stresses that death and dying may have an uneasy relationship with these models when older people are vulnerable and dependent on the care of others to provide this support at the end of life.

In the fullness of time, however, the majority of older people in the modern world negotiate this stage of life with a high level of support and care and surrounded by those significant people in life. The older person becomes the focus and locus of attention in the meeting of the physical and spiritual aspects of being, together with a continuum of meaning and existence through memory.

Conclusion

Care settings for older people are complex environments where the full range of social work skills will be brought to bear. Practice may move between a recognition of the real trauma that older people experience at a loss of independence and autonomy, and the alternative view that care settings provide a refuge, peace and contentment in later life. This latter effect may actually remove older persons from the trials of their lived experience and provide the environment within which they can grow and develop through the latter stage of life.

 Recommended Reading

Keenan, C. (2007) 'Group care', in J. Lishman (ed.) *Handbook for Practice Learning in Social Work and Social Care: Knowledge and Theory* (2nd ed.). London: Jessica Kingsley. A very good overview of the 'subjective reality' of individual experience and the range of potential interventions when working in this area.

Petch, A. (ed.) (2009) *Managing Transitions: Support for Individuals at Key Points of Change*. Bristol: The Policy Press. Research in practice for adults. A very useful section on the transitions for older people accessing a care setting.

Weinstein, J. (2008) *Working with Loss, Death and Bereavement: A Guide for Social Workers*. London: Sage. Particularly good on areas of 'disenfranchised grief' and the ethical considerations of working within these areas.

10

BEING A RESEARCH-PRACTITIONER

Learning Outcomes

This chapter looks at:

- Background to evidence-based practice.
- Emancipatory and participatory focus of research and how this informs the practice and experience of workers and older people.
- Becoming a research-practitioner and what this involves within an inclusive and collaborative context.
- The evidence-based research literature and how this may potentially inform and support effective practice.
- Mutuality of learning and how this is not a one-way process but one that should liberate practitioner and older people generally.
- Methodology and the practical application and appreciation of what works.

Background to evidence-based practice

Theoretical knowledge does not arrive fully formed from the minds of researchers but is premised by considerable time spent on research and evidence-based practice. To students who suggest that their own knowledge and experience is the critical faculty of their social work practice, I would ask them to exercise caution. If an individual knowledge and theory base is premised entirely on individual experience and these experiences have led to the development of your own individual value base then how can you stop your own inevitable prejudice impacting on how you work in the longer term? In effect, without this critical reflection of self within practice

(Schon, 1987) the likelihood is that individual experience may become filtered through the worker's dysfunctional experience, rationalisation and further reinforce inconsistent practice. There is an obligation therefore on practitioners to support this knowledge or evidence-based focus and to ensure that they are both accessing and assessing quality social work research that will support their knowledge and practice. While it is unlikely that the majority of practitioners in the field of social work with older people will become involved in regular active research, it is incumbent upon social workers to be aware of the areas in which research is being undertaken. This will also involve an ability to support a research-minded working environment (Phillips et al., 2006).

With regard to work on risk, we are attempting to address the degree of possibility there will be in any adverse event occurring with clients; but ultimately this can only be assessed at a higher or lower degree. Decisions, therefore, on the needs and potential risks in working with older people cannot be solely informed by personal experience but must be based on 'knowledge of the situation, practice wisdom and the valid research evidence that is available' (O'Sullivan, 1999: 137). At the same time that social work has sought to legitimise the knowledge base of the field (theory and intervention) as the most effective way to engage effectively with clients, this does not represent the totality of that social work experience. There are considerable numbers of clients who may fall outwith what some social workers consider a reasonable degree of engagement. These clients may be from disenfranchised backgrounds, ethnic groups or those who have committed crimes against vulnerable groups and find themselves the recipients of both social opprobrium and social work disapproval (Fook, 2000). This will only heighten an already developed sense of 'otherness' and make it more unlikely that social work services can reach or engage with these excluded groups, while at the same time increasing the stigmatisation and structural oppression of these clients.

In a climate where the care and support needs of older people may be increasingly viewed as 'problematic', it should not be a quantum leap to recognise that older people could easily fall within this 'problematic' focus rather than a consideration of the social construction of old age itself (Phillipson, 1982). If older people, then, are not included within those aspects of research that impinge upon them, it is difficult to see how older people generally can become part of that wider participatory paradigm. This may be analogous to wider structural oppression where other disadvantaged groups may be denied the power that governs services that impact on them. At a more functional and discriminatory level there will be wider unanswered questions about how people who are disadvantaged through disability or age are able to play a significant role in working with and influencing the decision-making process generally (Crawshaw, 2002).

Emancipation and participation

Fook (2000) states that the nature of research in relation to the reflective practitioner should be mutually emancipatory and participatory, where the ultimate outcome should be evaluated in terms of improved practice (Orme, 1997). What do we mean by emancipatory and participatory in this context? The *emancipatory* aspect is where the research actively improves the circumstances of the respondents being worked with. This could be in relation to an evaluation of a care service, or the role older people play in the running of any service that they have commissioned to provide them with care or something as fundamental as nutrition or social activity as part of a wider holistic need (Orme and Shemmings, 2010). Emancipatory research methods can be seen to fall within the social work focus of the exchange model of assessment (Smale et al., 2000) as well as the wider context of value-driven and ethical social work aspects of successful engagement.

The *participatory* element is where older people are actively leading the research material or where researchers are actively engaging with older people to assess their needs and wishes and the areas of research they would like addressed. This may involve a significant degree of communication (both open and closed) where older people may not be used to having their opinions elicited. They can be made anxious by the mechanics of the research itself or may have lost their capacity to communicate effectively due to illness or poor mental health.

Exercise

Can you speculate on areas of research that you think older people would be interested in researching? Consider areas of the lived experience of older people and what could be considered as meaningful and valid as a research topic. This could include issues of daily living, finances and resources generally

It should be clear that this emancipatory and participatory focus is one where the social worker either liberates or empowers the older person. Paradoxically, it is not in the gift of social work to do this other than through a supportive and advocacy role to ensure the older person achieves his/her own consideration of self-determination. Empowerment that is conferred may be done so at the behest of a professional (or others) who may have little or no understanding of the perceived needs and wishes of the older person. Furthermore, empowerment may be conferred within an environment that disadvantages the older person, particularly where there are significant aspects of structurally oppressive practice such as in institutional settings (Eastman, 1995). The research-practitioner has to consider the impact of the choice of research areas and whether this is really meaningful within the experience of older people at a micro or macro level.

The research learning experience

The practitioner, through the research, engages with the experiences and views of the older person and in the process learns more of the individual and collective needs of older people. The older person, through the participatory process, has the opportunity to state opinions, be heard, have expressed needs met and to feel valued. Critical reflection should encourage the practitioner to constantly review his/her practice, value base and engagement with older people. Alston and Bowles (2003) identify the key characteristics of any reflective practitioner as a person who can see clients as experts in the solution of their own identified problems; a person who recognises the dynamics of power and language; and who is self-critical and self-evaluative in the context of his/her own developing professional identity and that of the profession generally.

Becoming a research-practitioner

In the context of becoming and being a research-practitioner a consideration of time, expertise and the confidence to take on this expanded role will be extremely significant. Robson (2002: 535) identifies the anomalies that can exist within the research-practitioner context and identifies 'time, confidence, expertise' and what he refers to as the 'insider' problems. These latter problems are what I have previously referred to in the context of personal influence impacting adversely on any potential research and effectively skewing any potential validity, reliability and replicability of the research. There may also be ongoing problems due to lack of resources to support research within practice settings and the attitudes of staff who may feel threatened at a personal level by any discourse on care provision. This falls more within a consideration of loss and change and how practitioners manage transitions, than any raised awareness of the research focus. This may particularly be a problem in more specific settings that have become institutional through a neglect of training, indifferent management styles, lack of quality supervision and a reduction of positive advocacy for older people generally. It is quite easy to identify these settings as they are often characterised by an over-emphasis on rules, regulations and staff roles and frequently evidence more about staff than client need. In this context, evidence-based practice and research to support this is even more important. The net payoff is an engaged mutuality of relationships, a sharing of experience and an appreciation of the needs of a potentially disadvantaged group.

Research opportunities

Robson (2002) further states that there are significant opportunities for creating a research base within practice because of the potential opportunities practitioners may have in engaging with a specific client group and the availability of this group. This may be particularly so within research design areas where the practitioner will be best placed to determine the nature of how the research should be carried out to gain the most effective outcomes. While this may undoubtedly be the case, it has to be considered within a wider ethical perspective and take into account the fact that clients are not there to be experimented upon. This therefore needs to consider both ethical and value-driven practice. The more pragmatic aspects of research *reactivity* will also have to be included here: researchers themselves may intentionally or unwittingly influence the responses of the participants by using 'loaded' questions or attempting to research areas of practice where the researcher has been previously actively involved with the respondent group (Rosenthal and Rosnow, 1975).

To put this into focus, Arber and Ginn's (1991) research analysis of the General Household Survey clearly evidenced the significant role that older people play within the care of those over 65 years of age. This previously unreported and unacknowledged group would not have been brought to wider attention without this focus on research and evidence-based practice. The same is true of the very significant number of older people who are the primary carer for a son or daughter with a learning disability still resident at home. The evidence-based focus may have two strands. The first of these may be more related to *causality* where previously recognised and acknowledged theoretical bases of practice are utilised to try and make sense of a specific set of clients' needs or problems (Milner and O'Byrne, 2009). This of itself will pose problems. The practitioner may be effectively drawing upon their favourite theories to make sense of the needs of an older person who is taking part in a process where he/she may not understand the ground rules or even the language and perceived meaning of this language. This may become research practice that undermines rather than underpins good practice.

The second focus may be much more related to practice and particularly to the effectiveness of practice. It may be less involved with the assessment of need and more related to the evaluation of risk where the role of the social worker may be significantly different. There may be an over-emphasis here on attempting to legislate for every aspect of an older person's life at the expense of seeing the individual needs and wishes of that older person.

Exercise

You are asked to set up a short research project in a care setting for older people in relation to their satisfaction with the food available within the home.

- How would you carry out this research (individual interview, focus group or questionnaire)?
- What is the potentially positive or negative impact of this choice?
- How important do you think the venue and setting for the research is?
- What do you think your impact on the research could be?
- When you have addressed these issues you might like to consider the role of ethics and values (both research and social work) within this exercise.

Engagement with the research background

At a time when the language of care has increasingly become that of the marketplace with its concentration on best value, customer service and satisfaction, then the role of social work practitioner research may take on a more significant role (Jordan, 2007).

This is particularly so where it is becoming increasingly incumbent on practitioners to focus diminishing resources on an increasingly older population. As I have previously stated, it is not the nature of the ageing population itself that is the 'problem' here but the fact that there is an increasing likelihood that the longer a person lives the more likely he or she will be in receipt of support services. If this is the case then there is a clear need to ensure that research is directed *with* older people (able or otherwise) as part of a pre-emptive personalisation of the nature and shape of the services these individuals may want, both now and in the future.

Current social work training, with its emphasis on a more measured resource and output focus, may not be best placed to meet the evolving and individual needs of older people. Conversely, this may produce a more mechanised approach to practice where linear as opposed to engaged provision of services will become the norm. In this context it is much more likely that the 'problematisation' (Powell, 2001) of older people will become reinforced, as opposed to how, as a modern evolving society, we are able to meet the needs and well-being of a population with an increasing accumulation of years. As Jordan (2006) so profoundly states, the significant feature of any civilised society is its capacity to create value in terms of mutual appreciation of the diverse groups within that society. A Marxist perspective suggests that it is in the interests of capital to characterise older people as an increasing burden on society. This then leaves the way open to limit support resources for this 'non-productive' group, while the wider population will become increasingly unsympathetic to the needs of older people generally (Cunningham and Cunningham, 2012).

In essence, there needs to be an accrual of social capital through engagement with professionals and others by older people to ensure that their views and voices are both heard and acted upon. This can only be of benefit to the individual and society in general alike and research and evidence-based practice will be at the heart of this enquiry (Lymbery, 2001).

Social work research skills

Central to this is a well-educated and motivated workforce. In 2002 the Audit Commission indicated that practitioners were leaving the field of social work due to a combination of overwork, unmanageable workloads, unachievable targets and a general feeling that, as a profession, social workers were undervalued. As Ferguson (2012) states, the real problem is where 'contempt and blame' are routinely projected into social work. If social workers feel that they have lost their role as professionals with an associated knowledge base then there is much more likely to be a divide between theory and practice. Preston-Shoot (2003) argues that in an environment where outcomes are an increasing focus of social work practice and government policy, there should be an emphasis on the participation of clients and carers in the configuration of services as well as a more direct and active involvement in the research base itself. This is where the research-practitioner flourishes, particularly where there is that unique understanding of how environmental forces impact on individuals irrespective of their individual psychopathology. This global view will become the focus of future policy development.

The role of older people in research

Most research with older people and older people's services has been traditionally driven by full-time research professionals with a view to the future formulation of social policy directives. This research is only as good as the ethical and professional practice related to the research and, more importantly, how those results are defined and who or what is influencing how these findings are evaluated (Young, 1999).

Conversely, there is very little research generally completed by older people in relation to the effectiveness of the roles of social work practice. One exception can be found in the work of Older People Researching Social Issues (OPRSI Ltd, www. oprsi.co.uk). This organisation was founded after older participants were encouraged to research areas relevant to the experiences of older people after attending a research programme run by the University of Lancaster and the charity Counsel and Care. The primary focus of the OPRSI's work is to communicate the views of older people, through relevant research, to policy decision makers.

More recently, the OPRSI has collaborated with the Health Care Commission, the Audit Commission and the Commission for Social Care Inspection to assess how the standards of the National Service Framework for Older People (2001) were being met. The OPRSI has also collaborated with some prestigious research agencies such as Age UK and the Joseph Rowntree Foundation. Significantly, this organisation has produced publications with a range of social work researchers to assess the views of older people in relation to social workers themselves and their perceived effectiveness in carrying out their roles. This work was carried out as an evaluative aspect of how the National Service Framework for Older People was meeting its targets. In their research paper Manthorpe et al. (2008) speculate that while social workers are quick to refer to the importance of inclusion and empowerment this is not generally reflected in social workers actively seeking out the opinion of older people on social work effectiveness (Thompson and Thompson, 2001). This may be largely due to an unwillingness on the part of the profession to voluntarily place itself in the line of any further attention or attack. It comes at a time when the profession struggles to secure a more positive image in the face of extremely negative media depiction. Older people have also been characterised as a lower status group of clients than children, so concurrently any diminution in the professional role of social workers with older people will further disadvantage this group of individuals (Dwyer, 2005).

The findings of this research (Manthorpe et al., 2008) stated that older people were critical of poor assessment (the building block of any effective interaction), poor advice, lack of empathy as well as a poor knowledge base. Older people valued a skilled, informed, knowledgeable and empathic workforce. This is somewhat at odds with those who suggest that there should be a reduced role for professional social work practice when working with older people where the primary focus may be mainly concerned with meeting care needs (Lymbery, 2006). Another study, completed with over 1300 social workers and social care staff, indicated that fewer than 13% of respondents were able to identify a piece of research that emanated from a service user perspective. More surprisingly, 99% of the respondents were unable to refer directly to a randomised controlled trial (RCT) where results from research with a random sample of older people would be compared to another random group of similar respondents who receive no service or a lesser service (Sheldon and Chilvers, 2000).

Exercise

- Can you make a list of the ways in which older people might become involved in research you are interested in?
- How might you encourage older people to take part in this research?
- What do you think are the important social work skills you might need during this engagement?

The symbiotic evidence-based relationship

So why is it important that professionals utilise up-to-date research evidence as part of their working practice? Firstly, the research base will have been developed to meet a range of needs and policy issues that are current and that reflect the times we live in. This might be in the context of increasing structural inequality or those more psychological pressures that impact on individuals as part of an increasing range of stressors in old age (Trevithick, 2005). Such stressors may be related to finances, resources, health or a sense that the capacity for decision making and change may be slipping away. Secondly, and just as importantly, the research-practitioner role helps to create a new understanding of knowledge in practice where the research itself creates a new base of knowledge that can be assessed within individual and interprofessional practice. Unfortunately, as Preston-Shoot (2004) suggests, there is still not that commitment to view actual practice as a forum for the research paradigm. This is particularly the case where research with older people, as opposed to research that acts upon older people, may become the norm. The new focus is more likely to raise uncomfortable questions as to the older person's inherent view of age and ageing and how far this is being influenced by policy decision making and the social construction of ageing itself. Preston-Shoot (2007) argues against a more linear style of research where aims and objectives and the rationale are identified and then worked through and where the findings may meet the needs of the research but not necessarily the respondent group. Rather he advocates a more 'illuminative paradigm' (2007: 175) using a range of enquiries, dialogue and analyses to make sense of complicated needs or stressors of older people. These individuals may have become paralysed within the process of structural disadvantage and there will have been a negative impact on their capacity for engagement with the research process.

Social work and theoretical knowledge

Social work may therefore become the subject of research as well as an overall contributor to practice and clarify the social environment within which the research has taken place (Orme and Shemmings, 2010). This reiterates that view that an understanding of theoretical knowledge, without a commensurate understanding of the nature of structural and societal forces, is likely to have an adverse impact on working with older people. The current stratification of social work with a specific emphasis on outcome-driven results will only further delineate social work with older people in the context of the 'one size fits all'. It will miss the uniqueness of the individual as well as a critical analysis of the intellectual rigour of the research methodology.

Sources for Research Literature on Older People

- *Age and Ageing* www.ageing.oxfordjournals.org
- Age UK www.ageuk.org.uk
- *Ageing and Society* www.agingandsociety.com
- *British Journal of Social Work* www.basw.org
- *Community Care* www.communitycare.co.uk
- *Journal of Gerontological Social Work* www.tandfonline.com
- *Journal of Social Work Practice* www.tandfonline.com
- Sage Publications www.online.sagepub.com
- *Social Work Education* www.socialworkeducation.org.uk

An overview of the research literature

While there is an increasing emphasis on researching the role and place of older people within society there is still some way to go to ensure this is both inclusive and democratic. Significant numbers of research papers have focused on the nature of older age and dependency, with the result that older age has become fixed within the general societal consciousness as a time of dependency, need and illness (Phillipson and Walker, 1986). Even in more recent times, reviews of literature into the care of older people can concentrate on stress levels and satisfaction levels among staff as evidence (or indicators) of older people's well-being within care settings. Interestingly, in Powers et al. (1994) there was a direct correlation between the level of staff stress and the number of positive interactions with older clients. The speculation is that those staff who had invested more in an empathic relationship with older people were experiencing more distress at their inability to resolve presenting problems. The paradoxical position then suggests that the more investment there is in ethical engaged practice with older people the more potential there may be for a sense of frustration and powerlessness among staff. A radical change of focus is where the subjective experience of the older person becomes paramount and leads the research itself. Bowling (1996) reiterates this theme, suggesting that individuals are much more able, and should be encouraged, to define the nature of their own health and well-being. Research by Gabriel and Bowling (2004) clearly defines the nature of well-being in terms of the subjective perceptions of older people in the following areas: neighbourhood and environment, individual sense of well-being and positive outlook, health, finances and independent living skills. While there were fundamental issues of poor early life experiences and current problems related to poor communication and travel, it is significant that the older respondents in this study had a clear idea of what makes for a successful older age. It entails essentially the same aspects and attributes that younger people would also hold as important – financial security, friendships and a sense of ownership and belonging. So a fundamental truism of the nature of all people, irrespective of age or gender, is that wish to be well. This is reiterated within the work of Manthorpe et al. (2008) where older people clearly identified the inconsistencies of provision within social work practice. Also, some older people felt their individuality and care needs were being denied in the face of more organisational and structural needs. This was particularly the case when it came to the rationing of scarce resources irrespective of the care recommendations made by other support agencies. This research-practitioner focus clearly identifies areas of practice that could have a significant and positive impact on future work with older people.

Learning from older people

This should be at the heart of working towards policy making that potentially impacts on older people. If the old adage 'you can't buy a bicycle in a fish shop' holds true then the same is true of research into the needs of older people, i.e. ask older people. A significant feature of this will be the narrative approach where the direct qualitative responses of the older people themselves will act in an engaged and empathic way to both quantify individual well-being and to evidence individual need (Tanner, 2010). Implicit is the role of the wider sociological forces that can impact on older people. These include gender, ageism, ethnicity, stigma and that sense that older people 'live outside the grades or categories which the community regards as acceptable' (Galbraith, 1999: 235). Subsequently, feelings of 'otherness' are more likely to be reinforced among older people. Any research or learning that does not have at its core a rights-based agenda is unlikely to meet either practitioner learning or older person need. Interestingly, while work such as that of Banks (2006) refers to those Kantian and Utilitarian ethics of 'respect for persons' and 'the greatest good of the greatest number' respectively, policy decisions are frequently defined by political rhetoric or dogma. The focus of this 'welfare' approach may deny older people both a political and individual voice in meeting their needs in the longer term (Payne, 2006a). On a more fundamental level, a lack of research mindedness in relation to how older people develop psychologically will identify practitioners' lack of wider expertise in appreciating and challenging societal forces and structures (Kropf and Cummings, 2008). What is clear is that within the panoply of research texts related to the evidence base and narrative approaches there is very little reference to the 'rights' of older people within a global perspective. There is, however, much more emphasis on how older people could be treated within the process of the actual research itself. Why is that and does this buy into a more ageist perspective of research with older people?

Exercise

- What is the role of 'rights' in research with older people?
- What is the legislative and policy context within which you would think about this?
- What is the role of privacy and how does this conform with ethical and human rights understanding?

Combating ageism and negative stereotypes in research

Both 'elderly' and 'older people' are notoriously difficult terms to define. Firstly, practitioners would have to be aware that people age in different ways and different stages. Someone who is considered young today may have been considered as decrepit several hundred years ago. There is no natural correlation between age and need and some older people will make very little use of either health or social work services across their lifetimes (Reed et al., 2004). Even a consideration of the nature of independence and independent living can throw up some difficult considerations. Older people may not view independence simply as a lack of dependence on others but whether they have an individual role to play within their social context and society in general. It is, as Tanner (2001) so profoundly puts it, not just about meeting those mundane practical aspects of living but of 'ensuring the continuity of self' (Secker et al., 2003).

One of the most commonly held stereotypes of older people is that they have little to contribute. Their lives are characterised by an inability to engage with the wider community and to contribute to that community. If this is so then researchers need to be particularly careful as to how they both access older respondents and engage and use research findings (Bulmer, 2005). The former is related to a wider concern about the nature of privacy and how a loss of this may have a negative effect on the well-being of an older person. The latter is about how older people are considered generally and relates to issues of perceived passivity and submissiveness in the face of a research behemoth where individual identity may be lost in the process of the research itself.

Research, therefore, should have the same focus as the personalisation agenda. The initial premise for care and support services should be the older person him/herself. There should be an emphasis on making choices, feeling included and having one's wishes and aspirations met as far as possible (Social Care Institute for Excellence, 2010). Research-practitioners, and particularly young practitioners, should be aware of the socially constructed nature of older age and how negative stereotypes of older age can become part of practitioners' as well as the wider public's perception. Research shows that older people are traditionally portrayed in a negative light by the media (Robinson, 1998). Unsurprisingly, older people are depicted in the least favourable light within advertising directed at younger people. What do you think is the message, conscious or unconscious, that is being disseminated here?

> I'm young, you're old.
> I feel good therefore you must not.
> I feel better therefore you feel worse.
> It's better to be young than old.
> I don't want to be old.

While this may be overly simplistic in its application there is clearly a price to be paid for an environment where the personal image is paramount and where anything that offends against this ideal is a less worthy, deviant anomaly. Any practitioner imbued with this thinking will find it difficult to inhabit fully the research role in relation to older people. It denies the complexity of what it is to be old and, more importantly, to become old. It is, perhaps, not about an absolute term of being, but becoming. If this is the case then research-practitioners have to be adept at understanding, evaluating and analysing both psychosocial and biomedical knowledge in any research carried out with older people (Reed et al., 2006).

Research and dementia

This is particularly the case with those older people experiencing dementia. The fundamental question has always been, 'what is the potential for communication and engagement with those people experiencing dementia?' Feil (2002) writes on the nature of individual experience from a post-Freudian perspective, where the uniqueness of the individual is at the heart of her proposed intervention. She also speculates that the behaviour of older people cannot be changed unless they wish to change and that behaviour is defined by a multiplicity of life events. This is reinforced by the work of Sabat (2001, 2002), who argues that the individual's sense of self can still persist even when the more traditional forms of expression have been lost to a diagnosis of dementia. Again Sabat argues that it is the complex interplay of the totality of life experiences that has to be appreciated in any seeking or engagement with the 'self' of older people with dementia.

So what is the discourse we have with older people with dementia and how do we define it? Foucault (2002) identifies this discourse as those facets of experience and expression of the world that contribute to its complexity and totality for the individual. There are many discourses and therefore many ways of valuing the experiences of individuals, both from an ethical point of view and that of valuing the diversity of methods of engagement with sometimes hidden worlds. This is something of a challenge given the more biomedical approach to dementia, where it is defined almost exclusively within the realms of medicine. As research-practitioners we are therefore obligated to take a more pragmatic and wider ranging view of dementia itself and how this has the potential for being socially constructed in the same way that gender and old age are (Adams and Manthorpe, 2003).

Even within the field of health care there has been a tendency to view older people in these more negative ways. Health and social care staff may feel that their work is 'unglamorous' and this can be a contributory factor in how they view both themselves and older patients. The research-practitioner would have to consider this in any research that seeks to address the well-being of older people within a care setting. Working alongside this is the paradox of social work theory itself and how this can potentially undermine the needs of older people. I would refer here to the work of Cumming and Henry (1961) who argue that current practitioners may view disengagement theory as a natural progression of old age. This is as opposed to viewing the more individualistic and personalised presenting needs of the older person. Without this understanding, the deep-seated and continuing physical and emotional distress of older people may become masked within this theoretical focus and missed by social work practitioners.

Sadly, it is a truism that both student nurses and student social workers show a marked disinclination to pursue working with older people post-qualification (Wade, 2001). If the research-practitioner focus is to have any credibility then fundamental questions of why this should be the case need to be considered and addressed in any future research and policy making directed at older people.

Exercise

- What do you think you would need to consider in attempting any research with clients with dementia?
- How would you address issues of communication?
- Who else might you involve within this research?
- What agencies and information could you access to support this research?

Assessing and choosing a methodology

Skills needed

Both Preston-Shoot (1999) and Lymbery (2001) define the four key roles related to social work learning for practice as *political*, *values*, *leadership* and *solutions*. This congruency of themes defines how social work is increasingly inhabiting a more political milieu, where resources are often the focus of policy making. The same is no less true of values where a wider appreciation of the sociological forces that impact on older people should inform a more 'partnership'-based model of practice and research. The policy role is one where practitioners will have to actively advocate and challenge practice that is below an acceptable standard. This is particularly true within research where practitioners should not feel constrained by any organisational role conflict and where some practitioners effectively behave as agents of state control. Practitioner learning has also to be informed by the active participation of carers and service users as a means of defining the areas of importance for potential clients. Such participation should lead practitioners to appreciate the lived experience of those clients.

Advocacy/facilitation

Kelly (2010) has integrated the Kitwood (1997) person-centred approach to self-hood into a more fundamental aspect of how dementia sufferers can be supported to a sense of self, post-diagnosis. Practitioners who work in a more person-centred way are much more likely to have a successful outcome by becoming involved and appreciating the life experiences of the older person. There is also good evidence to show that staff who become involved at this level have a more positive outlook on their working practices and own sense of self. This is where the mutuality of learning lies and inherent is that sense of the uniqueness of individuals exemplified by Rogers (2002) and defined as 'unconditional positive regard'.

Methodologies

It is not possible here to give an overview of all the different methodologies for research that exist, so I intend to focus on social research and the role of the older person within this research. Any starting point has to be a consideration of the ethics that underpin and limit the breadth of research that can be carried out on human subjects (Bulmer, 2005). Both social work and the social sciences have their own codes of practice for research. These can be found on the websites of the British Association of Social Workers (BASW www.basw.co.uk), the Social Research Association (SRA www.the-sra.org.uk) and the British Sociological Association (BSA www.britsoc.co.uk).

The main areas of concern related to ethics for the research-practitioner are whether the research causes harm to participants; whether it is carried out without full and knowing consent; whether it invades the privacy of the respondents either knowingly or unknowingly; and whether there is any use of deception to gain access to respondents or information about them (Bryman, 2008). If older people are disadvantaged by age or infirmity it is likely to be much more difficult for them to fend off any third party expressing interest in their opinions for the purposes of research. This may be even more difficult if the groups carrying out research represent powerful agencies with a role in formulating policy. Research-practitioners need to acknowledge and be aware of the role of research in policy and how it can both liberate individuals and support and subscribe to more intrusive political forces. Concurrent with this is the question of what research sets out to do: whether it is to study the world in a more traditional way or seek to change the world through a more emancipatory focus. Orme (1997) suggests that this latter methodology may be particularly significant when the focus of social work research is to improve practitioner skills and practice. This 'action research' effectively seeks to change the world rather than simply studying it. Alston and Bowles (2003) define this action research and more importantly 'participatory' action research as challenging the more traditional norms of the researcher as 'expert' and the respondents as more passive recipients. This is a significant consideration for any research with older people. This research style also fits within an inclusive, collaborative and person-centred approach to social work practice.

Focus groups

At its most fundamental a focus group can provide more information than carrying out a series of individual interviews which may be time consuming and lead to a lot of analysis of the subjective experience of older individuals. The benefit of the focus groups is that it has a self-supporting and self-sustaining aspect. It allows for older respondents with similar interests and concerns to come together to discuss any gaps in service provision. It also has the benefit of reducing the power imbalance between the researcher and the individual older respondent who may be intimidated by the relationship or who may feel that his/her voice is unlikely to be heard anyway (Preston-Shoot, 2007). Focus groups, by their very nature, need to be structured in such a way that there is a clear directive of their intention and what it is that they aim to research. This will involve the use of a *facilitator* to lead and guide the discussion, although this intervention should be kept to a minimum and the group should be encouraged to become self-monitoring. Essentially, the more a facilitator intervenes the more likely it is that this will influence the responses of any older people taking part (Cronin, 2005). An understanding of the fundamental aspects of human development and psychology may also be an advantage where constituent members of the group may lack the confidence to participate or where other members seek to dominate (Whittaker, 2012).

Focus groups are particularly effective for ascertaining the views of a cohort of people in relation to an evaluation of the services provided within a care setting, for example. The most effective way to manage a group is to ensure the participants come from similar age ranges and experiences for validity of findings. Also the researcher has to consider the optimum number of older people who can be accommodated for their voices and opinions to be heard effectively. The venue too is important. Participants should be able find and access the location easily and they should be able to sit comfortably for the duration of the focus group. Lastly, there needs to be a strategy in place to ensure that any difficulties within the group can be addressed. This may involve some ground rules about who contributes and when and how any disputes can be resolved. An assertion of the importance and value of all contributions prior to the focus group starting is often an effective way to set the scene for a reasoned input from the respondents.

Qualitative data

Within any focus group the research-practitioner will be collecting a potentially wide range of older people's comments in the form of direct responses. These qualitative responses will have to be evaluated and analysed. The most effective way to do this is through a 'thematic analysis' (Bryman, 2008). Generally speaking this is where the responses from the older respondents are grouped into codes with specific key words to identify the broad scope of the responses of the older person. These codes are then themed together both for similarities and for differentials of sense and meaning. If, for example, key themes arise that suggest older people are very unhappy with their service provision this may mean several things. The services are below standard, the older people have not been included within the design and delivery of service provision, or there may be more general themes of a lack of engagement with older people. For further information on thematic analysis see Braun and Clarke (2006).

Qualitative methods work at a more individual and human level and are concerned with the interpretation that individuals bring to their own actions and lives. They tend to reside outwith more societal research and are less interested in abstract societal themes and more about how people think and feel. You can see here that this will be of specific interest to the research-practitioner. Individual and collective views of older people may then be utilised to inform practice if not longer term policy (Payne and Payne, 2004).

Narrative approaches

While qualitative research is based on the lived experiences and opinions of older individuals there is good evidence to suggest that these narrative approaches are a more fitting response to unanswered questions regarding the relationships that older people may have with their community, practitioners and with society in general.

Encouraging older people to take part in narrative work not only diminishes the power differential within the professional relationship but focuses the research clearly within the experience of the older person. Mishler (1986) states the importance of the personal narrative and how storytelling may be extremely significant in how respondents view their lives. Conversely, he speculates that within any power imbalance the researcher is likely to develop skills that actually 'suppress' stories as the he or she endeavours to get answers. The paradox is that answers are achieved rather than responses. This has serious implications for the whole nature of reliability of responses and whether these responses can ever be qualified as entirely valid.

The main forms of narrative approach are life history (sometimes referred to as the biographical method) and life story interview. The former is very much focused on the self-interpretation of the totality of an older person's life. The latter can be identified as a specific range of questions where the older person will be at the centre of an evaluation of the following themes: family, cultural background, education, relationships, retirement and what the future may hold (Atkinson, 2004). There is a direct correlation between the stories older people tell and an interpretation of the individual psychological development. The development itself may create the language within which the older person lives and interprets the world. It is unlikely that an older person who has not negotiated the vagaries of a dysfunctional human existence will be able to formulate these experiences into an optimistic narrative in later life. While resilience has a role to play here, the effects of these early life experiences may still be evident and driving behaviour in older age. But they may also act as a way of understanding the individual human condition (see Narrative Approaches in Chapter 7).

Conclusion

The role of the research-practitioner is a significant feature of any engagement that practitioners have with older people. It is at the core of any active interaction and functions with older people in a context that is meaningful to them. Pivotal to this whole concept is an appreciation of the role that power can play in research with any disadvantaged groups. An inclusive and collaborative approach will both liberate older respondents as well as have a potentially positive impact on any policy derived from this research.

 Recommended Reading

Bryman, A. (2008) *Social Research Methods* (3rd ed.). Oxford: Oxford University Press. A comprehensive overview of all the themes of effective research.

(Continued)

(Continued)

Elliot, J. (2007) *Using Narrative in Social Research: Qualitative and Quantitative Approaches*. London: Sage. Particularly useful for the inclusion and collaboration of respondents within the research-practitioner role.

Orme, J. and Shemmings, D. (2010) *Developing Research Based Social Work Practice*. Basingstoke: Palgrave Macmillan. An up-to-date and well-directed text that addresses ethical practice and the discourse in a way that will prove useful for any practitioner attempting research.

Whittaker, A. (2012) *Research Skills for Social Work* (2nd ed.). Exeter: Learning Matters. An excellent step by step approach to carrying out a social work research project.

CONCLUSION

It is a privilege to work with older people. Those people who are engaged with the world will take pleasure, not only in their own accomplishments, but in the accomplishments of others. Where better therefore than to engage with this repository of human experience and understanding developed across the lifetime of older people?

The main focus of this text is to focus and refocus on the individual experience, personal narratives and individuality of older people. Whereas I understand that social policy in relation to older people may have to have something of a generic nature, it is the process of how this is rolled out to meet individual need that is of most concern. It is certainly a truism that at times of societal stress and economic decline the vulnerable are more likely to be discriminated against. This incremental aspect of oppression can take on structural values where the common voice may ask 'why shouldn't older people contribute more' to their future care and well-being? Practitioners may then consider whether the nature of older people services needs to be re-evaluated within a modern world. It cannot be satisfactory for older people to have individual need and more generic support services tied into a boom and bust culture of care.

So what is the answer? Firstly there needs to be a more formal, considered affirmation of the role that older people have played within the formation of any modern society. Ironically, those older people who lived through post-Second World War society, with its limited resources and opportunities, may now be at the receiving end of increased poverty in older age. A significant step forward here would be to actively engage at a personal, cultural and structural (PCS) level (Thompson, 2006) with how older people are depicted generally. There could be a formal process of depicting older age as a time of opportunity and growth. This is particularly the case given the very significant contribution that older people make to society in terms of volunteering, caring for siblings and kinship care. Any practitioners who think that this draws undue attention to older people, even through positive discrimination, should ask themselves how wider ideas of discrimination on ethnicity, multiculturalism as well as sexual orientation have changed over the years. There is clear evidence that where discrimination is legislated for and discriminatory language addressed, this has a significant impact on the way society engages with those who may feel disenfranchised. Time will tell as to how this will develop.

The argument is certainly not helped by demonising the baby boomer generation. Nor is the suggestion that older people should contribute more to society to access their state pensions. There is certainly a deeper and more philosophical aspect here of when older people can expect to retire irrespective of any understanding of the social construct of retirement itself.

The most surprising aspect, from a pragmatic view, is how government agencies in the future hope to deal in a meaningful way with the ageing demographic, particularly in view of the fact that there will be an increased number of older voters. Agencies that hold older people in poor regard and particularly as net 'takers' from the public purse may find themselves at the receiving end of older people opprobrium as opposed to votes.

A key feature of any understanding of future support needs is a move away from the 'deficit model' (Ray et al., 2009) where older people are consistently viewed as the sum of their needs as opposed to their contribution. Unfortunately, this is frequently compounded by the poor status that working with older people has within society generally and, more specifically, within social work services. A recent straw poll of approximately 70 students identified only two who would consider working with older people as part of their future careers. It is therefore difficult for individual practitioners to pursue this when there is a lack of support within the profession.

Permeating all of this is the paradox that the process of engagement with older people may be more important than the outcome itself, whereas care management may be overly focused on process and driven by outcomes. So it is about finding more of a balance of the role and needs of older people generally. Neither can an evolving society deny the ageing demographic and the impact that this will have on resources and taxation generally. What is certain is that the demographic of itself raises serious questions about the future role that older people will play in political decision making. In a more optimistic world I would hope that the experiential knowledge that older people have acquired over a lifetime would engender a note of caution and reflection in how future state resources are accrued and utilised. Perhaps the only real certainty is that in the future uncertainty will exist (Brown and Rutter, 2006). Any contingency for this is likely to lessen a sense of defensiveness. The problem arises when this potential uncertainty begins to erode the ethical sense of who and what older people are. I am proposing a more radical rethinking of the nature of collective being with all that entails in the form of uncertainty and progress for the future. More important is the evolution of a collective and societal sense of belonging and a mutuality of support that the young and old should develop as different faces of the same societal coin.

An important part of this text is the consistent challenge identified in relation to a biological sense of ageing. This challenging of the 'common sense' view (Gaine, 2010) throughout the text will hopefully enable and encourage readers and practitioners to question any commonly accepted views of older people and older age. This rationale is couched within an understanding that commonly held views may prevail but are frequently wrong. A fairly typical theme is where older people are more often characterised as needy or a drain on finances when there is no evidence to support this.

While the role of older people may be constantly evolving in a changing world, the same is no less true of the role of the practitioner. Therefore a focus of these developing roles will be an engagement with continuous professional development particularly through evidence-based practice and research.

I hope that any readers find the format, case studies and questions a useful support in a consideration of the nature of working with older people in a modern world. As someone with a fair accumulation of years I have something of a vested interest here. I can only hope that the energy expended in writing this book will permeate the practice of all willing, current and future, practitioners.

REFERENCES

Abbott, S., Fisk, M. and Forward, L. (2000) 'Social and democratic participation in residential settings for older people: Realities and aspirations', *Ageing and Society*, 20 (3): 327–40.

Abendstern, M., Hughes, J., Clarkson, P. et al. (2011) 'The pursuit of integration in the assessment of older people with health and social care needs', *British Journal of Social Work*, 41 (3): 467–85.

Adams, T. and Manthorpe, J. (2003) *Dementia Care*. London: Arnold.

Age Concern (2008) *Later Life as an Older Lesbian, Gay or Bisexual Person*. London: Age Concern.

Age UK (2011a) *Changes to State Pension*. London: Age UK.

Age UK (2011b) *Lesbian, Gay or Bisexual, Planning for Later Life*. London: Age UK.

Age UK (2011c) *What the Health and Social Care Bill Means*. London: Age UK.

Age UK Factsheet 10 (2012) 'Paying for permanent residential care', www.ageuk.org.uk (last accessed 25 March 2013).

Age UK Factsheet 20 (2012) 'NHS continuing healthcare and NHS-funded nursing care', www.ageuk.org.uk (last accessed 25 March 2013).

Age UK Factsheet 29 (2012) 'Finding care home accommodation', www.ageuk.org.uk (last accessed 25 March 2013).

Ainsworth, M. (1962) *Deprivation of Maternal Care: A Reassessment of its Effects*. Geneva: World Health Organization.

Ainsworth, M., Blehar, M., Water, E. and Wall, S. (1978) *Patterns of Attachment*. Hillsdale, NJ: Lawrence Erlbaum.

Allen, P.D., Cherry, K.E. and Padmore, E. (2009) 'Self-reported ageism in social work practitioners and students', *Journal of Gerontological Social Work*, 52 (2): 124–34.

Alston, M. and Bowles, W. (2003) *Research for Social Workers: An Introduction to Methods* (2nd ed.). Abingdon: Routledge.

Alzheimer's Society (2012) *Leading the Fight Against Dementia: What is Dementia?* London: Alzheimer's Society.

Andersson, L. (ed.) (2003) *Cultural Gerontology*. Westport, CT: Auburn House.

Arber, S. (2004) 'Gender, marital status, and ageing: Linking material, health and social resources', *Journal of Aging Studies*, 18 (1): 91–108.

Arber, S. and Cooper, H. (2000) 'Gender and inequalities in women's health across the life course', in E. Annandale and K. Hunt (eds), *Gender Inequalities in Health*. Buckingham: Open University Press, pp. 123–49.

Arber, S. and Ginn, J. (1991) *Gender and Later Life: A Sociological Analysis of Resources and Constraints*. London: Sage.

Argyle, M. (2007) *Social Interaction*. London: Aldine Transaction.

Atchley, R.C. (1989) 'A continuity theory of normal ageing', *Gerontologist*, 29 (2): 183–90.

Atchley, R.C. (1999) *Continuity and Adaption in Ageing: Creating Positive Experiences*. Baltimore, MD: Johns Hopkins University Press.

Atkinson, D., Kim, A., Ruelas, S. and Lin, A. (1999) 'Ethnicity and attitudes towards facilitated reminiscence', *Journal of Mental Health Counseling*, 21 (1): 66–81.

Atkinson, P. (2004) 'Life story interview', in M.S. Lewis-Beck, A. Bryman and T.F. Liao (eds), *The Sage Encyclopedia of Social Science Research Methods* (Vols 1–3). Thousand Oaks, CA: Sage.

Audit Commission (2002) *Recruitment and Retention: A Public Service Workforce for the 21st Century*. London: The Stationery Office.

Baltes, P.B. and Smith, J. (2003) 'New frontiers in the future of ageing: From successful ageing of the young old to the dilemmas of the Fourth Age', *Gerontology*, 49 (2): 123–35.

Banford, C. and Bruce, E. (2000) 'Defining the outcomes of community care: the perspectives of older people with dementia and their carers', *Aging and Society*, 20 (5): 543–70.

Banks, S. (2006) *Ethics and Values in Social Work* (3rd ed.), Practical Social Work series. Basingstoke: Palgrave Macmillan.

Bano, B. and Benbow, S. (2010) 'Positive approaches to the fourth age', *Quality in Ageing – Policy, Practice and Research*, 11 (2): 29–34.

Barnes, S. (2002) 'The design of caring environments and the quality of life of older people', *Ageing and Society*, 22 (6): 775–89.

Barnes, S. (2005) 'The same old process? Older people, participation and deliberation', *Ageing and Society*, 25 (2): 245–59.

Barnett, E. (2000) *Including the Person with Dementia in Designing and Delivering Care: 'I Need to be Me'*. London: Jessica Kingsley.

Barrett, G., Sellman, D. and Thomas, J. (2005) *Interprofessional Working in Health and Social Care: Professional Perspectives*. Basingstoke: Palgrave Macmillan.

Barrett, M. and McIntosh, M. (1994) *The Anti-Social Family*. London: Verso.

Bartlett, H. and Burnip, S. (1998) 'Quality of care in nursing homes for older people: Providers' perspectives and priorities', *NT Research*, 3 (4): 257–68.

Beattie, A.M., Daker-White, G., Gilliard, J. and Means, R. (2005) 'They don't quite fit the way we organize our services': Results from a UK field study of marginalized groups and dementia care', *Disability and Society*, 20 (1): 67–80.

Bebbington, A., Darton, R. and Netten, A. (2001) *Care Homes for Older People, Volume 2. Admissions, Needs and Outcomes*. Canterbury: Personal Social Services Research Unit.

Beck, A.T. and Beck, J.S. (2005) *Cognitive Therapy for Challenging Problems*. New York: Guilford Press.

Beckett, C. and Maynard, A. (2005) *Values and Ethics in Social Work: An Introduction*. London: Sage.

Beresford, P. (2005) 'Social approaches to madness and distress: User knowledges and user experience', in J. Tew (ed.), *Social Perspectives in Mental Health: Developing Social Models to Understand and Work with Mental Distress*. London and Philadelphia: Jessica Kingsley.

Beresford, P. (2007) 'State of independence: Individual budgets, where social care users control the cash allocated to them, are being lauded: But are they just another attempt to cut costs?', *The Guardian*, 23 May.

Beresford, P. and Croft, S. (1993) *Citizen Involvement: A Practical Guide for Change*. Basingstoke: Macmillan.

Beveridge, W. (1942) *Social Insurance and Allied Services*, Cmd 6404. London: HMSO.

Bichard Inquiry Report (2004) London: The Stationery Office.

Biestek, F.P. (1961) *The Casework Relationship*. London: Unwin.

Biggs, S., Phillipson, C. and Kingston, P. (1993) *Old Age Abuse*. Buckingham: Open University Press.

Biltgard, T. (2000) 'The sexuality of elderly people on film – visual limitations', *Journal of Aging and Identity*, 5 (3): 169–83.

Bingham, J. (2012) 'Elderly ignored and treated as "objects" in care system', *The Telegraph*, 21 February.

Blanchard, M. (1996) 'Old age depression: a biological inevitability?', *Int. Rev. Psychiatry*, 8: 379–85.

Bland, R. (1999) 'Independence, privacy and risk: two contrasting approaches to residential care for older people', *Ageing and Society*, Cambridge: Cambridge University Press.

Blau, Z.S. (1981) *Aging in a Changing Society*. New York: Franklin Watts.

Bloustein, E. (1964) 'Privacy as an aspect of human dignity: an answer to Dean Prosser', *New York University Law Review*, 39 (6): 962–1007

Boffey, D. (2012) 'Sacked minister admits NHS cuts despite Cameron pledge', *The Observer*, 23 September.

Boise, L. (2009) 'Ethnicity and the experience of dementia', in M. Downs and B. Bowers (eds), *Excellence in Dementia Care: Research into Practice*. Maidenhead: McGraw-Hill/Open University Press.

Bond, J. and Corner, L. (2001) 'Researching dementia: Are there unique methodological challenges for health services research?', *Ageing and Society*, 21 (1): 95–116.

Bond, J. and Corner, L. (2004) *Quality of Life and Older People*. Maidenhead: Open University Press.

Bond, J. and Corner, L. (2006) 'The future of well-being: Quality of life of older people in the twenty-first century', in J. Vincent, C. Phillipson and M. Downes (eds), *The Futures of Old Age*. London: Sage, pp. 154–60.

Bowlby, J. (1969) *Attachment and Loss*, Volume 1. London: Pimlico.

Bowles, W., Collingridge, M., Curry, S. and Valentine, B. (2006) *Ethical Practice in Social Work: An Applied Approach*. Maidenhead: Open University Press.

Bowling, A. (1996) 'The effects of illness on quality of life', *Journal of Epidemiology and Community Health*, 50 (2): 149–55.

Boyd, D. and Bee, H. (2009) *Lifespan Development* (5th ed.). Upper Saddle River, NJ: Pearson Education.

Braun, V. and Clarke, V. (2006) 'Using thematic analysis in psychology', *Qualitative Research in Psychology*, 3 (2): 77–101.

Braye, S. and Preston-Shoot, M. (1995) *Empowering Practice in Social Care*. Buckingham: Open University Press.

Brearley, J. (2007) 'A psychodynamic approach to social work', in J. Lishman (ed.), *Handbook for Practice Learning in Social Work and Social Care: Knowledge and Theory* (2nd ed.). London: Jessica Kingsley.

Brearley, P. (1976) 'Social gerontology and social work', *British Journal of Social Work*, 6 (4): 433–47.

Brindle, D. (2012) 'There can be no "sticking plaster solution"', *The Guardian*, 22 February.

British Association of Social Workers (BASW) (2002) *Code of Ethics for Social Work*. Birmingham: BASW.

Brown, C. and Lowis, M.J. (2003) 'Psychosocial development in the elderly: An investigation into Erikson's ninth stage', *Journal of Ageing Studies*, 17 (4): 415–26.

Brown, K. and Rutter, L. (2006) *Critical Thinking for Social Work*. Exeter: Learning Matters.

Bryman, A. (2008) *Social Research Methods* (3rd ed.). Oxford: Oxford University Press.

Bulmer, M. (2005) 'The ethics of social research', in N. Gilbert (ed.), *Researching Social Life* (2nd ed.). London: Sage.

Bury, M. and Holme, A. (1991) *Life After Ninety*. London: Routledge.

Butler, F. (2004) *Human Rights: Who Needs Them? Using Human Rights in the Voluntary Sector*. London: Institute for Public Policy Research.

Bytheway, B. (1995) *Rethinking Ageing: Ageism*. Buckingham: Open University Press.

Bytheway, B., Keil, T., Allatt, P. and Bryman, A. (eds) (1990) *Becoming and Being Old: Sociological Approaches to Later Life*. London: Sage.

Bytheway, W. (1997) 'Talking about age: The theoretical basis of social gerontology', in A. Jamieson, S. Harper and C. Victor (eds), *Critical Approaches to Ageing and Later Life*. Milton Keynes: Open University Press.

Bywater, J. and Jones, R. (2007) *Sexuality and Social Work*. Exeter: Learning Matters.

Cann, P. (2009) 'Rewriting the story' in P. Cann, and M. Dean (eds), *Unequal Ageing: The Untold Story of Exclusion in Old Age*. Bristol: The Policy Press, pp.159–72.

Cann, P. and Dean, M. (eds) (2009) *Unequal Ageing: The Untold Story of Exclusion in Old Age*. Bristol: The Policy Press.

Care Quality Commission (2000) *National Minimum Standards for Care Homes for Older People*. London: Department of Health.

Carr, S. (2007) 'Participation, power, conflict and change: Theorizing dynamics of service user participation in the social care systems of England and Wales', *Critical Social Policy*, 27 (2): 266–76.

Cashdan, S. (1988) *Object Relations Therapy: Using the Relationship*. New York: W.W. Norton and Company.

Centre for Policy on Ageing (2007) *Action on Elder Abuse*. London: Centre for Policy on Ageing.

Challis, D. (1999) 'Assessment and care management: developments since the community care reforms', in M. Henwood and G. Wistow (eds), *With Respect to Old Age*, Research Volume 3, Cm 4192-11/3. London: Stationery Office. pp. 69-86.

Charles, K.K. and Sevak, P. (2005) 'Can family care-giving substitute for nursing home care', *Journal of Health Economy*, 24 (6): 1174–90.

Clare, L. (2003) 'Managing threats to self: Awareness in early stage Alzheimer's disease', *Social Science and Medicine*, 57 (6): 1017–29.

Clare, L., Roth, I. and Pratt, R. (2005) 'Perceptions of change over time in early-stage Alzheimer's disease: Implications for understanding awareness and coping style', *Dementia*, 4 (4): 487–520.

Clark, A. and Lynch, R. (2010) 'Older people', in S.J. Hothersall and M. Maas-Lowit (eds), *Need, Risk and Protection in Social Work Practice*. Exeter: Learning Matters.

Clark, A. (2009) *Ageism and Age Discrimination in Primary and Community Healthcare in the UK*. London: Centre for Policy on Ageing.

Clarke, C. (2006) 'Moral character in social work', *British Journal of Social Work*, 36 (1): 75–89.

Clarke, J., Newman, J., Smith, N. et al. (2007) *Creating Citizen-Consumers: Changing Publics and Changing Public Services*. London: Sage.

Clarkson, P., Hughes, J., Challis, D. et al. (2010) 'Targeting, care management and preventative services for older people: The cost-effectiveness of a pilot self-assessment approach in one local authority', *British Journal of Social Work*, 40 (7): 2255–73.

Cohen, M. (2003) *101 Ethical Dilemmas*. London: Routledge.

Cook, A. (2008) *Dementia and Well-being: Possibilities and Challenges*. Edinburgh: Dunedin.

Constable, G., (2009) 'Self-preservation', in A. Mantell (ed.) *Social Work Skills with Adults*. Exeter: Learning Matters.

Coulshed, V. and Orme, J. (2006) *Social Work Practice* (4th ed.). Basingstoke: Palgrave Macmillan.

Craig, G. (2004) 'Citizenship, exclusion and older people', *Journal of Social Policy*, 33 (1): 95–114.

Cranny-Francis, A., Waring, W., Stavropoulos, P. and Kirkby, J. (2003) *Gender Studies, Terms and Debates*. Basingstoke: Palgrave Macmillan.

Crawford, K. and Walker, J. (2008) *Social Work with Older People* (2nd ed.). Exeter: Learning Matters.

Crawshaw, M. (2002) 'Disabled people's access to social work education: Ways and means of promoting environmental change', *Social Work Education*, 21 (5): 503–14.

Crichton, J. and Koch, T. (2007) 'Living with dementia: Curating self-identity', *Dementia*, 6 (3): 365–81.

Crisp, R. (1995) 'Deontological ethics', in T. Honderich (ed.), *The Oxford Companion to Philosophy*. Oxford: Oxford University Press, pp. 187–8.

Cronin, A. (2005) 'Focus groups', in N. Gilbert (ed.), *Researching Social Life* (2nd ed.). London: Sage, pp. 164–77.

Cronin, A. (2006) 'Sexuality in gerontology: A heteronormative presence, a queer absence', in S. Daatland and S. Briggs (eds), *Ageing and Diversity: Multiple Pathways in Later Life*. London: Sage, pp. 107–22.

Cumming, E. and Henry, W. (1961) *Growing Old: The Process of Disengagement*. New York: Basic Books.

Cunningham, S. (2006) 'Demographic time bomb', or 'apocalyptic demography', in M. Lavalette and A. Pratt (eds), *Social Policy: Theories, Concepts and Issues* (3rd ed.). London: Sage.

Cunningham, S. and Cunningham, J. (2012) *Social Policy and Social Work: An Introduction*, Transforming Social Work Practice series. London: Sage/Learning Matters.

Dalley, G. (2000) 'Long-term care in the United Kingdom', *Journal of Aging and Social Policy*, 12: 1–5.

Dalrymple, J. and Burke, B. (1995) *Anti-oppressive Practice*. Buckingham: Open University Press.

Dalrymple, J. and Burke, B. (2006) *Anti-oppressive Practice: Social Care and the Law*. Maidenhead: Open University Press/McGraw-Hill.

Davey Smith, G. (ed.) (2003) *Health Inequalities: Lifecourse Approaches*. Bristol: The Policy Press.

Davies, J. and Gregory, D. (2007) 'Entering the dialogue: Marriage biographies and dementia care', *Dementia: The International Journal of Social Research and Practice*, 6 (4): 481–8.

Davis, N.A. (2000) 'Contemporary deontology', in P. Singer (ed.), *A Companion to Ethics*, *Blackwell Companions to Philosophy*. Oxford: Blackwell.

Dean, M. (2009) 'How social age trumped social class?', in P. Cann and M. Dean (eds), *Unequal Ageing: The Untold Story of Exclusion in Old Age*. Bristol: The Policy Press.

De Beauvoir, S. (1972) *Old Age*. London: Penguin Books.

De Hennezel, M. (2008) *The Warmth of the Heart Prevents the Body from Rusting: Ageing Without Growing Old*. Carlton North, Victoria: Scribe.

Department of Health (1989) *Caring for People: Community Care in the Next Decade and Beyond*, London: HMSO.

Department of Health (1991a) *Care Management and Assessment: Manager's Guide*. London: DH

Department of Health (1991b) *Care Management and Assessment: Practitioner's Guide*. London: DH.

Department of Health (2000a) *No Secrets: Guidance on Developing and Implementing Multi-agency Policies and Procedures to Protect Vulnerable Adults from Abuse*, DH Circular HSC 2000/007.

Department of Health (2000b) *NHS Plan: A Plan for Investment, A Plan for Reform*. London Stationery Office.

Department of Health (2001a) *Care Homes for Older People: National Minimum Standards*. London: Department of Health.

Department of Health (2001b) *National Service Framework for Older People*. London: Department of Health.

Department of Health (2002a) *Fair Access to Care Services: Guidance on Eligibility Criteria for Adult Social Care*, LAC (2002) 13. London: The Stationery Office.

Department of Health (2002b) *Guidance on the Single Assessment Process for Older People*, HSC 2002/001: LAC (2002)1. London: Department of Health.

Department of Health (2002c) *Women's Mental Health: Into the Mainstream*. London: Department of Health.

Department of Health (2003) *Guidance on the Single Assessment Process for Older People: Implementation Guidance for April 2004*. London: Department of Health.

Department of Health (2004) *The National Service Framework for Older People*. London: Department of Health.

Department of Health (2005) *Independence, Well-being and Choice*. London: Department of Health.

Department of Health (2006) *Our Health, Our Care, Our Say: Making it Happen*. London: Department of Health.

Department of Health (2007a) *Putting People First: A Shared Vision and Commitment to the Transformation of Adult Social Care*. London: Department of Health.

Department of Health (2007b) *Putting People First: Transforming Adult Social Care*. London: Department of Health.

Department of Health (2007c) *Modernising Adult Social Care: What's Working?* London: Department of Health.

Department of Health (2008a) *Transforming Social Care*. London: Department of Health.

Department of Health (2008b) *Carers at the Heart of 21st Century Families and Communities*. London: Department of Health.

Department of Health (2008c) *Health and Care Services for Older People: Overview Report on Research to Support the National Service Framework for Older People*. London: Department of Health.

Department of Health (2009a) *The Common Assessment Framework for Adults: A Consultation on Proposals to Improve Information Sharing around Multi-disciplinary Assessment and Care Planning*. London: Department of Health.

Department of Health (2009b) *Shaping the Future of Care Together*. London: The Stationery Office.

Department of Health, (2009c) *The National Dementia Strategy*. London: HMSO.

Department of Health (2010) *Mental Health and Well-Being*. London: DH.

Department for Work and Pensions (2008a) *Income-related Benefits: Estimates of Take-up in 2006–2007*. London: DWP Analytical Services Division.

Department for Work and Pensions (2008b) *Households below Average Income – 1994/5 to 2006/7*. London: DWP, Information Analysis Directorate.

Department for Work and Pensions (2009a) *Opportunity Age Indicators – 2008 Update*. London: DWP, Older People and Ageing Society Division.

Department for Work and Pensions (2009b) *Building a Society for All Ages: Choice for Older People*. London: DWP.

Dewey, J. (1939) 'Introduction', in E.V. Cowdrey (ed.), *Problems of Ageing*. Baltimore, MD: Williams and Wilkins.

Dilworth-Anderson, P. and Gibson, B.E. (2002) 'The cultural influence of values, norms, meanings and perceptions in understanding dementia in ethnic minorities', *Alzheimer's Disease and Related Disorders*, 16 (2): 56–63.

Doel, M. and Marsh, P. (1992) *Task-centred Social Work*. Aldershot: Ashgate.

Doel, M. and Marsh, P. (2005) *The Task Centred Book*, Social Work Skills series. London: Routledge.

Doel, M. and Shardlow, S. (2005) *Modern Social Work Practice: Teaching and Learning in Practice Settings*. Aldershot: Ashgate.

Doka, J.K. (ed.), (2002) *Disenfranchised Grief: New Directions, Challenges, and Strategies for Practice*. Champaign, IL: Research Press.

Dominelli, L. (2002) 'Anti-oppressive practice in context', in R. Adams, L. Dominelli and M. Payne (eds), *Social Work: Themes, Issues and Critical Debates* (2nd ed.). Basingstoke: Palgrave Macmillan.

Dominelli, L. (2003) 'Feminist theory', in M. Davies (ed.), *Companion to Social Work*. Oxford: Blackwell.

Donald, I.P. and Bown, H. (2003) 'Independent multidisciplinary review before entry to institutional care', *British Journal of Social Work*, 33 (5): 689–97.

Dowling, B., Powell, M. and Glendinning, (2004) 'Conceptualising successful partnerships', *Health and Social Care in the Community*, 12 (4): 309–17.

Dreher, B.B. (2001) *Communication Skills for Working with Elders* (2nd ed.). New York: Springer.

Duffy, S. and Gillespie, J. (2009) *Personalisation and Safeguarding*. London: In Control.

Dwyer, S. (2005) 'Older people and permanent care: Whose decision?', *British Journal of Social Work*, 35 (7): 1080–92.

Eastman, M. (1995) *User First: Implications for Management*. London: Chapman Hall.

Egan, G. (2007) *The Skilled Helper: A Systematic Approach to Effective Helping*. Pacific Grove, CA: Brooks/Cole.

Erikson, E.H. (1995) *Childhood and Society*. London: Vintage.

Fairbairn, W.R.D. (1954) *An Object Relations Theory of the Personality*. New York: Basic Books.

Feil, N. (2002) *The Validation Breakthrough: Simple Techniques for Communicating with People with Alzheimers-type Dementia* (2nd ed.). Baltimore, MD:Health Professions Press.

Ferguson, H. (2012) 'Social workers deserve recognition rather than this endless criticism', *The Guardian*, 13 November.

Ferguson, I. (2007) 'Increasing user choice or privatizing risk? The antinomies of personalization', *British Journal of Social Work*, 37 (3): 387–403.

Ferri, C.P., Prince, M., Brayne, C. et al. (2005) 'Global prevalence of dementia: A Delphi consensus study', *Lancet*, 366: 2112–17.

Finch, J. and Groves, D. (1980) 'Community care and the family', *Journal of Social Policy*, 9 (4): 487–514.

Fisher, M. (1991) 'Defining the practice content of care management', *Social Work and Social Sciences Review*, 2 (3): 204–30.

Fook, J. (1995) 'Social work: Asking the relevant questions', paper presented at the 24th National AASW Conference, Launceston.

Fook, J. (ed.) (2000) 'Deconstructing and reconstructing professional expertise', in B. Fawcett, B. Featherstone, J. Fook and A. Rossiter (eds), *Practice and Research in Social Work*. London: Routledge, pp. 104–19.

Fook, J. (2003) *Social Work: Critical Theory and Practice*. London: Sage.

Foucault, M. (1980) *Power/Knowledge: Selected Interviews and Other Writings 1972–1977*. New York: Pantheon Books.

Foucault, M. (1988) 'Technologies of the self', in L. Martin, H. Gutman and P. Hutton (eds), *Technologies of the Self: A Seminar with Michel Foucault*. London: Tavistock.

Foucault, A. (2002) *Primer: Discourse, Power and the Subject*, trans. A. McHoul and W. Grace. Melbourne: Melbourne University Press.

Fraser, M. (1999) *Improving Services for Older People: Staff Development in Dementia Care*. Cheltenham: Stanley Thorne.

Fries, J.F. (1980) 'Aging, natural death and the compression of morbidity', *New England Journal of Medicine*, 303: 130–35.

Froggatt, K. (2004) *Palliative Care in Care Homes for Older People*. London: The National Council for Palliative Care.

Gabriel, Z. and Bowling, A. (2004) 'Quality of life from the perspectives of older people', *Ageing and Society*, 24 (5): 675–91.

Gaine, C. (ed.) (2010) *Equality and Diversity in Social Work Practice*. Exeter: Learning Matters.

Galbraith, J.K. (1999) *The Affluent Society*. London: Penguin Books.

Gallo, L.C., Bogart, L.M., Vranceanu, A. and Matthews, K.A. (2005) 'Socioeconomic status, resources, psychological experiences and emotional responses: A test of the reserve capacity model', *Journal of Personality and Social Psychology*, 88 (2): 386–99.

Galpin, D. and Bates, N. (eds) (2009) *Social Work Practice for Adults: Post-qualifying Social Work Practice*. Exeter: Learning Matters.

Gana, K., Alaphilippe, D. and Bailly, L. (2004) 'Positive illusions and mental and physical health in older age', *Aging and Mental Health*, 8 (1): 58–64.

Gardner, A. (2011) *Personalisation in Social Work: Transforming Social Work Practice*. Exeter: Learning Matters.

Garstka, T.A., Schmitt, M.T., Branscombe, N.R. and Hummert, M.L. (2004) 'How young and older adults differ in their responses to perceived age discrimination', *Psychology and Ageing*, 19 (2): 326–35.

Gay and Grey in Dorset (2006) *Lifting the Lid on Sexuality and Ageing*. Bournemouth: Help and Care Development.

General Social Care Council (2002) *Codes of Practice for Social Care Workers and Employers*. London: GSCC.

Giddens, A. (2009) *Sociology*. Cambridge: Polity Press.

Gilleard, C. and Higgs, P. (2000) *Cultures of Ageing: Self, Citizen and the Body*. Harlow: Prentice-Hall.

Gillies, V. and Edwards, R. (2006) 'A qualitative analysis of parenting and social capital: Comparing the work of Coleman and Bourdieu', *Qualitative Sociology Review*, 11 (2): 42–60.

Gilligan, R. (2001) *Promoting Resilience: A Resource Guide on Working with Children in the Care System*. London: British Association for Adoption and Fostering.

Ginn, J. and Arber, S. (1999) 'The politics of old age in the UK', in A. Walker and G. Naegele (eds), *Rethinking Ageing: The Politics of Old Age in Europe*. Buckingham and Philadelphia: Open University Press, pp. 152–67.

Glendinning, C., Challis, D., Fernandez, L. et al. (2008) *Evaluation of the Individual Budgets Pilot Programme: Final Report*. York: Social Policy Research Unit.

Goffman, E. (1961) *Asylums: Essays on the Social Situation of Mental Patients and Other Inmates*. London: Penguin Books.

Goffman, E. (1990) *Stigma: Notes on the Management of Spoiled Identity*. London: Penguin Books.

Goldsmith, M. (1996) *Hearing the Voice of People with Dementia: Opportunities and Obstacles*. London: Jessica Kingsley.

Gordon, D.S. and Spicker, P. (1997) *Planning for the Needs of People with Dementia*. Aldershot: Avebury.

Gould, M. (2008) 'Liberation theory', *The Guardian*, 30 January.

Grenier, A. (2007) 'Constructions of frailty in the English language, care practice and lived experience', *Ageing and Society*, 27 (3): 425–55.

Grief, C. and Myran, D. (2006) 'Bereavement in cognitively impaired older adults: Case series and clinical considerations', *Journal of Geriatric Psychiatry and Neurology*, 19 (4): 209–15.

Griffiths Report (1988) *Community Care: An Agenda for Action*. London: HMSO.

Gwilliam, C. and Gilliard, J. (1996) 'Dementia and the social model of disability', *Journal of Dementia Care*, 4 (1): 14–15.

Haber, D. (2009) 'Adding an empowerment paradigm', *Journal of Applied Gerontology*, 28 (3): 283–97.

Hanmer, J. (1997) 'Women and reproduction', in V. Robinson and D. Richardson (eds), *Introducing Women's Studies* (2nd ed.). Basingstoke: Macmillan.

Hanson, E., Kaur, N. and Wyncoll, K. (2002) *Culturally Competent Care: A Good Practice Guide for Care Management*. Maidstone: Kent County Council.

Harlow, R.E. and Cantor, N. (1996) 'Still participating after all these years: A study of life task participation in later life', *Journal of Personality and Social Psychology*, 71 (6): 1235–49.

Havinghurst, R.J., Neugarten, B.L. and Tobin, S.S. (1963) 'Disengagement, personality and life satisfaction in the later years', in P. Hansen (ed.), *Age with a Future*. Copenhagen: Munksgoasrd, pp. 419–25.

Healthcare Commission (2009) *Equality in Later Life: A National Study of Older People's Mental Health Services*. London: Healthcare Commission.

Healy, K. and Mulholland, J., (2007), *Writing Skills for Social Workers*. London: Sage.

Help the Aged (2006) *My Home Life: Quality of Care in Care Homes*. London: Help the Aged.

Heywood, F., Oldman, C. and Means, R. (2002) *Housing and Home in Later Life*. Buckingham: Open University Press.

Higham, P. (2006) *Social Work: Introducing Professional Practice*. London: Sage.

Hill, M. (1997) *Understanding Social Policy*, (5th ed.). Oxford: Blackwell.

Hill, M. (2003) *Understanding Social Policy* (7th ed.). Oxford: Blackwell.

HM Government (2008) 'The case for change: Why England and Wales needs a new care and support system', 12 May.

Holloway, F. (2010) 'Rehabilitation psychiatry in an age of austerity', *Journal of Mental Health*, 19 (1): 1–7.

Hothersall, S. (2006) *Social Work with Children, Young People and their Families in Scotland*. Exeter: Learning Matters.

Howe, D. (1995) *Attachment Theory for Social Work Practice*. Basingstoke: Macmillan.

Howe, D. (2002) 'Relating theory to practice', in M. Davies (ed.), *The Blackwell Companion to Social Work* (2nd ed.). Oxford: Blackwell.

Howe, D. (2009) *A Brief Introduction to Social Work Theory*. Basingstoke: Palgrave Macmillan.

Howe, D. (2011) *Attachment Across the Life Course: A Brief Introduction*. Basingstoke: Palgrave Macmillan.

Hughes, B. (1995) *Older People and Community Care: Critical Theory and Practice*. Buckingham: Open University Press.

Hugman, R. (2005) *New Approaches in Ethics for the Caring Professions*. Basingstoke: Palgrave Macmillan.

Hugman, R. and Smith, D. (1995) *Ethical Issues in Social Work*. London: Routledge.

Hunter, S. and Ritchie, P. (eds) (2008) *Co-production and Personalisation in Social Care*. London: Jessica Kingsley.

Huppert, F.A., Baylis, N. and Keverne, B. (2005) *The Science of Well-being*. Oxford: Oxford University Press.

Iliffe, S., De Lepeliere, J., Hout, H. et al. and the Diadem Group (2005) 'Understanding obstacles to the recognition of and response to dementia in different European countries: A modified focus group approach using multi-national, multi-disciplinary expert groups', *Aging and Mental Health*, 9 (1): 1–6.

Innes, A. (2009) *Dementia Studies*. London: Sage.

Irvine, R., Kerridge, I., McPhee, J. and Freeman, S. (2002) 'Interprofessionalism and ethics: Consensus or clash of cultures?', *Journal of Interprofessional Care*, 16 (3): 199–210.

Jewell, A. (ed.) (2004) *Ageing, Spirituality and Well-being*. London: Jessica Kingsley.

Johns, R. (2011) *Social Work, Social Policy and Older People*. Exeter: Learning Matters.

Johnson, P. (1998) 'Historical readings of old age and ageing', in P. Johnson and P. Thane (eds), *Old Age from Antiquity to Post-Modernity*. London: Routledge, pp. 1–18.

Johnson, M. (ed.) (2005) *The Cambridge Handbook of Age and Ageing*. Cambridge: Cambridge University Press.

Jolley, D., Jefferys, P., Katona, C. and Lennon, S. (2011) 'Enforced relocation of older people when care homes close: A question of life and death?', *Age and Ageing*, 40 (5): 534–7.

Jonas-Simpson, C.M. (2001) 'From silence to voice: Knowledge, values, and beliefs guiding health-care practices with persons living with dementia', *Nursing Science Quarterly*, 14 (4): 304–10.

Jones, I.R., Hyde, M., Victor, C.R. et al. (2008) *Ageing in a Consumer Society: From Passive to Active Consumption in Britain*. Bristol: The Policy Press.

Jordan, B. (2006) 'Rewarding company, enriching life: The economics of relationships and well-being', www.billjordan.co.uk.

Jordan, B. (2007) *Social Work and Well-being*. Lyme Regis: Russell House Publishing.

Kadushin, A. and Kadushin, G. (1997) *The Social Work Interview* (4th ed.). New York: Columbia University Press.

Keady, J., Williams, S. and Hughes-Roberts, J.H. (2005) 'Emancipatory practice development through life-story work: Changing care in a memory clinic in North Wales', *Practice Development in Health Care*, 4 (4): 203–12.

Keenan, C. (2007) 'Group care', in J. Lishman (ed.), *Handbook for Practice Learning in Social Work and Social Care: Knowledge and Theory* (2nd ed.). London: Jessica Kingsley, Chapter 17.

Kellaher, L.A. (1986) 'Determinants of quality of life in residential settings for old people', in K. Judge and I. Sinclair (eds), *Residential Care for Elderly People*. London: HMSO.

Kelly, F. (2010) 'Recognising and supporting self in dementia: A new way to facilitate a person-centred approach to dementia care', *Ageing and Society*, 30 (1): 103–24.

Killick, J. and Allan, K. (2002) *Communication and the Care of People with Dementia*. Buckingham: Open University Press.

The Kings Fund, (2012) *The Health and Social Care Act 2012: The Tale in a Timeline*. London: The King's Fund.

Kitwood, T. (1987) 'Explaining senile dementia: The limits of neuropathological research', *Free Associations*, 10 (1): 117–40.

Kitwood, T. (1989) 'Brain, mind and dementia, with particular reference to Alzheimer's disease', *Ageing and Society*, 9 (1): 1–15.

Kitwood, T. (1993) 'Towards a theory of dementia care: The interpersonal process', *Ageing and Society*, 13 (1): 51–67.

Kitwood, T. (1995) 'Studies in person-centred care: building up the mosaic of good practice', *Journal of Dementia Care*, 3 (5): 12–13.

Kitwood, T. (1997) 'The uniqueness of people persons with dementia', in M. Marshall (ed.), *State of the Art in Dementia Care*. London: Centre for Policy on Ageing.

Kitwood, T. (1999) *Dementia Reconsidered: The Person Comes First*. Buckingham: Open University Press.

Knapp, M. and Prince, M. (2007) *Dementia UK*. London: Alzheimer's Society.

Knapp, M. et al. (2007) *Dementia UK: Report to the Alzheimer's Society*. London: Kings College London and London School of Economics and Political Science.

Koprowska, J. (2008) *Communication and Interpersonal Skills in Social Work* (2nd ed.). Exeter: Learning Matters.

Kropf, N. and Cummings, S. (2008) 'Evidence-based interventions with older adults: Concluding thoughts', *Journal of Gerontological Social Work*, 50 (SI): 345–55.

Lander, V. (2010) 'Race and ethnicity', in C. Gaine (ed.), *Equality and Diversity in Social Work Practice*. Exeter: Learning Matters, pp. 88–101.

Lapid, M.I., Rummans, T.A., Boeve, B.F. et al. (2011) *What is the Quality of Life in the Oldest Old?* Northfield, IL: International Psychogeriatric Association.

Larkin, M. (2009) *Vulnerable Groups in Health and Social Care*. London: Sage.

Laslett, P. (1996) *A Fresh Map of Life* (2nd ed.). London: Macmillan.

Law, J., Laidlaw, K. and Peck, D. (2010) 'Is depression viewed as an inevitable consequence of age? The "understandability phenomenon" in older people', *Clinical Gerontologist*, 33 (3): 194–209.

Lawton, M.P., Weisman, G., Sloane, P. et al. (2000) 'A "professional environmental assessment procedure" for special care units for elders with dementing illness and its relationship to the "therapeutic environment screening schedule"', *Alzheimer Disease and Associated Disorders*, 14 (1): 28–38.

Leadbetter, C. (2004) *Personalisation through Participation: A New Script for Public Services*. London: Innovation Unit of the Department for Education and Skills.

Lee, D., Woo, J. and Mackenzie, A. (2002) 'A review of older people's experiences with residential care placement', *Journal of Advance Nursing*, 37 (1): 19–27.

Lee, M. (2006) *Promoting Mental Health and Well-being in Later Life: A First Report from the UK INQUIRY into Mental Health and Well-being in Later Life*. London: Age Concern and the Mental Health Foundation.

Leese, D. and Leese, J. (2006) 'Direct payments: Creating a two tiered system in social care?', *British Journal of Social Work*, 36 (8): 1379–93.

Lefrancois, G.R. (1999) *The Lifespan* (6th ed.). Belmont, CA: Wadsworth.

Levy, C.S. (1976) *Social Work Ethics*. New York: Human Science Press.

Lewin, F.A. (2001) 'Gerotranscendence and different cultural settings', *Ageing and Society*, 21 (4): 395–415.

Lewis, L. (2009) 'Introduction: Mental health and human rights: social policy and sociological perspectives', *Social Policy and Society*, 8 (2): 211–14.

Lewis, P. (2010) 'Forced to choose eating or heating, family burns furniture to keep warm', www.guardian.co.uk, 17 January.

Lindsay, T. and Orton, S. (2008) *Groupwork Practice in Social Work*. Exeter: Learning Matters.

Lishman, J. (2009) *Communication in Social Work* (2nd ed.). Basingstoke: Palgrave Macmillan.

Lister, R. (1997) *Citizenship: Feminist Perspectives*. Basingstoke: Palgrave Macmillan.

Lloyd, J. (2009) *Caring in the Older Population*. London: ILC.

Lloyd, L. (2004) 'Mortality and morality: Ageing and the ethics of care', *Ageing and Society*, 24 (2): 235–56.

Lloyd, M. and Taylor, C. (1995) 'From Florence Hollis to the Orange Book: Developing a holistic model of social work assessment in the 1990s', *British Journal of Social Work*, 25 (6): 691–710.

Loretto, W. (2010) 'Work and retirement in an ageing world: The case of older workers in the UK, twenty-first century society', *Journal of the Academy of Social Sciences*, 5 (3): 279–294.

Lowe, G.R. (1993) *The Growth of Personality: From Infancy to Old Age*. London: Penguin Books.

Lymbery, M. (2001) 'Social work at the crossroads', *British Journal of Social Work*, 31 (3): 369–84.

Lymbery, M., (2005) *Social Work with Older People: Context, Policy and Practice*, London: Sage.

Lymbery, M. (2006) 'United we stand? Partnership working in health and social care and the role of social work in services for older people', *British Journal of Social Work*, 36 (7): 1119–34.

Lymbery, M. (2007) *Social Work with Older People, Context, Policy and Practice*. London: Sage.

Lymbery, M. (2010) 'A new vision for adult social care? Continuities and change in the care of older people', *Critical Social Policy*, 30 (1): 5–26.

Lynch, R. (2010) in S. Hothersall and J. Bolger (eds), *Social Policy for Social Work, Social Care and the Caring Professions: Scottish Perspectives*. Farnham: Ashgate.

Lyonette, C. and Yardley, L. (2003) 'The influence on carer wellbeing of motivations to care for older people and the relationship with the care recipient', *Ageing and Society*, 23 (4): 487–506.

McAdams, D. (1997) *Stories We Live By: Personal Myths and the Making of the Self*. New York: Guilford Press.

McAdams, D.P. and Janis, L. (2004) 'Narrative identity and narrative therapy', in I.E. Angus and J. McLeod (eds), *The Handbook of Narrative and Psychotherapy*. London: Sage.

McCaffrey, T. (1998) 'The pain of managing', in A. Foster and Z. Roberts (eds), *Managing Mental Health in the Community*. London: Routledge.

McIntyre, S. (1977) 'Old age as a social problem', in R. Dingwall, C. Heath, M. Reid and M. Stacey (eds), *Health Care and Health Knowledge*. London: Croom Helm.

Mackenzie, J., Bartlett, R. and Downs, M. (2005) 'Moving towards culturally competent dementia care: Have we been barking up the wrong tree?', *Reviews in Clinical Gerontology*, 15: 39–46.

McLean, T. (2007) 'Interdisciplinary practice', in J. Lishman (ed.), *Handbook for Practice Learning in Social Work and Social Care: Knowledge and Theory* (2nd ed.). London: Jessica Kingsley.

McNair, S., Flynn, M. and Dutton, N. (2007) *Employers' Responses to an Ageing Workforce: A Qualitative Study*, Research Report No. 455. Leeds: DWP.

McNamara, B. (2004) 'Good enough death: Autonomy and choice in Australian palliative care', *Social Science and Medicine*, 58 (2): 929–38.

Macionis, J.J. and Plummer, K. (2008) *Sociology: A Global Introduction* (4th ed.). Harlow: Pearson/Prentice Hall.

Mantell, A. and Scragg, T. (eds) (2009) *Safeguarding Adults in Social Work*. Exeter: Learning Matters.

Manthorpe, J. and Iliffe, S. (2008) 'The mental health of older people: Taking a long view', *Journal of Integrated Care*, 16 (5): 4–13.

Manthorpe, J. and Iliffe, S. (2009) 'Policy and practice in the promotion of mental health and well-being in later life', in M. Cattan (ed.), *Mental Health and Well-being in Later Life*. Maidenhead: McGraw-Hill/Open University Press, pp. 48–63.

Manthorpe, J., Moriarty, J., Rapaport, J. et al. and OPRSI (Older People Researching Social Issues) (2008) '"There are wonderful social workers but it's a lottery": Older people's views about social workers', *British Journal of Social Work*, 38 (6): 1132–50.

Manton, K., Stallard, E. and Corder, L. (1995) 'Changes in morbidity and chronic disability in the US elderly population: Evidence from the 1982, 1984 and 1989 National Long Term Care Survey', *Journal of Gerontology*, 50B: S104–S204.

Marchbank, J. and Letherby, G. (eds) (2007) *Introduction to Gender: Social Science Perspectives*. Harlow: Pearson Longman.

Marcoen, A., Coleman, P.G. and O'Hanlon, A. (2007) 'Psychological Ageing', in J. Bond, S. Peace, F. Dittmann-Kohli and G. Westerhof (eds), *Ageing in Society* (3rd ed.). London: Sage, pp. 38–67.

Markson, E. (2003) *Social Gerontology Today*. Los Angeles: Roxbury.

Marshall, M. and Tibbs, M.-A. (2006) *Social Work and People with Dementia: Partnerships, Practice and Persistence* (2nd ed.). Bristol: BASW/The Policy Press.

Martin, R. (2011) *Social Work Assessment, Transforming Social Work Practice*. Exeter: Learning Matters.

Martin-Matthews, A. (2000) 'Intergenerational caregiving', in E. Gee and G. Gutman (eds), *The Overselling of Population Ageing*. Ontario: Oxford University Press.

Maslow, A. (1987) *Motivation and Personality* (3rd ed.). New York: Harper and Row.

Mathews, I. (2009) *Social Work and Spirituality*. Exeter: Learning Matters.

Mauk, K.L. (2006) *Gerontological Nursing, Competence for Care*. Burlington, MA: Jones and Bartlett Publishers.

Maynard, C. (2003) 'Differentiate depression from dementia', *Nurse Practitioner*, 28 (3): 18–27.

Mearns, D. (2003) *Developing Person-centred Counselling* (2nd ed.). London: Sage.

Michael, Sir J. (2008) *Healthcare for All*. London: Department of Health.

Midwinter, E. (2005) 'How many people are there in the third age?', *Ageing and Society*, 25 (1): 9–18.

Mill, J.S. ([1861] 1998) *Utilitarianism*. Oxford: Oxford University Press.

Miller, C. and Freeman, M. (2003) 'Clinical teamwork: The impact of policy on collaborative teamwork', in A. Leathard (ed.), *Interprofessional Collaboration: From Policy to Practice in Health and Social Care*. Hove: Brunner-Routledge.

Milner, J. and O'Byrne, P. (2009) *Assessment in Social Work* (3rd ed.). Basingstoke: Palgrave Macmillan.

Mishler, E.G. (1986) *Research Interviewing: Context and Narrative*. Cambridge, MA: Harvard University Press.

Modood, T., Beishon, S. and Virdee, S. (1998) 'Changing ethnic identities in Britain', in A. Giddens (ed.), *Sociology: Introductory Readings*. Cambridge: Polity Press, pp. 211–18.

Morgan, K. (1992) *Gerontology: Responding to an Ageing Society*. London: Jessica Kingsley.

Morris, J. (1993) *Community Care or Independent Living*. York: Joseph Rowntree Foundation.

Morris, N. (2012) 'Outrage as former head of benefits agency Lord Bichard says the retired should take up community service or have their pensions docked', *The Independent*, 24 October.

Morton, I. (1999) *Person-centred Approaches to Dementia Care*. New York: Winslow Press.

Mowlan, A., Tennant, R., Dixon, J. and McCreadie, C. (2007) *UK Study of Abuse and Neglect of Older People: Qualitative Findings*. London: National Centre for Social Research, Kings College.

Moyle, W. (2008) 'Complementary therapies: Do they have a role in the treatment of disruptive behaviours?', presentation delivered at University of Wollongong, NSW for Eastern Australia Dementia Training and Study Centre, 27 February.

Mullender, A. (1996) *Rethinking Domestic Violence: The Social Work and Probation Response*. London: Routledge.

Mullender, A. and Ward, D. (1991) *Self-directed Groupwork: Users Take Action for Empowerment*. London: Whiting and Birch.

Murphy, S. (2011) 'Older people suffering under "poorly publicised" fuel poverty scheme', www.guardian.co.uk, 16 December.

Murray Parkes, C. (1987) *Bereavement: Studies of Grief in Adult Life*. London: Tavistock Publications.

Murray Parkes, C., Stevenson-Hinde, J. and Marris, P. (1991) *Attachment Across the Life Cycle*. London and New York: Routledge.

Musingarimi, P. (2008) *Health Issues Affecting Older Gay, Lesbian and Bisexual People in the UK. A Policy Brief*. London: International Longevity Centre UK.

Muthesius, D. (1997) 'Reminiscence and the relationship between young and old', cited in H. Bee and D. Boyd, *Lifespan Development* (3rd ed.), (2003). Harlow: Allyn and Bacon.

Nabors, N.A., Hall, R.L., Miville, M.L. et al. (2001) 'Multiple minority group oppression: Divided we stand?', *Journal of the Gay and Lesbian Medical Association*, 5 (3): 101–105.

Naegele, G. and Walker, A. (1999) 'Conclusion', in A. Walker and G. Naegele (eds), *Rethinking Ageing: The Politics of Old Age in Europe*. Buckingham: Open University Press.

National Assembly for Wales (2000) *In Safe Hands*. Available at: http://wales.gov.uk/docrepos/40382/dhss/socialservices/reportsenglish/safehands_e.pdf;jsessionid=EDF35952999361C1111251B90DB61608?lang=en

Naylor, L. (2010) 'Safeguarding adults for community care', in K. Brown (ed.), *Vulnerable Adults and Community Care* (2nd ed.). Exeter: Learning Matters, pp. 113–26.

Neal, M. and Briggs, M. (1999) 'Validation therapy for dementia', *The Cochrane Library*, Issue 4, Oxford.

Netuveli, G., Wiggins, R.D., Montgomery, S.M. et al. (2008) 'Mental health and resilience at older ages: Bouncing back after adversity in the British Household Panel Survey', *Journal of Epidemiology and Community Health*, 62 (1): 987–91.

Neuberger, Baroness J. (2009) 'What does it mean to be old?', in P. Cann and M. Dean (eds), *Unequal Ageing: The Untold Story of Exclusion in Old Age*. Bristol: The Policy Press.

Neumann, C.V. (2000) *Sources of Meaning and Energy in the Chronically Ill Frail Elder*. Milwaukee: The University of Wisconsin-Milwaukee.

Newbronner, L., Chamberlain, R., Bosanquet, K. et al. (2011) *Keeping Personal Budgets Personal: Learning from the Experiences of Older People, People with Mental Health Problems and Their Carers*, SCIE Report 40. London: Social Care Institute for Excellence.

Nusberg, C. (1995) 'Preface', in D. Thursz, C. Nusberg and J. Prather (eds), *Empowering Older People: An International Perspective*. London: Cassell.

O'Connor, D., Phinney, A., Smith, A. et al. (2007) 'Personhood in dementia care: Developing a research agenda for broadening the vision', *Dementia*, 6 (1): 121–42.

O'Hagan, K. (2000) 'Crisis intervention', in M. Davies (ed.), *Blackwell Encyclopaedia of Social Work*. Oxford: Blackwell.

O'Hara, M. (2012) 'Better Life project allows older people to tell it like it is', *The Guardian*, 21 February.

O'Keeffe, M., Hills, A., Doyle, M. et al. (2007) *UK Study of Abuse and Neglect of Older People: Prevalence Survey Report*, prepared for Comic Relief and the Department of Health.

Older People Steering Group (2004) *Older People Shaping Policy and Practice*. York: Joseph Rowntree Foundation.

Oliver, R.W. (1993) *Psychology and Health Care*. Oxford: Bailliere Tindall.

Office for National Statistics (2008) *National Population Projections, 2006-based*. Basingstoke: Palgrave Macmillan.

Office of Population Censuses and Surveys (OPCS) (1991) *Population Projections 1987–2027*. London: HMSO.

Oppenheim, C. and Harker, L. (1996) *Poverty: The Facts* (3rd ed.). London: Child Poverty Action Group.

Orme, J. (1997) 'Research into Practice', in G. McKenzie, J. Powell and R. Usher (eds), *Understanding Social Research: Perspectives on Methodology and Practice*. Hove: Falmer Press.

Orme, J. and Shemmings, D. (2010) *Developing Research Based Social Work Practice*. Basingstoke: Palgrave Macmillan.

O'Sullivan, T. (1999) *Decision Making in Social Work*. Basingstoke: Palgrave Macmillan.

Ovretveit, J., Mathias, P. and Thompson, T. (eds) (1997) *Interprofessional Working for Health and Social Care*. Basingstoke: Palgrave Macmillan.

Oyebode, J. (2009) 'Grief and bereavement', in M. Downs and B. Bowers (eds), *Excellence in Dementia Care: Research into Practice*. Maidenhead: McGraw-Hill/Open University Press, pp. 379–94.

Parekh, B. (2000) *Report of the Commission on the Future of Multi-ethnic Britain*. London: Runnymede Trust.

Park, A. (2000) 'The generation game', in R. Jowell, J. Curtice, A. Park et al. (eds), *British Social Attitudes*, Report No. 17. London: Sage, pp. 1–19.

Parker, J. and Bradley, G. (2010) *Social Work Practice: Assessment, Planning, Intervention and Review* (3rd ed.). Exeter: Learning Matters.

Parker, S., Fook, J. and Pease, B. (1999) 'Empowerment: The modern social work concept *par excellence*' in B. Pease and J. Fook (eds), *Transforming Social Work Practice: Postmodern Critical Perspectives*. London and New York: Routledge, pp. 150–60.

Parrott, L. (2002) *Social Work and Social Care* (2nd ed.). London and New York: Routledge.

Parrott, L. (2010) *Values and Ethics in Social Work Practice* (2nd ed.). Exeter: Learning Matters.

Patsios, D. (2006) 'Pensioners, poverty and social exclusion', in C. Pantazis, D. Gordon and R. Levitas (eds), *Poverty and Social Exclusion in Britain: The Millennium Survey*. Bristol: The Policy Press.

Payne, G. and Payne, J. (2004) *Key Concepts in Social Research*. London: Sage.

Payne, M. (2005) *Modern Social Work Theory* (3rd ed.). Basingstoke: Palgrave Macmillan.

Payne, M. (2006a) *Narrative Therapy* (2nd ed.). London: Sage.

Payne, M. (2006b) *What is Professional Social Work?* (2nd ed.). Bristol: BASW/The Policy Press.

Peace, S. (1998) 'Caring in place', in A. Brechin, J. Walmsley, J. Katz and S. Peace (eds), *Care Matters*. London: Sage.

Peace, S. and Holland, C. (2001) 'Homely residential care: A contradiction in terms?', *Journal of Social Policy*, 30 (3): 393–410.

Peace, S., Kellaher, L. and Willocks, D. (1997) *Re-evaluating Residential Care*. Buckingham: Open University Press.

Peace, S.M., Kellaher, L. and Holland, C. (2005) *Environment and Identity in Later Life*. Buckingham: Open University Press.

Pearce, A., Clare, L. and Pistrang, N. (2002) 'Managing sense of self: Coping in the early stages of Alzheimer's disease', *Dementia: The International Journal of Social Research and Practice*, 1 (2): 173–92.

Pease, B. and Fook, J. (1999) 'Postmodern critical theory and emancipatory social work practice', in B. Pease and J. Fook (eds), *Transforming Social Work Practice: Postmodern Critical Perspectives*. London and New York: Routledge.

Pensions Commission (2005) *Pensions: Challenges and Choices*. London: The Stationery Office.

Percival, J. and Hanson, J. (2006) 'Big brother or brave new world? Telecare and its implications for older people's independence and social inclusion', *Critical Social Policy*, 26 (4): 888–909.

Perry, E. (2009) 'Working with older people: managing risk and promoting independence', in D. Galpin and N. Bates (eds), *Social Work Practice with Adults*. Exeter: Learning Matters.

Phillips, J. (1992) *Private Residential Care: The Admission Process and Reactions of the Public Sector*. Aldershot: Avebury.

Phillips, J. and Waterson, J. (2002) 'Care management and social work: A case study of the role of social work in hospital discharge to residential or nursing home care', *European Journal of Social Work*, 5 (2): 171–86.

Phillips, J., Bernard, M., Phillipson, C. and Ogg, J. (2002) 'Social support in later life: A study of three areas', *British Journal of Social Work*, 30 (6): 837–54.

Phillips, J., Ray, M. and Marshall, M. (2006) *Social Work with Older People* (4th ed.). Basingstoke: Palgrave Macmillan.

Phillips, J., Ajrouch, K. and Hillcoat-Nalletamby, S. (2010) *Key Concepts in Social Gerontology*. London: Sage.

Phillipson, C. (1982) *Capitalism and the Construction of Old Age*. London: Macmillan.

Phillipson, C. (1993) 'The sociology of retirement', in J. Bond, P. Coleman and S. Peace (eds), *Ageing and Society: An Introduction to Social Gerontology*. London: Sage.

Phillipson, C. (1998) *Reconstructing Old Age: New Agendas in Social Theory and Practice*. London: Sage.

Phillipson, C. (2007) 'The "elected" and the "excluded": sociological perspectives on the experience of place and community in old age', *Ageing and Society*, 27: 321–42.

Phillipson, C. and Baars, J. (2007) 'Social theory and social ageing', in J. Bond, S. Peace, F. Dittman-Kohli and G. Westerhof (eds), *Ageing in Society: European Perspectives on Gerontology*. London: Sage.

Phillipson, C. and Walker, A. (eds) (1986) *Ageing and Social Policy*. Aldershot: Gower.

Pilgrim, D. (2007) *Key Concepts in Mental Health*. London: Sage.

Pillemer, K., Suitor, J.J. and Wethington, E. (2003) 'Integrating theory, basic research and intervention: Two case studies from caregiving research', *The Gerontologist*, 43 (Special Issue 1): 19–28.

Plummer, K. (1995) 'Social work with older people', in V.E. Cree and A. Davis (2007), *Social Work: Voices from the Inside*. London: Routledge, pp. 127–47.

Polizzi, K.G. and Millikin, R.J. (2002) 'Attitudes towards the elderly: Identifying problematic usage of ageist and overextended terminology in research instructions', *Educational Gerontology*, 28: 367–77.

Post, S. (2000) *The Moral Challenge of Alzheimer Disease* (2nd ed.). Baltimore, MD: Johns Hopkins University Press.

Postle, K. (2002) 'Working "between the idea and the reality": Ambiguities and tensions in care managers' work', *British Journal of Social Work*, 32 (3): 335–51.

Powell, J.L. (2001) 'Theorizing gerontology: The case of old age, professional power and social policy in the United Kingdom', *Journal of Aging and Identity*, 6 (3): 117–35.

Powell, J. (2008) 'Promoting older people's voices', *Social Work in Health Care*, 44 (1–2): 111–26.

Powell, J., Robison, J., Roberts, H. and Thomas, G. (2007) 'The single assessment process in primary care: Older people's accounts of the process', *British Journal of Social Work*, 37 (6): 1043–58.

Powers, A.R., McPherson, M. and Treebus, S.L. (1994) 'Staff psychological well-being and quality of care', *Quality Health Care Research*, 2: 46–52.

Powers, B.A. and Watson, N.M. (2011) 'Spiritual nurturance and support for nursing home residents with dementia', *Dementia*, 10 (1): 59–80.

Prasher, V.P. (2005) *Alzheimer's Disease and Dementia in Down's Syndrome and Intellectual Disabilities*. Oxford: Radcliffe Publishing.

Preston-Shoot, M. (1999) 'Recreating mayhem? Developing understanding for social work with mentally disordered people', in D. Webb and R. Harris (eds), *Mentally Disordered Offenders: Managing People Nobody Owns*. London: Routledge.

Preston-Shoot, M. (2003) 'Changing learning and learning change: Making a difference in education, policy and practice', *Journal of Social Work Practice*, 17 (1): 9–23.

Preston-Shoot, M. (2004) 'Evidence: The final frontier? Star Trek, groupwork and the mission of change', *Groupwork*, 14 (3): 18–43.

Preston-Shoot, M. (2007) *Effective Groupwork* (2nd ed.). Basingstoke: Palgrave Macmillan.

Pritchard, J. (2003) *Training Manual for Working with Older People in Residential and Day Care Settings*. London: Jessica Kingsley.

Pugh, S. (2005) 'Assessing the cultural needs of older lesbians and gay men: Implications for practice', *Practice*, 17 (3): 207–18.

Pugh, R. and Cheers, B. (2010) *Rural Social Work: An International Perspective*. Bristol: The Policy Press.

Rankin, J. (2004) *Mental Health in the Mainstream: Developments and Trends in Mental Health Policy*, Institute for Public Policy Research Working Paper 1.

Ray, M. and Phillips, J. (2002) 'Older people', in R. Adams, L. Dominelli and M. Payne (eds), *Critical Practice in Social Work*. Basingstoke: Palgrave Macmillan, pp. 199–209.

Ray, M., Bernard, M. and Phillips, J. (2009) *Critical Issues in Social Work with Older People*. Basingstoke: Palgrave Macmillan.

Reamer, F.G. (2006) *Social Work Values and Ethics* (3rd ed.). New York: Columbia University Press.

Reed, J., Stanley, D. and Clarke, C. (2004) *Health, Well-Being and Older People*. Bristol: The Policy Press.

Reed, J., Cook, M., Cook, G. et al. (2006) 'Specialist services for older people: Issues of negative and positive ageism', *Ageing and Society*, 26 (6): 849–65.

Reid, W.J. (1978) *The Task-Centred System*. New York: Columbia University Press.

Rentz, C., Krikorian, R. and Keys, M. (2005) 'Grief and mourning from the perspective of the person with a dementing illness: Beginning the dialogue', *Omega*, 50: 165–79.

Riddell, M. (2007) 'But not everyone can grow old gracefully', *The Observer*, 10 June.

Rimmer, E., Wojciechowska, M., Stave, C. et al. (2005) 'Implications of the Facing Dementia Survey for the general population, patients and caregivers across Europe', *International Journal of Clinical Practice*, 59 (supplement 146): 17–24.

Robins, R.W., Trzesniewski, K.H., Tracy, J.L. et al. (2002) 'Global self-esteem across the life span', *Psychology and Aging*, 17 (3): 423–34.

Robinson, T.E. (1998) *Portraying Older People in Advertising: Magazines, Television and Newspapers*. New York: Garland.

Robson, C. (2002) *Real World Research* (2nd ed.). Oxford: Blackwell.

Rogers, C. (1959) 'A theory of therapy, personality and interpersonal relationships, as developed in the client-centred framework', in S. Koch (ed.), *Psychology: A Study of a Science, Vol. 3. Formulations of the Person and the Social Context*. New York: McGraw-Hill, pp. 184–256.

Rogers, C. (1961) *On Becoming a Person*. Boston: Houghton Mifflin

Rogers, C.R. (1980) *A Way of Being*. Boston: Houghton Mifflin.

Rogers, C. (2002) 'The interpersonal relationship in the facilitation of learning', in H. Kirschenbaum and V.L. Henderson (eds), *The Carl Rogers Reader* London: Constable.

Rosenthal, R. and Rosnow, R.L. (1975) *The Volunteer Subject*. New York: Wiley.

Rowson, R. (2006) *Working Ethics: How to be Fair in a Culturally Complex World*. London: Jessica Kingsley.

Rutter, M. (1975) *Helping Troubled Children*. London: Penguin Books.

Rutter, M. (1987) 'Psychosocial resilience and protective mechanisms', *American Journal of Orthopsychiatry*, 57 (3): 316–31.

Ryckman, R.M. (2008) *Theories of Personality* (8th ed.). Belmont, CA: Thomson/Wadworth.

Sabat, S. (2001) *The Experience of Alzheimer's Disease: Life Through a Tangled Veil*. Oxford: Blackwell.

Sabat, S. (2002) 'Surviving manifestations of selfhood in Alzheimer's disease', *Dementia*, 1 (1): 25–36.

Saleebey, D. (2009) *The Strengths Perspective in Social Work Practice* (5th ed.). London: Allyn and Bacon.

Sandman, C.A. (1993) 'Memory rehabilitation in Alzheimers disease', *Clinical Gerontologist*, 13(4): 19–33.

Sands, R. (1996) 'The elusiveness of identity in social work practice with women', *Clinical Social Work Journal*, 24 (2): 167–86.

Sands, R.G. and Nuccio, K. (1992) 'Postmodern feminist theory and social work', *Social Work*, 37 (6): 489–94.

Scharf, T. (2009) 'Too tight to mention: unequal income in older age', in P. Cann and M. Dean (eds), *Unequal Ageing – The Untold Story of Exclusion in Old Age*. Bristol: The Policy Press, p. 25–52.

Scharf, T., Phillipson, C., Smith, A.E. and Kingston, P. (2002) *Growing Older in Socially Deprived Areas: Social Exclusion in Later Life*. London: Help the Aged.

Scheffler, M.J. (1988) *Consequentialism and its Critics*. Oxford: Oxford University Press.

Schlesinger, B. (1996) 'The sexless years of sex rediscovered', *Journal of Gerontological Social Work*, 26 (1–2): 117–31.

Schon, D.A. (1987) *Educating the Professional Practitioner*. San Francisco: Jossey-Bass.

Schreuder, J.N. (1997) 'Post-traumatic re-experiencing in old age: Working through or covering up?', in L. Hunt, M. Marshall and C. Rowlings (eds), *Past Trauma in Late Life: European Perspectives on Therapeutic Work with Older People*. London: Jessica Kingsley.

Schwartz, L.K. and Simmons, J.P. (2001) 'Contact quality and attitudes towards the elderly', *Educational Gerontology*, 27 (2): 127–37.

Scott, J. and Clare, L., (2003) 'Do people with dementia benefit from psychological interventions offered on a group basis?' *Clinical Psychology and Psychotherapy*, 10(3): 186–96.

Scourfield, P. (2007) 'Helping older people in residential care remain full citizens', *British Journal of Social Work*, 37 (7): 1135–52.

Scourfield, P. (2008) 'Going for brokerage: A task of "independent support" or social work?', *British Journal of Social Work*, 40 (3): 858–77.

Scourfield, P. and Burch, S. (2010) 'Ethical consideration when involving older people in public service participation processes', *Ethics and Social Welfare*, 4 (3): 236–53.

Secker, J., Hill, R., Villeneau, L. and Parkman, S. (2003) 'Promoting independence: But promoting what and how?', *Ageing and Society*, 23 (3): 375–91.

Sheldon, B. and Chilvers, R. (2000) *Evidence-based Social Care: A Study of Prospects and Problems*. Lyme Regis: Russell House Publishing.

Seymour, J., Bellamy, G., Gott, M. et al. (2002) 'Using focus groups to explore older people's attitudes to end of life care', *Ageing and Society*, 22 (4): 517–26.

Sharkey, P. (2007) *The Essentials of Community Care* (2nd ed.). Basingstoke: Palgrave Macmillan.

Sheach-Leith, V., Sutherland, M. and Gibson, N. (2011) 'Gender', in C. Yuill and A. Gibson (eds), *Sociology for Social Work: An Introduction*. London: Sage, 45–68.

Silverman, P. (1987) *The Elderly as Modern Pioneers*. Bloomington, IL: Indiana University Press.

Slater, R. (1995) *The Psychology of Growing Old: Looking Forward*. Milton Keynes: Open University Press.

Smale, G. (1996) *Mapping Change and Innovation*. London: HMSO.

Smale, G., Tuson, G., Biehal, N. and Marsh, P. (1993) *Empowerment, Assessment, Care Management and the Skilled Worker*. London: NISW and the Stationery Office.

Smale, G., Tuson, G. and Statham, D. (2000) *Social Work and Social Problems: Working Towards Social Inclusion and Social Change*. Basingstoke: Palgrave Macmillan.

Small, J., Geldart, K., Gutman, G. and Scott, M. (1998) 'The discourse of self in dementia', *Ageing and Society*, 18 (3): 291–316.

Snell, J. (2011) 'I still have a lot to give', Social care interview, 19 October *Society Guardian*.

Social Care Institute for Excellence (2010) *Personalisation: A Rough Guide*. London: SCIE.

Social Care Institute for Excellence (2011). *Report 40: Keeping Personal Budgets Personal: Learning from the Experiences of Older People, People with Mental Health Problems and their Carers*. London: SCIE.

Social Exclusion Unit (2005) *Excluded Older People: Social Exclusion Unit Interim Report*. London: Office of the Deputy Prime Minister.

Social Exclusion Unit (2006) *A Sure Start to Later Life: Ending Inequalities for Older People*. London: Office of the Deputy Prime Minister/Social Exclusion Unit.

Social Work Task Force (2009) *Building a Safe, Confident Future: The Final Report of the Social Work Task Force, November 2009*. London: DSCF.

Spector, A., Orrell, M., Davies, S. and Woods, R.T. (1999) 'Reminiscence therapy for dementia', *The Cochrane Library*, Issue 4, Oxford.

Stanley, L. and Wise, S. (1990) *Feminist Praxis: Research, Theory and Epistemology in Feminist Sociology*. London: Routledge.

Statham, D. and Kearney, P. (2007) 'Models of assessment', in J. Lishman (ed.), *Handbook for Practice Learning in Social Work and Social Care: Knowledge and Theory*. London: Jessica Kingsley, 101–14.

Stevenson, O. (2001) 'Old people at risk', in P. Parsloe (ed.), *Risk Assessment in Social Care and Social Work*. London: Jessica Kingsley, pp. 201–16.

Stuart-Hamilton, I., (1998) 'Women's attitudes to ageing: some factors of relevance to educational gerontology', *Education and Ageing*, 13(1): 67–88.

Stuart-Hamilton, I. (2006) *The Psychology of Ageing: An Introduction* (4th ed.). London: Jessica Kingsley.

Stuart-Hamilton, I. and Mahoney, B. (2003) 'The effect of ageing awareness training on knowledge of and attitude towards, older adults', *Educational Psychology*, 29 (3): 251–60.

Sugarman, L. (1986) *Life Span Development Concepts, Theories and Interventions*. London: Routledge.

Sullivan, M. (2008) 'Social workers in community care practice: Ideologies and interactions with older people', *British Journal of Social Work*, 39 (7): 1306–25.

Sulmasy, D. (2008) 'Dignity, rights, health care and human flourishing', in D.N. Weisstub and G.D. Pintos (eds), *Autonomy and Human Rights in Health Care*. Dordrecht, Netherlands: Springer. pp. 25–36.

Tanner, D. (2010) *Managing the Ageing Experience: Learning from Older People*. Bristol: The Policy Press.

Tanna, S. (2004) '*A Public Health Approach to Innovation*', Alzheimer's Disease, 'Opportunities to address Pharmaceutical Gaps'. Geneva: World Health Organization.

Taylor, B.J. and Donnelly, M. (2006) 'Professional perspectives on decision making about the long-term care of older people', *British Journal of Social Work*, 36 (5): 807–26.

Teyber, E. and McClure, F.H. (2006) *Interpersonal Process in Therapy: An Integrative Model* (6th ed.). Pacific Grove, CA: Brooks/Cole.

The Guardian (2012) 'Health and social care bill: In need of radical surgery', Editorial, 5 March.

Thomas, D. (1998) *Dylan Thomas – Collected Poems 1934–1953*. London: Phoenix Paperbacks.

Thompson, N. (1992) *Existentialism and Social Work*. Aldershot: Avebury.

Thompson, N. (1998) *Promoting Equality: Challenging Discrimination and Oppression in the Human Services*. London: Macmillan.

Thompson, N. (2000) *Theory and Practice in Human Services*. Buckingham: Open University Press.

Thompson, N. (2002) *People Skills* (2nd ed.). Basingstoke: Palgrave Macmillan.

Thompson, N. (2003a) *Promoting Equality: Challenging Discrimination and Oppression*. Basingstoke: Palgrave Macmillan.

Thompson, N. (2003b) *Communication and Language: A Handbook of Theory and Practice*. Basingstoke: Palgrave Macmillan.

Thompson, N. (2006) *Anti-discriminatory Practice* (4th ed.). Basingstoke: Palgrave Macmillan.

Thompson, N. (2009) *Understanding Social Work* (3rd ed.). Basingstoke: Palgrave Macmillan.

Thompson, N. (2011) *Effective Communication: A Guide for the People Professions* (2nd ed.). Basingstoke: Palgrave Macmillan.

Thompson, N. (2012) *Grief and its Challenges*. Basingstoke: Palgrave Macmillan.

Thompson, N. and Thompson, S. (2001) 'Empowering older people: Beyond the care model', *Journal of Social Work*, 1 (1): 61–76.

Thorson, J.A. (2000) *Ageing in a Changing Society* (2nd ed.). New York: Brunner/Mazel.

Tilford, S. (2009) 'Theoretical perspectives on ageing and health promotion', in M. Cattan (ed.), *Mental Health and Well-being in Later Life*. Maidenhead: Open University Press, pp. 30–47.

Timmins, N. (2012) *Never Again? The Story of the Health and Social Care Act 2012*. The Kings Fund.

Tornstam, L., (1996) 'Gerotranscendence: the contemplative dimension of aging', *Journal of Aging Studies*, 11 (2): 143–154.

Townsend, P. (1964) *The Last Refuge: A Survey of Residential Institutions and Homes for the Aged in England and Wales*. London: Routledge and Kegan Paul.

Townsend, P. (1979) *Poverty in the United Kingdom: A Survey of Household Resources and Standards of Living*. London: Allen Lane.

Townsend, P. (1981) 'The structured dependency of the elderly: The creation of social policy in the twentieth century?', *Ageing and Society*, 1 (1): 5–28.

Townsend, P. (2007) 'Using human rights to defeat ageism: Dealing with policy-induced "structured dependency"', in M. Bernard and T. Scharf (eds), *Critical Perspectives in Ageing Societies*. Bristol: The Policy Press.

Trevithick, P. (2005) *Social Work Skills: A Practice Handbook* (2nd ed.). Maidenhead: Open University Press.

Tulle, E. and Lynch, R. (2011) 'Later life', in C. Yuill and A. Gibson (eds), *Sociology for Social Work: An Introduction*. London: Sage, pp. 116–37.

UK Commission for Employment and Skills (2008) *Working Futures, 2007–2017*. Institute for Employment Research, University of Warwick.

Ungerson, C. (1990) 'The language of care', in C. Ungerson (ed.), *Gender and Caring*. Hemel Hemstead: Harvester Wheatsheaf, pp. 8–33.

United Nations Department of Economic and Social Affairs, Population Division (2009), www.un.org/esa/population/publications (last accessed 25 March 2013).

Victor, C. (2005) *The Social Context of Ageing: A Textbook of Gerontology*. Abingdon: Routledge.

Victor, C.R. and Yang, K. (2012) 'The prevalence of loneliness among adults: A case study of the United Kingdom', *The Journal of Psychology: Interdisciplinary and Applied*, 146 (1–2): 85–104.

Victor, C., Scambler, S. and Bond, J. (2009) *The Social World of Older People: Understanding Loneliness and Social Isolation in Later Life*. Maidenhead: McGraw-Hill/Open University Press.

Vincent, J. (2003) *Old Age*. London: Routledge.

Vincent, J., Phillipson, C.R. and Downs, M. (eds) (2006) *The Future of Old Age*. London: Sage.

Wade, S. (2001) 'Combating agism: An imperative for contemporary health care', *Reviews in Clinical Gerontology*, 11 (3): 285–94.

Wadensten, B. and Hagglund, D. (2006) 'Older people's experience of participating in a reminiscence group with a gerotranscendental perspective: Reminiscence group with a gerotranscendental perspective in practice', *International Journal of Older People Nursing*, 1 (3): 159–67.

Waite, L. and Das, A. (2010) 'Families, social life, and well-being at older ages', *Demography*, 47 (supplement): S87–S109.

Walker, A. (1981) 'Towards a political economy of old age', *Ageing and Society*, 1: 73–94.

Walker, A. (1990) 'Poverty and inequality in old age', in J. Bond and P. Coleman (eds), *Ageing in Society*. London: Sage, pp. 280–303.

Walker, A. (1992) 'The social construction of dependency in old age', in M. Loney, R. Bocock, J. Clarke et al. (eds), *The State of the Market*. London: Sage/Open University.

Walker, A. (ed.) (1996) *The New Generational Contract: Intergenerational Relations, Old Age and Welfare*. London: UCL Press.

Walker, A. (2009) 'Why is ageing so unequal', in P. Cann and M. Dean (eds), *Unequal Ageing: The Untold Story of Exclusion in Old Age*. Bristol: The Policy Press.

Walker, S. and Beckett, C. (2003) *Social Work Assessment and Intervention*. Lyme Regis: Russell House Publishing.

Walker, A. and Maltby, T. (1997) *Ageing Europe*. Buckingham: Open University Press.

Walker, A., Guillemard, A.-M. and Alber, J. (1993) *Older People in Europe: Social and Economic Policies*. Brussels: EC Commission.

Wang, H.-X., Wahlberg, M., Karp, A. et al. (2012) 'Psychosocial stress at work is associated with increased dementia risk in late life', *Alzheimer's and Dementia*, 8 (2): 114–20.

Wanless, D. (2006) *Securing Good Care for Older People: Taking a Long-term View*. London: King's Fund.

Ward, R.A., (1984) *The Aging Experience*. New York: Harper and Row.

Ward, R., River, L. and Fenge, L.-A. (2008) 'Neither silent nor invisible: A comparison of two participative projects involving older lesbians and gay men in the United Kingdom', *Journal of Gay and Lesbian Social Services*, 20 (1–2): 147–65.

Warren, J. (2007) *Service User and Carer Participation in Social Work*. Exeter: Learning Matters.

Watson, D. and West, J. (2006) *Social Work Process and Practice: Approaches, Knowledge and Skills*. Basingstoke: Palgrave Macmillan.

Weaver, J. (1999) 'Gerontological education: A new paradigm for the 21st century', *Educational Gerontology*, 25 (6): 479–90.

Webb, S.A. (2006) *Social Work in a Risk Society: Social and Political Perspectives*. Basingstoke: Palgrave Macmillan.

Weinstein, J. (2008) *Working with Loss, Death and Bereavement: A Guide for Social Workers*. London: Sage.

Wenger, G.C. and Tucker, I. (2002) 'Using network variation in practice: Identification of support network type', *Health and Social Care in the Community*, 10 (1): 28–35.

Westerhof, G.J. and Tulle, E. (2007) 'Meanings of ageing and old age: discursive contexts, social attitudes and personal identities', in J. Bond, S. Peace, F. Dittman-Kohli and G. Westerhof (eds), *Ageing in Society, European Perspectives on Gerontology*. London: Sage Publications. pp. 235–54.

Westius, A., Andersson, L. and Kallenberg, K. (2009) 'View of life in persons with dementia', *Dementia*, 8 (4): 481–99.

Whalley, L. (1997) 'Early onset dementia', in S. Hunter (ed.), *Dementia: Challenges and New Directions, Research Highlights in Social Work 31*. London: Jessica Kingsley, pp. 71–8.

Wharton, A.S. (2005) *The Sociology of Gender: An Introduction to Theory and Research*. Malden, MA and Oxford: Blackwell.

White, J. (2002) in M. Davies (ed.), *The Blackwell Companion to Social Work* (2nd ed.). Oxford: Blackwell.

Whittaker, A. (2012) *Research Skills for Social Work: Transforming Social Work Practice*. Exeter: Learning Matters.

Wilkinson, H., Kerr, D. and Cunningham, D. (2005) 'Equipping staff to support people with an intellectual disability and dementia in care home settings', *Dementia*, 4 (3): 387–400.

Williams, A. and Nussbaum, J.F. (2001) *Intergenerational Communication Across the Lifespan*. Mahwah, NJ: Erlbaum.

Williams, J., Netten, A. and Ware, P. (2007) 'Managing the care home closure process: Care managers' experiences and views', *British Journal of Social Work*, 37 (5): 909–24.

Williams, S. and Keady, J. (2006) 'Editorial: The narrative voice of people with dementia', *Dementia*, 5 (2): 163–68.

Williams, S.J. and Bendelow, G. (1998) *The Lived Body: Sociological Themes, Embodied Issues*. London and New York: Routledge.

Wilson, K., Ruch, G., Lymbery, M. et al. (2008) *Social Work: An Introduction to Contemporary Practice*. Harlow: Pearson Longman.

Windle, G., Markland, D. and Woods, B. (2008) 'Examination of a theoretical model of psychological resource', *Ageing and Mental Health*, 12 (3): 285–292.

Windle, K., Wagland, R., Lord, K. et al. (2008) *National Evaluation of Partnerships for Older People Projects: Interim Report of Progress*. Canterbury: University of Kent, Personal Social Services Research Unit.

Windle, K., Wagland, R., Forder, J. et al. (2010) *National Evaluation of Partnerships for Older People Projects*. London: Department of Health.

Wolff, J. (2011) *Ethics and Public Policy: A Philosophical Inquiry*. Abingdon: Routledge.

Woods, R.T. (1996) 'Psychological "Therapies" in Dementia', in R.T.Woods (ed.), *Handbook of the Clinical Psychology of Ageing*. John Wiley and Sons. p.575–600.

World Health Organization (2013) *Health Statistics and Health Information Systems, Definition of an Older or Elderly Person*. Geneva: World Health Organization.

Yang, K. and Victor, C. (2011) 'Age and loneliness in 25 European nations', *Ageing and Society*, 31(8): 1–21.

Young, J. (1999) *The Exclusive Society*. London: Sage.

Young, M. and Schuller, T. (1991) *Life After Work: The Arrival of the Ageless Society*. London: HarperCollins.

Yuill, C., Gibson, A. and Thorpe, C. (2011) 'Sociology for social work – an overview', in C. Yuill and A. Gibson (eds), *Sociology for Social Work: An Introduction*. London: Sage, pp. 1–25.

Zaidi, A. (2006) *Poverty of Elderly People in EU25*. Vienna: European Centre.

Zautra, A.J., Hall, J.S. and Murray, K.E. (2010) 'Resilience: A New Definition of Health for People and Communities', in J.W. Reich, A.J. Zautra and J.S. Hall (eds), *Handbook of Adult Resilience*. New York and London: Guilford Press, pp. 3–34.

INDEX